*To the Rangers and Naturalists
of California's Desert Lands*

Borrego Palm Canyon

The Anza-Borrego Desert Region

A Guide to the State Park and Adjacent Areas of the Western Colorado Desert

Lowell & Diana Lindsay

Cartography by Casey Cook

Published in Cooperation with
the California Department of Parks and Recreation,
the Anza-Borrego Desert Natural History Association, and
the U.S. Department of the Interior, Bureau of Land
Management, California Desert District

WILDERNESS PRESS
BERKELEY

First Edition October 1978
First Edition October 1978
Second Edition November 1985
Third Edition July 1991
FOURTH EDITION October 1998
Second printing April 2000

Cover photos © 1998 by Larry Ulrich
Book design by Margaret Copeland, Terragraphics
Cover design by Larry B. Van Dyke

Library of Congress Card Number 98-10340
ISBN 0-89997-187-3

Printed in the United States of America

Published by: **Wilderness Press**
1200 5th Street
Berkeley, CA 94710
(800) 443-7227; FAX (510) 558-1696
mail@wildernesspress.com

Contact us for free catalog
Visit our web site at **www.wildernesspress.com**

♻ Printed on recycled paper, 20% post-consumer waste

Cover photos: *(front)* **Bigelow's monkey-flower and ocotillo, Southwest Grove, Mountain Palm Springs, Anza-Borrego Desert State Park;**
(back) **Dune primrose, desert sunflower, and desert sand verbena.**

Library of Congress Cataloging-in-Publication Data

Lindsay, Lowell.
    The Anza-Borrego Desert region : a guide to the state park and adjacent areas of the western Colorado Desert/Lowell and Diana Lindsay.—4th ed.
        p.   cm.
    "Published in cooperation with the California Department of Parks and Recreations [sic], the Anza-Borrego Desert Natural History Association, and the U.S. Department of the Interior, Bureau of Land Management, California Desert District."
    Includes bibliographical references (p.) and index.
    ISBN 0-89997-187-3 (alk. paper)
    1. Hiking—California—Anza-Borrego Desert State Park—Guidebooks.
2. Outdoor recreation—California—Anza-Borrego Desert State Park
—Guidebooks. 3. Desert survival. 4. Anza-Borrego Desert State Park
(Calif.)—Guidebooks. I. Lindsay, Diana, 1944-   . II. Title.
GV199.42.C22A594   1998
917.94'98—dc21   98-10340
                                                                                        CIP

Contents

Part II—Road And Trail Guide By Area

Appendices

Read This

Hiking in the backcountry entails unavoidable risk that every hiker assumes and must be aware of and respect. The fact that a trail is described in this book is not a representation that it will be safe for you. Trails vary greatly in difficulty and in the degree of conditioning and agility one needs to enjoy them safely. On some hikes, routes may have changed or conditions may have deteriorated since the descriptions were written. Also, trail conditions can change even from day to day, owing to weather and other factors. A trail that is safe on a dry day or for a highly conditioned, agile, properly equipped hiker may be completely unsafe for someone else or unsafe under adverse weather conditions.

You can minimize your risks on the trail by being knowledgeable, prepared and alert. There is not space in this book for a general treatise on safety in the mountains, but there are a number of good books and public courses on the subject and you should take advantage of them to increase your knowledge. Just as important, you should always be aware of your own limitations and of conditions existing when and where you are hiking. If conditions are dangerous, or if you are not prepared to deal with them safely, choose a different hike! It's better to have wasted a drive than to be the subject of a mountain rescue.

These warnings are not intended to scare you off the trails. Millions of people have safe and enjoyable hikes every year. However, one element of the beauty, freedom and excitement of the wilderness is the presence of risks that do not confront us at home. When you hike you assume those risks. They can be met safely, but only if you exercise your own independent judgment and common sense.

Outline of Trips by Area

(Including major points of interest and side trips)

List Of Maps And Illustrations

Preface

I first saw Anza-Borrego from the cockpit of a Navy helicopter, operating off the USS Hornet (CV-12). We were between Vietnam deployments and were practicing high-speed search and rescue missions inland. Although the altimeter showed 6000', we were about 2000' above ground level (AGL) eastbound over McCain Valley. Then the bottom dropped out. Suddenly altitude and AGL matched, and the ground was very, very far away. Only years later did I understand that we had just shot over the Laguna escarpment, far above one of the greatest desert preserves of America.

"Look down there," I yelled into the mike. "I don't see anything," crackled Steve. "Right! I've never seen so much nothing anywhere. We gotta get in there ASAP." Within days, Diana and I and some squadron buddies were deep in the Carrizo Badlands and, not knowing it at the time, embarked on a life-long quest to know Anza-Borrego and the Colorado Desert. In a way, we went into the desert in 1967 and have never returned.

—Lowell Lindsay

After twenty years in three editions and many more printings, this is a completely revised, expanded, and updated book from the ground up. This new road and trail guide offers the following highlights:

- Comprehensive, coordinated, and detailed road and trail logs, with interpretive background, which treats the region as a unified whole: paved and dirt roads, 4WD and mountain bike routes, hiking and equestrian trails.
- Integrated, coordinated system of highway logs, utilizing official post mileage and post mile markers where available, supplemented by conventional odometer mileages.
- Introduction to field use of portable Global Positioning System (GPS) units and the Universal Transverse Mercator (UTM) system to enhance conventional map and compass techniques in the Anza-Borrego region.
- A reference table for the backpocket regional map which gives the 7.5' USGS topographic map name for each gridded quadrangle on the regional map. Sites on the regional map or in its alphabetical index can thus be located on their corresponding detailed topographic map.
- Expanded Desert Directory of recreational and public safety agencies, organizations, accommodations, and facilities in the Anza-Borrego/Yuha region.
- Table of Trips by mode of travel: auto, 4WD, mountain bike, horseback, nature walk, hike, and backpack.
- Comprehensive list by title of interpretive panels and monuments, incorporated into the roadlogs and including UTM coordinates and many latitude-longitude coordinates, to enable practice of the powerful new GPS technology for land navigation.
- A Table of 100 Common Plants in Anza-Borrego by Family listing current scientific names (standardized with the Jepson manual), common names,

and reference to the page numbers found in leading plant guides for more detailed study.

The companion volume to this guidebook, *Anza-Borrego from A to Z: People, Places, and Things*, is being prepared by Sunbelt Publications. It will provide a single source for the cultural and natural history of the region as encountered on-site on its highways and byways. It will also include an overview of the epic historical events that transpired here including the Fages and Anza expeditions, the discovery and development of the Southern Emigrant Trail, and the fabled Butterfield Overland Mail. Together with this guidebook, *A to Z* will be another contribution in the Sunbelt Natural History series which includes *Geology of Anza-Borrego: Edge of Creation* by Paul Remeika and *Desert Lore of Southern California* by Choral Pepper, soon to appear in a new California State Sesquicentennial edition.

About the Authors

Diana and Lowell Lindsay have been desert naturalists for over twenty years, and have written several books including *Our Historic Desert* for Copley Press. Diana received her master's degree from San Diego State University, specializing in history and geography of the Southwest, and she holds a lifetime California teaching credential. Lowell is a former navy helicopter pilot and wilderness survival instructor. He received his master's degree from West Texas State University in Public Administration, specializing in Environmental Education.

The Lindsays own Sunbelt Publications, a regional book and map wholesale company serving booksellers throughout the Southwest and Baja. They teach natural-history classes and lead field trips for several organizations including Grossmont College, San Diego Natural History Museum, and the Anza-Borrego Foundation.

Acknowledgments

We originally dedicated this book to "The Rangers and Naturalists of California's Desert Lands." Some of them have "gone to the golden hills," to use the terminology of E Clampus Vitus, a California historical fraternity. Others are continuing to make great contributions in their chosen fields. Many have been an important part of our life, work and play. To each of them, including the staff and volunteers of our desert public lands, we are deeply grateful and renew our original dedication.

Acknowledgments to the 1st Edition (a reprint)

The authors wish to express sincere appreciation to the following for their invaluable assistance and encouragement, without which the *Guide to the Anza-Borrego Desert Region* would have remained an incomplete set of weathered notes buried variously in backpacks, jeep glove compartments and among mislaid letters.

To Maurice H. (Bud) Getty, manager of Anza-Borrego Desert State Park, for extensive, in-depth support of field work, review of text, encouragement and for many years of warmest friendship.

To Jack Welch, manager of San Diego Coast Area of the California State Park System, who provided highly detailed and extensive ranger patrol reports from the 1950s and who checked descriptions along the Anza trail.

To the many California State Park Rangers stationed at Anza-Borrego Desert State Park who have provided information and have taken us out on numerous patrols, including Gar Salzgeber, John McBride, Glenn Mincks, Terry Brann, Dan Tuttle, Ken Jones, Mark Jorgensen and naturalist Paul Johnson, with particular thanks to Ranger George Leetch, who has provided us years of cooperation and wisdom in our desert travels.

To the staff of the El Centro office of the Bureau of land Management for their assistance and review of the text, especially former El Centro Resource Area Manager Cliff Yardley, current area manager David Mari and their staffs.

For official sanction of the book by the following agencies and organizations: California Department of Parks and Recreation; U.S. Dept of the Interior, Bureau of Land Management, Riverside District Office; and the Anza-Borrego Desert Natural History Association.

To Dr. Robert Sawvell, professor of geography at West Texas State University, for extensive assistance and advice in the preparation of the maps for the text.

To William Knyvett, publisher of *Desert Magazine*, for permission to use Marshal South's "Tracks of the Overland Stage" in its entirety.

To Carl Bullock, associate director of the Santa Ana-Tustin YMCA, who has provided extensive field-work support and encouragement through the years.

To Thomas Winnett and Jeff Schaffer at Wilderness Press, who have carefully edited the text, provided invaluable technical assistance and developed an attractive format.

And to all the other friends and relatives who have helped to gather information.

—*Lowell and Diana Lindsay*
Amarillo, Texas
January 5, 1978

Acknowledgments to the 4th Edition

Sincere thanks to the following superintendents who facilitated the review of this edition: Dave Van Cleve of the Colorado Desert District; John Quirk of Anza-Borrego Desert State Park; and Curt Itogawa of Ocotillo Wells State Vehicular Recreation Area. In particular we appreciate the in-depth reviews by rangers Paul Remeika, Jim Meier, and Bob Theriault.

Much of the new material in this edition derives from areas under the stewardship of the U.S. Bureau of Land Management. El Centro Area Manager Terry Reed compiled many pages of comments from his staff to assist us. Lead Recreation Planner Arnie Schoeck is particularly recognized, not only for detailed review of this and other manuscripts, but for extensive time in the field above and beyond the call of duty, helping us to get it right.

Our six years as natural history instructors, through Grossmont College Extension and as volunteers at the San Diego Natural History Museum, enabled us to completely field-test and update our original work as well as to research and present new findings. Sincere thanks to our hundreds of students and in particular, those who worked with us from the beginning—Pam and Charlie Watson, Roberta and Ray Wisniewski, and Eric Mustonen. Co-instructor Bill Howell has not only provided invaluable information but has also modeled a highly effective style of presenting this information. Sincere thanks to Jim Dice, plant ecologist from the California Dept. of Fish and Game, for reviewing the plant list in the Appendix. We are also thankful to cartographer Casey Cook, intern from the Geography Department of San Diego State University, who updated and computerized our maps.

Similar to our sentiments of twenty years ago, we deeply appreciate the contribution of Wilderness Press staff to our success. Editor Tom Winnett remains the mentor emeritus of rigorous field work, careful research, and precise verbal expression. Publisher Caroline Winnett has helped to insure that our final work matches the interests and needs of our readers.

Finally, as we shared at his memorial service this year, thanks again to George Leetch. It was he who, at our first encounter with the desert in 1967, let us know loud and clear that jeep tires weren't for running over his desert plant friends. If our subsequent work has contributed to saving some of his friends, then we're on the right track.

—*Diana and Lowell Lindsay*
San Diego, California
October 18, 1998

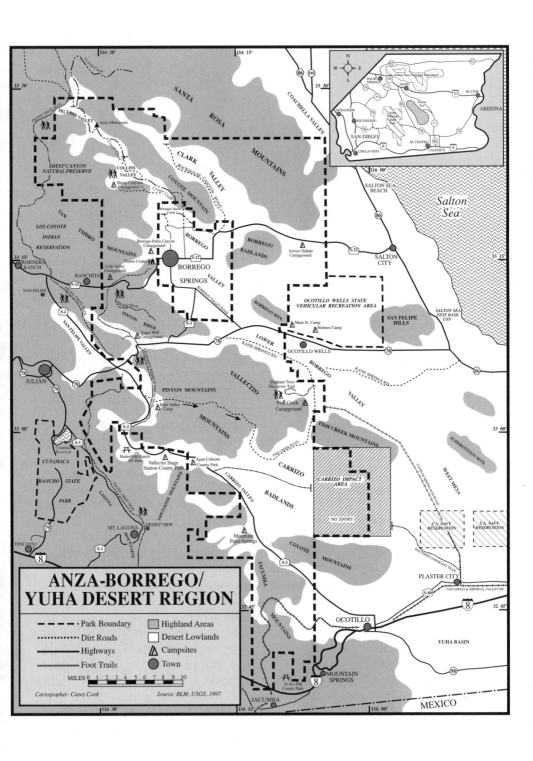

ANZA-BORREGO/
YUHA DESERT REGION

- - - Park Boundary   Highland Areas
.... Dirt Roads   Desert Lowlands
——— Highways   Campsites
∞∞∞∞∞ Foot Trails   Town

MILES 0 1 2 3 4 5 6 7 8 9 10

Cartographer: Casey Cook   Source: BLM, USGS, 1997

CHAPTER 1
Areas, Access, and Outdoor Activities

The Anza-Borrego and Western Colorado Desert region is a vast and intriguing land covering much of San Diego County and parts of Riverside and Imperial counties from the Coachella Valley to the Mexican border. From prehistoric Native Americans through weekend vacationers, people have called this desert home, some for all of their lives, others for some part of their lives. From piney mountain crags to a windy inland sea, a rich variety of desert plants and animals dwell in habitats as different as their inhabitants.

In some one million acres or sixteen hundred square miles, this region appeals to a broad range of visitors. Recreationists include off-highway vehicle explorers, backpackers, hikers, equestrians, mountain bikers, nature seekers and campers. Researchers and students in the natural and cultural sciences span the gamut from archaeology to zoology. This desert region is within two to three hours' travel time from most major population centers of southern California, especially the three million souls of San Diego County.

The name "Anza-Borrego" symbolizes the relationship of people and the natural environment in the deserts of the California borderlands. Juan Bautista de Anza was the Spanish captain of the epic 1775-76 San Francisco colonial expedition which passed through the region. *Borrego* is Spanish for sheep, and the peninsular bighorn sheep is the very symbol of desert mountain wilderness in the Californias. Geologist William Phipps Blake, of the U.S. Pacific Railroad Survey (1853), named the entire area for "the desert bordering the Great Colorado of the West," referring to the watershed area of the lower Colorado River and Salton Basin. The Colorado Desert portion of the Sonoran Desert occupies part of four states: Alta California, Arizona, Baja California, and Sonora.

This book is a guide to the county, state, and federal public lands of the Western Colorado Desert that are west of the Salton Sea and New River, north of the international border, east of the Peninsular Ranges crest, and south of the Santa Rosa Mountains National Recreation Area in Riverside County. These are almost the exact boundaries foreseen early in the 20th century, by a group of prominent San Diegans, for a million-acre public park that was even considered for U.S. National Park status in 1936.

Seven decades later, this desert regional preserve exists, albeit under several public land stewards. The California Department of Parks and Recreation (CDPR) manages about two-thirds of it in the 620,000-acre Anza-Borrego Desert State Park (ABDSP) and the ultimate 75,000-acre Ocotillo Wells State Vehicular Recreation Area (OWSVRA). Most of the remaining third is administered by the U.S. Bureau of Land Management (BLM). This third, in the 1975 BLM Management Plan, was named the Yuha Desert Planning Unit, and it shows on current USGS maps as "Yuha Desert Recreation Lands." BLM today applies the term "Yuha Desert" specifically to the 41,000-acre Yuha Basin south of old Highway 80. Other BLM areas in the region include the Jacumba Wilderness, the Elliott Mine area and Table Mountain of southeast San Diego County, Coyote Mountains Wilderness, West Mesa, Fish Creek Mountains Wilderness, Superstition Mountain, San Sebastian Marsh, and San Felipe Hills. Additional public land managers in the region include the San Diego County Parks Department and the U.S. Forest Service. Adjacent BLM areas to the west will be included in a future edition of this guidebook including McCain Valley, the Carrizo Gorge Wilderness, and the Sawtooth Mountains Wilderness.

In defining and describing the region covered by this guidebook, two terms are used synonymously: "The Anza-Borrego and Yuha Desert Region" or "The Anza-Borrego and Western Colorado Desert Region." The former is shorter and snappier; the latter is geographically and administratively more correct, especially from a BLM perspective, which considers the Western Colorado Desert Ecosystem to extend east to the Chocolate Mountains.

Anza-Borrego Desert State Park (ABDSP), containing 386,000 acres of state wilderness "where man himself is a visitor who does not remain," includes almost 1,000 square miles. It is California's largest state park, the nation's largest desert state park, and one of the very largest parks in North America. Combined with adjacent BLM wilderness areas totaling about 100,000 acres, this is a vast natural laboratory for research and wilderness values in which human impact is minimized in a 750-square-mile nearly contiguous desert and desert mountain preserve.

Little known to most, there are three piney, montane areas in the western portion of this region, all of which are portions of designated wildernesses, and two of which are traversed by the Pacific Crest Trail. The northwest montane area crests over 6000' at Combs Peak on Bucksnort Mountain. The central montane area rises to over a mile high, reaching the Sunrise Highway in the Laguna Mountains. The southern montane area centers on 4040' Table Mountain near Jacumba.

DIVISION OF THE REGION INTO SEVEN AREAS

This guide to the Anza-Borrego and Western Colorado Desert region is organized into seven areas, each of which is aligned along the major corridor of travel through the area. These areas are roughly equivalent to ranger patrol sectors of the public land management agencies. The agencies include ABDSP in eastern San Diego County and a portion of Riverside County, BLM areas in western Imperial County and a corner of southeast San Diego County, and OWSVRA, which straddles the county line. (References to "county line" alone throughout this book refer to San Diego and Imperial counties. Other county lines will always be specified.) The designations of the seven areas (e.g., Southeastern, Western, Central) derive from their relative positions in the region as defined above, with Harper Flat in the Vallecito Mountains being the center of the defined region.)

Trips are numbered according to their area. Points of interest, un-numbered side trips, and hikes are described when reached en route. The major trip through the area corridor of travel, generally the only paved road,is listed first as Trip "#A" with numbered branch trips following (e.g., AREA 4—CENTRAL: Trip 4A—Hwy 78, Trip 4B—Grapevine Canyon.) The trip titling standard is "from-to-via" (from an origin to a destination via a route).

Paved roads, dirt roads, 4WD roads and trails, and riding/hiking trails and routes are portrayed as integrated route elements of a whole region rather than as separate segments by mode of travel. The concept is that a typical desert explorer may drive along a paved road, transition to a dirt road, go into 4WD on a jeep trail, reach a trailhead and then hike from there. (See Appendix 3 for trips displayed by mode of travel: auto, 4WD, nature walk, hike, mountain bike, horse.) It also recognizes that visitors are less concerned with land management boundaries than they are with getting from point A to point B.

Route narratives are aligned to match the prevailing direction of travel of most visitors: generally west to east, north to south. Visitors typically travel east or southeast from the urban areas of San Diego and Los Angeles, explore a while, and then return home expeditiously. Wherever choices had to be made in order to classify a trip, the prime criterion was the perspective of most of the visitors along a particular route. For example, although Pinyon Mountain Road and upper Fish Creek through Split Mountain can be done from west to east, few are so inclined or even able. The Squeeze and the Pinyon Mountain Dropoff preclude all but the boldest and best equipped off-highway drivers and mountain bikers. So upper Fish Creek and Harper Flat are treated in Area 5 (Eastern), accessible from Split Mountain, rather than Area 6 (Southwestern), accessible from Hwy S-2.

CLASSIFICATION OF PUBLIC LANDS

Public-land managers use varying terms to describe vehicle access and usage in their units and areas of responsibility. Here is an overview, ranked from emphasis on resource protection to emphasis on multiple use. See the Desert Citizenship section for rules and regulations on vehicle access. Contact rangers for details on the area of your choice (see Desert Directory).

Closed Area: This classification ranges from Carrizo Impact Area (absolutely no public access) to a BLM ACEC, such as San Sebastian Marsh (closed to vehicles, open to hikers).

Wilderness Area: This classification is closed to vehicles, generally open to hikers, although seasonal closures may apply (e.g., Coyote Canyon in ABDSP is closed to all access in the summer season).

ABDSP nonwilderness and BLM Limited Access areas: These classifications make up the majority of vehicle routes in the region. Vehicle travel is OK on established paved and dirt roadways (ABDSP) and approved Routes of Travel (BLM). No cross-country vehicle travel allowed. An unusual example of an approved route of travel through a Closed Area is the service road paralleling the U.S. Gypsum railroad. Mountain bikes are treated the same as other vehicles with some rare exceptions by management decision (e.g., Middle Willows in Coyote Canyon OK for bike but not motor vehicle.) Some BLM closed routes to vehicles may be open to bikes.) Again, check with your local ranger for details.

OWSVRA or BLM Open Area: Legal vehicle travel generally unrestricted including non-street-legal "green sticker" vehicles.

CLASSIFICATION BY ROUTE CONDITION

The route condition for a trip is classified according to the most difficult portion of the road or trail along that route. **THESE ARE APPROXIMATIONS ONLY** because conditions change constantly due to flash floods,mud and rock slides, growth of vegetation, and road work by jeep clubs. What is passable by family car today may be jeep-only tomorrow. Contact ABDSP visitor center, OWSVRA headquarters, BLM El Centro, or rangers for latest information. (See Desert Directory Appendix 2.)

Routes are described in this guidebook as follows:

Paved or dirt road—generally passable by conventional auto and recreational vehicles (RVs). "Truck trail" is an old term which indicates dirt roads suitable for light trucks or 4WD.

4WD road or route—generally passable by off-highway vehicle (OHV), four-wheel-drive (4WD) vehicles and mountain bicycle. Off-road vehicle (ORV), Jeep, 4WD, sport utility vehicles (SUVs) and "sport utes" are generally synonymous terms.

Horse trails—no vehicles. Only Coyote Canyon has designated horse trails in this desert region. (Adjacent Cuyamaca Rancho State Park has an extensive horse trail system.)

Hiking trail or route—foot travel only. While nature walks and some hikes are maintained and posted (signed), most in this region are cross-country routes requiring land navigation skills. (See Chapter 3 on topographic map, compass, and GPS/UTM use.)

MILEAGE SYSTEM FOR ROAD AND TRAIL NARRATIVES

Roadway checkpoints are referenced in either of two ways: conventional cumulative odometer mileages and the "post mile" system, used by public highway and safety agencies. The post mile system is an external reference and is absolute for all users. The odometer method is an internal reference and is relative to one's own journey. Each has its advantages.

Although the odometer system requires no new learning, few odometers agree exactly and even the same one will vary from time to time due to ambient conditions, tire inflation, road surface, and weather effects. This is especially true on dirt roads, where sand and mud traps induce variations. On the other hand, dirt roads have no post mile markers so odometer references are necessary.

"Post mile" refers to the actual mileage of a checkpoint from a designated mile zero when the highway was constructed. This mile zero is generally a county line or the beginning of the numbered highway. Post miles generally increase northward and eastward. County Hwy S-2 is a good example. Although it trends southeastward, it is numbered with miles increasing to the east from its origin at Warner Junction (Hwys S-2 and 78) to post mile 56.5 at the San Diego/Imperial County line. There it returns to zero, increasing to post mile 8 in Ocotillo.

Be clear that a given "post mile" is not the same as a "post mile marker". Every point on a highway is a certain *post mile* or fraction thereof. A *post mile marker* is a physical object that displays the post mile number. (The informal but common term "mile post" is synonymous with the formal term "post mile marker.") Baja travelers are far more familiar than U.S. travelers with the concept of fixed distance markers because of the ubiquitous kilometer posts on all paved roads. (Be patient—the U.S. is trying to catch up.)

Be aware also that realignment, shortening or lengthening of a highway does not change post mileages along the entire highway. The letter "R" is added only to the affected post mile marker(s) to indicate a realignment. Such realignments, rare in the Anza-Borrego region, are of little consequence in using post miles to locate checkpoints.

Post miles are portrayed on a variety of objects such as post mile marker signs ("paddle-board markers"), labels on bridges, and signs on emergency telephone call boxes. Many San Diego County highways, especially in rural recreational areas such as the Laguna Mountains and Anza-Borrego Desert State Park, are very clearly posted with large green post mile markers. State highways are posted with vertical white paddle-shaped markers which give the highway name, county code, and post mileage, generally every half mile.

Call boxes are the most standardized of all post mile markers and are now found on almost all freeways and major rural highways every one or two miles. Numbers on the call-box sign give the post mile as follows: the lower left number is the highway number. A hyphen separates this from the lower right number, which is the post mile to one-tenth of a mile. (Note: You must add the decimal point to this post mile display.) Example: 8-685 means Interstate 8, post mile 68.5 miles east from mile zero at Mission Bay; 78-790 means State Highway 78, post mile 79.0 east from mile zero in Oceanside; 5-5 means Interstate 5, post mile 0.5 mile north from mile zero at the international border.

In this guide stated mileages have been carefully calculated on the basis of several sources, including topographic, BLM, state-park and auto-club maps, and multiple transits of each route by the authors. However, off-highway travelers should continually cross-check map, guidebook, odometer, and compass references with the terrain. Cardinal points of the compass are generally used instead of "left" and "right" to eliminate confusion on approach directions. Be sure to reverse any left-right designations when proceeding in the opposite direction from that logged herein.

Lacking signs, hiking-trail and cross-country checkpoints are best given in terms of prominent terrain features, elevations, map and compass fixes, sectional references on topographic maps, or GPS readings in conjunction with a UTM grid on a topo map. UTM and Latitude/Longitude (Lat/Lon) fixes are offered for almost all historical monuments to give users a chance to practice using the GPS system in a safe environment before venturing off-highway or into the wilderness.

CAMPING IN THE REGION

There are several kinds of camping in the region: developed public and private campgrounds including RV parks, group camps (Borrego Palm Canyon and Vallecito County Park), a horse camp (Coyote Canyon), backcountry or primitive campgrounds, and open campsites. The latter type of camping is an exception in public parks and the fact that it is permitted in ABDSP is dependent upon continued good outdoor-citizenship practices of visitors. See the Desert Citizenship section below for rules and regulations on camping and vehicle use off-highway. All of OWSVRA and BLM public land is open camping, unless posted closed.

Elevations are given throughout this book as guides for seasonal trip planning. Only the hard-core desert rat and the fully prepared camper should plan campsites below 2000' from July through September. Peak-use desert season is considered to be November through April. Flash floods tend to occur in August and September. Rain, if any, tends to be November through February. The peak of the wildflower season, if any, tends to be March for low desert and is progressively later as elevations increase through June for high desert and mountains.

Developed Campgrounds

See Desert Directory in Appendix 2 for reservation phone numbers. Fees for individual sites range from $10 to $25 depending on services, season, and distance from town. There is surprisingly little difference in price between private and public campgrounds. In addition to the listings below, many motels offer RV camping, some with hookups.

Developed Campgrounds in Borrego Valley

ABDSP Borrego Palm Canyon (elev. 775') 2.5 miles west of Borrego Springs just off Hwy S-22. 117 individual sites including 52 RV hookup sites (no tents), each site maximum 8 people. Five group sites (no RVs), each maximum 24 people, youth group minimum is one supervising adult per 12 campers. Drinking water, telephone, restrooms with showers, picnic tables, shade ramadas, seasonal campfire programs, nature trail, one mile northwest from

Borrego Palm Canyon campground entrance

park headquarters and visitor center. During the winter-spring season, reservations are a must, far ahead.

Palm Canyon Resort (elev. 790') On Hwy S-22 in west Borrego Springs. 40 RV sites with hookups. Store, restaurant, laundromat, swimming pools and jacuzzis. Drinking water, telephone, restrooms with showers, picnic tables, shade ramadas, seasonal campfire programs, 1/2 mile from park headquarters and visitor center.

ABDSP Vernon Whitaker Horse Camp (elev. 960') About 8 miles north of Borrego Springs off Henderson Canyon Rd. 10 individual sites (equestrians only), RVs must be self-contained, each site maximum 8 people, 4 horses. 40 corrals, drinking water, restrooms with showers, picnic tables, many miles of horse trails in Coyote Canyon, Collins Valley, Fig Tree Valley. See the Desert Citizenship section for rules and regulations on horseback riding.

Developed Campgrounds Along Hwy S-2

Banner Store and Recreation Ranch (elev. 2,755') On Hwy 78 between Julian and Hwy S-2, about 5 miles west of Scissors Crossing. Tents and RVs. Oak-shaded campgrounds. RV sites with hookups, tent sites. Store, fuel, telephone. Drinking water, restrooms, picnic tables. Good base to explore Chariot and Rodriguez canyons mining area.

Stagecoach Trail RV Resort (elev. 2,304') On Hwy S-2 4 miles southeast of Scissors Crossing in Shelter Valley. RVs and tents. Store. Drinking water, restrooms with showers, picnic tables, shade ramadas. Pacific Crest Trail (PCT) passes nearby. A higher, cooler elevation than the low desert.

Butterfield Ranch (2,040') On Hwy S-2 about 13 miles southeast of Scissors Crossing. 300 RV sites with hookups, 200 tent sites. Store and fuel, restaurant, laundromat. Drinking water, restrooms with showers, picnic tables, shade ramadas, swimming pool and jacuzzi, duck pond, playground.

Vallecito Regional Park (elev. 1,600') On Hwy S-2 about 18 miles southeast of Scissors Crossing. 44 individual sites, RVs must be self-contained. Drinking water, restrooms, playground, picnic tables, shade ramadas, seasonal campfire programs, picnic area with tables. Group site (tents only), maximum capacity 45 campers. Closed July-September. Restored site of Butterfield Stage Station, active 1858-1861.

Agua Caliente Regional Park (elev. 1,350') On Hwy S-2 about 21 miles southeast of Scissors Crossing. 104 RV hookup sites, 36 campsites. Drinking water, restrooms with showers, picnic tables,shade ramadas, seasonal campfire programs, indoor mineral bath and an outdoor wading pool. Store, paved air strip. Pets are not permitted at Agua Caliente.

ABDSP Bow Willow (elev. 950') On Hwy S-2 31 miles southeast of Scissors Crossing. 16 individual sites, RVs must be self-contained, each site maximum 8 people. Drinking water, chemical toilets, picnic tables, shade ramadas, 55 miles from park headquarters.

Developed Campgrounds In The Central And East Hwy 78 Area

ABDSP Tamarisk Grove (elev. 1,400') Near intersection of Hwys 78 and S-3 Yaqui Pass Road. 27 individual sites, RVs must be self-contained, each site maximum 8 people. Drinking water, restrooms with showers, picnic tables, shade ramadas, seasonal campfire programs, nature trail, 13 miles from park headquarters.

Desert Ironwoods RV Park and Motel (elev. 454') On Highway 78 about 3 miles west of Ocotillo Wells and OWSVRA. 106 RV sites with hookups, tent sites. Motel, store, laundromat, swimming pool, telephone, picnic tables.

Split Mountain Park and Country Store (elev. 400') On Split Mountain Rd about 1 mile south of Hwy 78. 50 RV sites. Store, laundromat, swimming pool, telephone, picnic tables.

Leapin' Lizard RV Ranch (elev. 400') On Split Mountain Rd about 1 mile south of Hwy 78 and west on Kunkler Rd. 60 RV sites w/hookups, many tree-shaded. Laundromat, pool and spa (new in 1998), picnic area, tiled restrooms w/showers.

Blu-In (elev. 26') On Hwy 78 between Ocotillo Wells and Trifolium (Hwy 86). 10 RV sites with hookups, tent sites. Supplies, cafe, drinking water, restrooms with showers, picnic tables.

Other RV Campgrounds In The Region

Salton City Spa & RV Park (elev. -87') At junction of Hwys 86 and S-22. 250 RV sites with hookups, no tents. Swimming pool and jacuzzi, mineral spa, sauna, restrooms with showers, laundromat, tennis courts, playground, cable TV and store.

Rio Bend RV Resort Ranch (elev. -50') At Drew Road offramp from I-8 at Seeley, 7 miles west of El Centro on the New River. 230 RV sites with hookups.

Swimming pool and jacuzzi, restrooms with showers, laundromat, sport facilities, cable TV and store, fishing lakes. Good base to explore Yuha Desert and Superstition Mountain.

Kamp Anza RV Resort (elev. 4,100') About 3 miles southeast of Anza, which is on Hwy 371. Good base to explore northern Coyote Canyon and the northern mountain areas of ABDSP along the PCT. 106 tent or RV sites, many with hookups. Swimming pool and jacuzzi, restrooms with showers, laundromat, sport facilities, store, fishing pond.

Backcountry (Primitive) Campgrounds

Backcountry (formerly called primitive) campgrounds are long-established sites that are scattered throughout ABDSP and OWSVRA in areas of high visitation. A few have pit or chemical toilets. None have water or trash cans (therefore please "pack it in, pack it out"—that goes for toilet paper too). Park use fee applies in ABDSP. Reservations not available, first-come first-served, although most have a very lot of lebensraum.

Culp Valley (3,400') On Hwy S-22 between Ranchita and Borrego Springs. 10 miles from park HQ. Accommodates RVs. Good option for hot weather.

Sheep Canyon (1,500') In Collins Valley area of Coyote Canyon. Pit toilets, picnic tables, shade ramadas. 14 miles from park HQ. Rugged 4WD road up Lower Willows Bypass, which has eaten many vehicles. Ideal for riders and hikers.

Arroyo Salado (880') On Hwy S-22 between Borrego Springs and Salton City. 19 miles from park HQ. RVs beware of sand traps.

Yaqui Pass (1,730') On Hwy S-3 between Hwy 78 and Borrego Springs. 12 miles from park HQ. Accommodates RVs. Good option when Borrego Palm Canyon is full.

Yaqui Well (1,400') Just west of the junction of Hwys 78 and S-3, Yaqui Pass Rd. Pit toilets. RVs beware of sand traps. Light RVs only recommended. Nature trail. 13 miles from park HQ. Good option when Tamarisk Grove is full.

OWSVRA The Quarry and Main St. (elev. 170') In the lee of East Butte, Borrego Mountain, northwest of Ocotillo Wells (Hwy 78). Chemical toilets, shade ramadas, fire rings.

OWSVRA Holmes Camp (elev. 176') About 1.5 miles east of Ocotillo Wells and just north of Hwy 78 via Wolfe Well Rd. Chemical toilets, shade ramadas, fire rings.

Fish Creek (280') Off Hwy 78, south of Ocotillo Wells. Some picnic tables, fire rings. 30 miles from park HQ. Light RVs only recommended; beware of sand traps.

Blair Valley (2,500') Off Hwy S-2 about 7 miles southeast of Scissors Crossing (Hwys 78 and S-2). 32 miles from park HQ. A huge, sheltered area that accommodates RVs and large groups.

Mountain Palm Springs (760') Off Hwy S-2 about 25 miles southeast of Scissors Crossing (Hwys 78 and S-2). Accommodates RVs. Chemical toilets. 54 miles from park HQ.

OUTDOOR ADVENTURE AND NATURAL HISTORY IN THE REGION

The table of Recommended Trips by Mode of Travel in Appendix 3 tabulates the following information into: nature walks, trail hikes, cross-country hikes, backpacks, horseback routes, mountain bike routes and motor vehicle trips via paved road, dirt road, or 4WD road.

The following walks and hikes are suggested in state park and BLM literature and are all described in this guidebook (see table of contents and index). These and other walks, hikes, and backpacks are marked by symbol in this guidebook.

Borrego Palm Canyon Area: BPC Nature Trail, Panoramic Overlook Trail, Visitor Center Trail, Hellhole Canyon/Maidenhair Falls Trail.

Coyote Canyon and Borrego Badlands: Alcoholic Pass, Truckhaven Rocks, Calcite Mine.

Culp Valley Area: Pena Spring, Lookout Point, California Riding and Hiking Trail (Hellhole/Dry Canyon Ridge Trail).

Tamarisk Grove Area: Cactus Loop Trail, Yaqui Well Nature Trail, Bill Kenyon Overlook, Narrows Earth Trail.

Split Mountain Area: Elephant Trees Discovery Trail, Wind Caves Trail,

Blair Valley Area: Ghost Mountain (Marshal South Home/Yaquitepec), Morteros Trail, Pictograph/Smugglers Canyon, Oriflamme Canyon.

Agua Caliente Hot Springs: Moonlight Trail, Desert Overlook Trail.

Bow Willow Area: Pygmy Grove, Southwest Grove, Mary's Bowl Grove, Palm Bowl.

Jacumba Wilderness: Smugglers Cave, Elliott Mine, Valley of the Moon, Boulder Canyon, Davies Valley, Skull Valley.

Nature Walks and Interpretive Services

The nature walks noted in the Table of Recommended Trips includes not only those which are self-guiding via signs or brochures (e.g., The Narrows Earth Trail) but also those which have exceptional value as natural or historical sites (e.g., Pena Spring in Culp Valley and San Sebastian Marsh). The detailed Borrego Palm Canyon narrative in Area 1 describes many common desert plants and features that apply broadly throughout the region. Most visitors start their first tour of the Anza-Borrego Desert in Borrego Palm Canyon.

A full array of interpretive services are offered by the various public land managers and public service organizations in the region. The ABDSP visitor center (the "VC") is the hub of these activities for the park. It is open from 9 a.m. to 5 p.m. daily except during the summer months, when it is weekends-only. It offers exhibits, displays, and a book store with many naturalist talks and walks from there.

The ranger station in OWSVRA provides similar services for that area while the Imperial Valley College Museum (IVCM) is being developed in Ocotillo to service the southern desert area. The San Diego Natural History Museum (SDNHM) in Balboa Park has a decades-long presence in this region and offers both permanent and rotating desert exhibits as well as an extensive field trip selection. In addition, the SDNHM Canyoneers conduct guided nature walks and hikes in Anza-Borrego and the Yuha Desert region. Community colleges

Visitor Center

such as Grossmont offer similar programs. See the Desert Directory in the Appendix for contact information.

All interpretive monuments and markers in the region are listed by name at their respective checkpoints in the text of this guidebook. In some cases, particularly pertinent information on the marker is repeated in italics in the text. Italics are also used to quote relevant citations.

Hiking and Backpacking

The Table of Recommended Trips includes: nature walks (discussed above), trail hikes, cross-country hikes, and backpack routes. All of these are indicated in the text of this guidebook with a "hiker" symbol. Trail hikes are those on developed trails or, in many cases, closed or abandoned 4WD routes that are now dedicated to hiking. Cross-country hikes comprise the majority of opportunities for foot travel in the region. These require a higher level of preparation, fitness, and land navigation skills.

This book does not recommend hikes and backpacks on dirt roads and 4WD routes that are used by motor vehicles. This particularly applies to long trudges in sandy washes where a passing jeep cavalcade is fun only for the wheelies. There's such an offering of hiking trails and cross-country routes available— why mix it up with the sport utes? Walk the stream sides, canyons and ridges that the ute can only pine for.

Backpacking in this region is a form of cross-country hiking, requiring similar expertise and additional knowledge of backcountry campcraft. Almost all backpacks recommended herein are in the Coyote Canyon area or in the

Borrego Valley west-side canyons where water is available. A popular introductory desert backpack for groups is Hellhole Canyon from the staging area
on Hwy S-22 between mile markers 16 and 17. (Be aware that the frequency of
mountain lion contact has increased here in recent years.) Another popular
backpack is Borrego Palm Canyon. A few other backpacks are suggested in the
Santa Rosas where sparse water supplies may be available.

Additional backpacking opportunities exist in BLM Wilderness areas
including the Fish Creek Mountains, Carrizo Gorge, Coyote Mountains,
Sawtooth Mountains, and the Jacumba Mountains, Davies Valley being a particular feature of the latter.

The serious challenge of exposure to wind and sun plus water deficit is discussed at length in the "How To and What Not" section below. Sadly, there is
barely a season that goes by without one or more fatalities in the western
Colorado Desert region directly related to violations of exposure and water
rules. These rules apply just as surely to casual nature walks as to backcountry
treks. In summary, carry and drink way more water than you think you need,
up to a gallon per person per day. (Actual need for water varies greatly
between individuals. More than a gallon per day may be needed.) Tank up like
a camel before the trek and drink often en route. Be sure that others in your
party are doing the same. Sun and wind protection is provided by brimmed
hats, abundant lotion, and light, loose, layered clothing. Wear sturdy footwear
for protection from rough terrain and cactus spines. Tell somebody responsible
where you are going and when you will return. Make phone contact with that
person as soon as possible after the trek.

Horseback Riding

Thanks substantially to volunteer Vern Whitaker, Anza-Borrego is now a
popular destination for equestrians. Originating from Horse Camp, many
miles of designated horse-only trails now thread Coyote Canyon. See Camping
section above for horse camp information and the Desert Citizenship section
below for rules and regulations on horseback riding in the park. Private stables
in Borrego Springs also offer riding opportunities. Contact the Chamber of
Commerce (see Appendix 2).

Mountain Biking and Recommended Routes

As rapidly as the 4WD phenomenon burst forth in the early 1970s, so did
mountain biking in the latter 1980s. Bicycles are regulated by the vehicle code
and must follow the same access rules as motor vehicles. This specifically
means that bikes are allowed on established paved and dirt roadways within
ABDSP (some 500 miles worth) and on approved routes of travel in BLM areas
(hundreds more miles). What bikes don't have to be, is licensed or registered.
What they can't do is the same any off-roader shouldn't do: make new vehicle
routes or re-open closed routes. This includes paralleling an existing route in
search of firmer ground.

The primary guideline for cyclists is to use roads that are posted (signed) on
either ABDSP or BLM land. Wilderness areas are, of course, completely closed

to all vehicles including bicycles. Conversely, access rules are minimal in OWSVRA and BLM Open Areas. Adjacent Cuyamaca Rancho State Park has an excellent system of mountain bike routes including several from which where motor vehicles are excluded.

The table of Recommended Trips in Appendix 3 lists dozens of routes suitable for mountain bikes in the region, all of which have been ridden by the authors. These are generally 4WD routes that avoid deep sand in washes, the latter being a nemesis for bikers.

The following routes are recommended for mountain bike treks. Don't forget that these are shared with 4WD vehicles. Use caution. See road narratives for mileage and details:

Hwy S-22 west: Jasper Trail/Grapevine Canyon—Be wary of upward-bound 4WD traffic on the steep, tight curves of Jasper south of the "four-way" junction with Old Culp Valley Road.

Borrego Valley north: Coyote Canyon—Any or all of the dirt road/4WD route is serene. Much of it parallels the creek. The 3.1-mile vehicle-closed portion between Middle and Upper Willows is open to cyclists by park management directive.

Hwy S-22 east: Clark Valley to Rockhouse Canyon—Generally hardpack dirt, although there are sand traps near Alcoholic Pass. Bikes can travel farther toward the roadhead than most, even gnarley vehicles.

Hwy S-22 east: Thimble Trail/Short Wash—Generally hardpack dirt in the Borrego Badland highlands, although sand may require some walking out in Fonts Point Wash or Palo Verde Wash. Fonts Point and Vista del Malpais—sometimes uncomfortable riding in soft sand, other times OK. Try it but be prepared to divert to a nearby option.

Hwy S-22 east: Calcite Mine—Another case of bikes able to go where jeeps should fear to tread. A steeply pitched washout is no problem for a bike.

Hwy 86 north: Wonderstone Wash—Have plenty of water and permission from the quarry operator. Otherwise a rocky but hardpacked route.

Borrego Valley south: Glorietta Canyon—A good sundowner if you're based in Borrego Valley.

Hwy 78 central: Old Borrego Valley Road—After lunching in Nude Wash, take this somewhat sandy loop back into Borrego Valley.

Hwy 78 central: Borrego Mountain—Good hardpack in the uplands but avoid dropping into the very sandy San Felipe Wash. Explore the overlook, Buttes Pass, Hawk Canyon, and Goat Trail down to the OWSVRA ranger station.

Hwy 78 east: Harper Flat/Pinyon Mtns—Carry the bike on a 4WD vehicle to Hapaha Flat, then walk or ride the rugged, rarely traveled 4WD route up the Pinyon Mtn dropoff to serene Pinyon Valley. Exit via an idyllic dirt descent to Hwy S-2 in Earthquake (Shelter) Valley.

Hwy 78 east: San Felipe Hills—Travel the Pole Line Road and explore Artesian Well and the Gas Domes.

Hwy S-2: Blair and Little Blair valleys—Classic, fairly flat introductory mountain biking with many points of interest.

Hwy S-2: Oriflamme/Chariot/Rodriguez Canyons loop—steep climbing 2,000' but good loop ride, or exit to a pickup at Banner, Hwy 78.

I-8: Table Mtn—excellent network of old mining roads in rarely biked corner of San Diego County. 3,500' elevation cooler than deserts.

I-8: Elliott Mine Area—take a 4WD route to the saddle and then ride the many loop trips and side routes of this fascinating area. Hike to Smugglers Cave or into Valley of the Moon.

I-8: Painted Gorge—Hardpack dirt into colorful area with little elevation gain. From Coyote Wash, interesting route works west to Fossil/Shell Canyon.

Hwy 94: Yuha Rim/Geoglyphs—Good hardpack dirt all around the rim. Avoid dropping into sandy washes of Yuha Basin.

ABBREVIATIONS USED IN THIS BOOK

Abbreviations, unless obvious, will be defined when first introduced in the text. Abbreviations found herein but not included below are used only once and defined. Public land managers may have specific definitions for terms that vary between agencies. Check with rangers for regulations in your area of interest.

ABDNHA	Anza-Borrego Desert Natural History Association
ABDSP	Anza-Borrego Desert State Park
ABF	Anza-Borrego Foundation (a non-profit land trust)
ACEC	Area of Critical Environmental Concern (BLM)
AVE	Avenue
BM	Bench Mark (elevation)
BLM	U.S. Dept. of the Interior, Bureau of Land Management
CDCA	California Desert Conservation Area (BLM)
CDPA	California Desert Protection Act, 1994 (BLM)
CDFG	California Dept. of Fish and Game
CDPR	California Dept. of Parks and Recreation
CDMG	California Dept. of Conservation, Division of Mines and Geology
CDOG	California Division of Oil, Gas and Geothermal Resources
CDF	California Dept. of Forestry
CRHT	California Riding and Hiking Trail
DAG	Desert Access Guide (BLM map series)
GPS	Global Positioning System
HWY	Highway, generally paved and numbered
IVC(M)	Imperial Valley College (Museum)
LACM	Los Angeles County Museum
LAT, LON	Latitude and Longitude
MVTT	Mason Valley Truck Trail
OWSVRA	Ocotillo Wells State Vehicular Recreation Area
PCT	Pacific Crest Trail
RT	Route, generally 4WD very rough
RD	Road, generally dirt or 4WD required
SJFZ	San Jacinto fault zone, also

SAFZ	San Andreas, EFZ Elsinore
SDAG	San Diego Association of Geologists
SCGS	South Coast Geological Society
SDNHM	San Diego Natural History Museum
SDSU	San Diego State University
SVRA	State Vehicular Recreation Area
UCSD	University of California, San Diego
USNPS	U.S. Dept. of the Interior, National Park Service
USD	University of San Diego
USGS	U.S. Dept. of the Interior, Geological Survey
UTM	Universal Transverse Mercator (map grid system)
VC	ABDSP Visitor Center

CHAPTER 2

How-tos and What-Nots of Desert Exploring

PRE-TRIP PREPARATION

For there are two deserts: One is a grim desolate wasteland. It is the home of venomous reptiles and stinging insects, of vicious thorn-covered plants and trees and unbearable heat...visualized by those children of luxury to whom any environment is intolerable which does not provide all the comforts and luxuries of a pampering civilization.

The other desert—the real desert—is not for the eyes of the superficial observer or the fearful soul of the cynic. It is a land which reveals its true character only to those who come with courage, tolerance, and understanding. For those the desert holds rare gifts.
—Randall Henderson, *On Desert Trails*

For those who would seek "the real desert" in the Anza-Borrego region, the following pages cover the basics of what to do and what not to do out there, by vehicle and afoot, in camp and on the trail.

Telephone, write or personally visit public-land personnel to determine current conditions in the area you will visit, including weather conditions, road and route conditions, latest entry regulations for vehicle, fire hazard, recommended camping, availability and potability of water. (See Desert Directory in Appendix 2.)

Let somebody know where you are going, what you are going to do there, and when you will return. Be sure it is someone who would notice that you were overdue and would notify the proper authorities. This is particularly true of backpacking trips. Backpack permits are required for Borrego Palm Canyon.

Note: If you tell BLM or park rangers that you will check out with them at the end of your trip, be sure you do. If officers or contact stations are closed when you come out, leave a note, well anchored, in a prominent place nearby.

Good luck and happy adventuring in the Anza-Borrego!

VEHICLE SAVVY

Unlike many mountain, forest and beach recreation areas, the desert allows the motorist to reach remote areas far from well-traveled roads and concentrations of people. The allure of the desert wilderness, however, can lead to a situation wherein a simple mechanical problem may be compounded into a serious, life-threatening emergency. It is essential, therefore, that off-highway travelers be familiar with their machine, check and stock it well before their trip, be prepared to deal with the most common emergencies and breakdowns, and be experienced in sandy-wash, rocky-road and steep-slope driving.

Pre-trip preparation includes a thorough check of all systems (electrical, cooling, lubricating, fuel, brake and suspension) as well as main and spare tires. If maintenance work on anything is almost due, do it before the trip.

While on the trip, make a daily check of the following:

1. fluid levels in the battery, radiator, crankcase and automatic transmission;
2. condition of fan belts, coolant hoses, tires, oil pan, gas tank, springs, steering gear and engine mounts;
3. battery terminals (tight and free of corrosion);
4. mounting of accessories, including air cleaner, carburetor, generator, battery box, pumps;
5. no evidence of fresh oil, gas, coolant or transmission leaks.

Desert Driving Techniques

Beyond proper pre-trip planning, the single most important concern in desert off-roading is the possibility, even the probability, of getting stuck in sand, mud or soft dirt, or on high-centered ruts or on rocks. If possible, practice driving on such surfaces before the trip, with another vehicle standing by to tow as necessary.

If vehicle footing is at all uncertain, the minutes spent walking ahead to check it out may mean hours saved digging out. The same applies to turning around at a dead end or backing out a long stretch. When proceeding over a soft surface, gear down before entry. Then maintain adequate forward momentum, without letting the wheels spin. So long as the wheels are not spinning, you're not going to dig in. Be aware, however, that the lower the gear, the greater the likelihood of spinning. The trick is to achieve a balance between sufficient power and speed to get through and not so much that you lose traction. Partly deflated tires can increase traction, but don't deflate them so far as to cause the tire to slip on the rim. Building up a questionable route with rocks or hard earth may be more minutes spent wisely against the possibility of having to dig out later on. Avoid sudden motions of starting, stopping and turning.

Beware of your particular vehicle's clearance. Just because a route looks well traveled doesn't mean that your vehicle can make it. High centers, sharp angles of descent and ascent in washes, and rocks can hang up vehicles with low clearance, long overhangs, or long wheel bases. The difference between a little bobtail rig and a long, heavy pickup camper or motor home becomes painfully obvious on many off-road pitches.

Here too the advantage of posi-traction or limited-slip differential becomes significant. With a conventional differential, one stuck drive wheel will cause

Damage by jeep cavalcade

the other to spin freely, leading to dig-in. The limited slip tends to keep the other wheel driving should its mate get stuck.

But then comes the inevitable time(s) when the road wins, and your vehicle loses. You're stuck. The first action is no action. Rather than immediately trying to fight your way through and getting hopelessly stuck, get out and survey the problem. Generally you will want to plan your exit in reverse. Where you came from was clearly negotiable. Where you're going may not be. Dig away the sand or mud from in front of and behind the tires to form a ramp to harder ground. It will also be necessary to dig out for the differential, pans, and other low hangers underneath. If available, put rocks, blankets, carpets, chicken wire or whatever under the tires and on the exit route to improve traction. You may want to jack up the stuck wheels to get these materials beneath them. Brush may work too, as a last resort. First of all, it's illegal to destroy vegetation in any park or protected area, and second, that brush didn't grow there for the purpose of compensating for your lack of off-road expertise. Finally, nature may laugh last if the vegetation you use under wheel happens to have a thorny appetite for rubber.

Then you can either decide to rock back and forth between low gear and reverse, or move directly out in the selected direction. Slowly apply the gas and/or slowly engage the clutch to see if there's sufficient traction for the wheels to take hold without slipping. If so, continue moving out decisively, but not so fast as to start slipping. Continue to gain momentum until you reach firm ground. Don't get overconfident before you reach firm footing, or you'll be starting the whole process all over again.

Should none of this work, you have two choices: continue engineering the road for traction, and perhaps also deflate tires to 12-15 pounds, or wait for an assisting vehicle with rope or chain. In the latter case, there are three concerns: don't let the assist vehicle also get stuck during rescue; beware of possible parting of the line under tension and a vicious backlash; attach the line to firm structural points on both vehicles (which, for example, steering tie rods and VW bumpers are not). If you've deflated the tires, don't forget to reinflate them prior to hard-road or pavement travel.

Some final notes on off-roading:

1. Beware of side-slanting routes. A vehicle can easily negotiate a steep incline straight ahead, up or down, that would send it rolling should it get sideways. If you start sliding sideways, attempt to turn downhill if at all possible. Better to get stuck into the side of a dugway facing downward than to roll to the bottom.

2. Travel with at least one other vehicle in company.

3. Don't push beyond the limits of your vehicle to display your macho.

4. Obey the rules and regulations of the park and the BLM, which are based on common sense and on a sense of responsibility on the part of every desert visitor, to protect our remaining park lands and natural preserves for future generations.

5. Respect dry washes if there is any possibility of rain, even in far distant mountains. Many true tales are told of campers, cars and even settlements being swept to their ruin in what appeared to be a dry wash. Flash floods are just that. They don't give warning.

6. Speed, promptness and precise scheduling are required attributes of our urban world. When off-road, however, the only real deadline you have is to get out, safely. Mañana is soon enough if it means just being a few hours late rather than leaving behind a broken hulk of metal and rubber. Today's excellent suspension systems and tires mask the terrific beating that vehicles take when speeding along dirt roads or trails. You may not feel the damage being done by high-speed off-road travel, but your vehicle certainly does. And sooner or later it will inform you in no uncertain terms.

7. Always stop and walk ahead to survey any hazardous condition. Then plan your route to negotiate the section carefully.

8. Be considerate of fellow campers and desert people and wandering children, especially around campsites. Motorcycles and many of today's OHVs are extremely loud and unnerving when revved up. Nothing can shatter the pleasure of desert recreation faster than the blast of a tailpipe. Both ear damage and accidents have been caused by such sound pollution. What may be music to the ears of the driver is madness to the minds of others. Fifteen miles per hour is the absolute maximum speed around campsites.

Vehicle Equipment Checklist

The following checklist is adapted from the "What to take on the tour" section of the 1921 edition of the Automobile Green Book. Why not? The conditions of today's off-road travel are much the same as the conditions of yesterday's road touring. What grandpa knew about his horseless carriage is still good horse sense for grandson's off-roading.

Tool kit
- Set of wrenches (open, box, socket, and adjustable)
- Large and small screw drivers (including Phillips and slotted)
- Pliers (clamp, needle nose, channel, locking vice grips)
- Spotlight or trouble lamp, flashlight with spare bulb and batteries
- Wire cutters and tin snips
- Spade or collapsible shovel
- Crowbar
- Large hammer (when all else fails)

Tire and traction equipment
- At least one extra mounted and inflated spare tire in good condition (two extra are even better—it's almost impossible for the average motorist to repair today's tires)
- Air-pressure gauge
- Hand pump or engine pump
- Jack (at least one but two are better. One should be a bumper jack or "come along," which can substitute for a power winch)
- Tow chain or two-hooked nylon spring line
- Roll of chicken wire, flat boards, canvas strips, strip of carpet or any material to provide traction in soft sand
- Tire air jumper or canned compressed filter

Fuel, oil, coolant equipment
- 2- to 5-gallon can of spare gas
- 5 quarts of spare oil
- Minimum of 5 gallons of water for vehicle only (drinking and cooking water are in addition to this)
- Funnel
- Various cans of sealant, fuel treatment, oil conditioner, WD-40

Repair materials
- Bag of assorted nuts, bolts, lock washers, screws, cotter pins
- Electrical tape
- Assorted lengths and sizes of electrical wiring
- Cake of soap (to plug pan punctures)
- Assorted fuses and lamp bulbs
- Radiator hoses and hose clamps
- Spare set of keys
- Credit cards, checkbook, and spare cash (works when nothing else will)
- Portable radio and extra batteries (for latest weather in emergencies)

WEATHER, WATER AND PERSONAL EQUIPMENT

The special conditions of desert camping and travel include unexpected climate extremes, great sun and wind exposure, and a greater water need despite the smaller natural supply. The common view of the desert is that of a hot and dry place. The wise desert visitor will temper this view. Daily temperature ranges of 50° from high to low are not uncommon. Both Yuma and Palm Springs have record daily ranges of 81°, from 120°F to 39°F in one 24-hour period!

Exposure to sun and wind during outdoor activities in the desert is due to a general lack of cloud cover and of natural vegetation. Low humidity, direct sun and high temperatures require a person to drink a lot of water at the very time that most of the desert's few streams, water holes and springs are drying up. Yet, by contrast, during August 1977, the hottest month of the year, 2.53 inches of rain were dumped on Borrego Springs in less than six hours, and 4.5 inches in two days, during the disastrous "50-year storm" of Hurricane Doreen. A station in Coyote Canyon recorded 5.25 inches one night during this storm! (This storm confounded the annual averages, which would lead one to expect less than five inches of rain in an entire year.) Severe sand and dust storms, especially in the spring, are other weather hazards. So the rule in the desert is to prepare for weather extremes, and enjoy anything less.

None of this is to say that the desert is not the place to vacation. On the contrary, over a million visitor-use days per year in the Anza-Borrego region prove just the opposite. The point is that the special environmental conditions of the desert require special planning and foresight to ensure a peasant stay, especially in remote areas. The following 21-year averages in Borrego Valley provide a guide to planning.

	January	April	August	November
High temperature (°F)	68	83	106	78
Low temperature (°F)	43	53	75	51
Rainfall (inches)	1.36	.28	.58	.71

High elevations will have lower temperatures overall, lower daily temperature ranges, greater rainfall and lower surface wind velocity. Wind velocity may, however, be significantly higher on mountain peaks and high plateaus, such as Ranchita and the Santa Rosas.

Wind, Water and You

As noted above, temperatures can drop as much as 50° from a hot day to a frigid, windy night. A pre-trip check with rangers or law-enforcement officials will give you a good idea of what to expect. The wind-chill factor can cause the effective temperature on exposed flesh to be far lower than the actual air temperature. For example, at an air temperature of 40°F with a wind speed of 20 miles per hour (not unusual on the desert), the flesh is experiencing an effective temperature of 16°F. An air temperature of 32°F with a 28-mile-per-hour wind results in an effective temperature of 0°F. Plan clothing and shelter accordingly.

At the other end of the temperature scale, the body copes with heat by sweating, which produces evaporation and subsequent cooling, all of which is beautifully designed to maintain a normal body temperature of 98.6°F. At air temperatures above 92°F the body will absorb heat directly from the atmosphere, and at lower temperatures it will absorb heat from direct sunlight on the skin. Furthermore, the body produces its own heat as a result of activity, work, eating and exercise.

The implications of all this lead to...

The Water Maxims

Rule 1: Store Water in Your Belly, Not your Canteen. Drink on demand and in sufficient quantities to amply satisfy thirst. Tank up like a camel before the trek and whenever you encounter natural water supplies. Treat the water if necessary.

Rule 2: Conserve Sweat, Not Water. Reduce sweating by rest and proper protective clothing. Travel during the cool of the day, before 10 a.m. or after 4 p.m., even at night (if light and terrain permit it), resting 10 minutes or more each hour. Rest often, in the shade, any available shade. Rest off the ground if possible. Temperatures may be 30-40° cooler one foot of the ground. Wear light-colored, light-weight, long-sleeved and long-legged, loose, layered clothing and a broad-brimmed hat. These will reduce sweat loss, reflect heat and permit circulative cooling between the layers, all of which reduce water needs.

Rule 3: Keep Your Mouth Shut when in trouble due to lack of water. Great things will happen. If you breathe through your nose, you won't smoke, talk, drink booze, gripe or eat. That way, you will reduce water loss from the large mucous membranes of the mouth and upper throat, and you will minimize the need for water to metabolize alcohol and food.

Not enough can be said about the need for an adequate water supply in arid areas. Parents who carefully guard the welfare of their children in the city may think nothing of letting junior jump on his minibike and ride miles and hours out into desolate desert badlands without a drop of water. The false security of the familiar family car, and no extra water supply, has led to many a sad end of a Search and Rescue operation, even on paved roads in the lonely out-there. Some seasoned hikers have tragically neglected the potential realities of a long trek—burning midday sun, dehydration and delirium. Adequate water is therefore the single most important thing in wise desert travel.

All natural water supplies should be suspected. Any standard purification method is suitable:

1. Water-purification tablets—follow directions on container. Usually one tablet per quart of clear water or two tablets per quart of cloudy water are sufficient. Shake and let stand for 30 minutes.

2. Iodine—3-6 drops per quart is sufficient, depending on purity. Add iodine, shake and let stand for 30 minutes.

3. Boiling—bringing to a boil will do the job.

Note: These three methods will treat biological impurities only. Chemical impurities cannot be removed except by distilling. Fortunately, there are no known chemically hazardous natural water supplies in the Anza-Borrego area.

4. Sun still. This ingenious device, developed by the U.S. Department of Agriculture, produces up to 3 pints of water per day. Details are available in most survival books. Practice the technique before you actually need the water. In a practice situation it can be an enjoyable and educational outdoor activity.

Basically the technique begins with digging a hole about 18 inches deep at the center and 36 inches across. Place a collecting vessel at the center of the hole. Completely cover the hole with an impermeable (waterproof) plastic sheet (tube tent, rain coat, etc.), anchored around the edges with soil or sand, such that it's air-tight. Put a weighting object (rock, soil, etc.) in the center of the plastic sheet so that the sheet forms an inverted cone with the apex over the container. During the day, water will condense on the underside of the sheet, run down to the center, and drop into the container. Fleshy plants, cactus or impure water may be placed in the hole to accelerate the process.

Desert Hiking and Getting Unlost

In desert canyons, brush-covered hillsides, rocky outwash slopes and sandy washes, distances can be very deceiving. Here the hiker's normal 2-to-3 miles per hour pace on a trail may become 1/2-1 mile per hour. Dry waterfalls and precipitous mountainsides may cause lengthy and unexpected detours. Plan your trip and water supply accordingly.

If lost or stranded with a disabled vehicle, you should generally stay with it, even a motorcycle. It's a lot easier to spot than a lone walker on the desert. If lost afoot or with a functioning vehicle, stop, reflect, and make a plan. Know where you're going, and why. Should you decide to travel afoot in hot weather, walk only during the cool of the day, around dawn or dusk, and only if you have water. Rest at least 10 minutes out of every hour. Be prepared to signal searching aircraft or ground parties. Basically, you want to produce an unusual or unnatural effect in the terrain: smoke, fire, mirror flashes, flashes from mirror substitutes like glass or aluminum, noise, sudden movements, pieces of clothing waved, or whatever is available that contrasts with the natural terrain. Remember that most washes in the Anza-Borrego region lead east downstream to a paved road or habitation where help can be obtained. An exception is in the Carrizo Wash area between Highways S-2 and the Carrizo Impact Area. In this area travel up-wash west to the highway. **REFER TO A MAP** and **HAVE A PLAN!**

Personal Equipment Checklist

This section is oriented toward light-weight, minimum-space, multipurpose equipment for an individual. Adapt as necessary to your particular needs. See the Vehicle Equipment Checklist above for automotive equipment.

Climate determines clothing. A basic rule for outdoor wear is "lightweight, light-colored, layered and loose." Light-colored outer layers minimize heat absorption and provide best visibility in most Southwest environments. Several layers of lightweight garments, such as a sweater, a sweatshirt, a light jacket and "fishnet" or thermal underwear are better than a single heavy coat. A person who starts a hike early in the cool of morning will soon be generating

substantial body heat, and the air will be getting warmer. Then, into the afternoon and evening the temperature decreases, perhaps to a deep chill. Using the
layered system enables one to adapt to successive changes rather than be limited to the all-or-nothing of a single heavy garment. Since insulation from heat or
cold depends on the amount of dead air trapped in the small spaces of the material between the body and the outside air, layering also increases insulation.

The Ten Essentials

Credit the Sierra Club for widely popularizing this list as the very basic
items that no one should ever be without while engaged in outdoor activities,
whether in camp or on the trail.

Pathfinding
1. Map of area (study it and the guidebook before the trip)
2. Compass (practice using it)
3. Flashlight (with spare batteries and bulb)

Protection
4. Sunglasses (plus sunscreen, insect repellent and chapstick)
5. Spare food and water (carry a full canteen even for short desert walks and
   one gallon of water per person per day for extended travel)
6. Extra clothing (appropriate for expected low temperatures. Use "layered"
   system)

Emergencies
7. Waterproof matches or a propane lighter
8. Candle for fire starting
9. Pocket knife
10. First-aid kit (antiseptic and assorted band-aids as a minimum)
"11." Toilet paper (also good for starting fires)

Clothing (includes what is worn)
- 1-2 pairs of trousers (one can be shorts or swimsuit)
- Shirts, sweaters, sweatshirts (one heavy and long-sleeved)
- Jacket or parka (windproof and water-repellent)
- Socks (one change per day. Heavy socks for boots)
- Visored or brimmed hat (for sun and rain protection)
- Wool cap (unless parka has hood)
- 1 pair heavy shoes or boots, well broken in
- Bandanas (good for many uses)
- Mittens or gloves
- Raincoat or poncho (lightweight plastic or coated nylon)

Bedding and Shelter
- Sleeping bag (goose-down filler best, but expensive. Inexpensive bag
  may be supplemented by extra blankets.)
- Ground cloth (many things are suitable—extra poncho, plastic sheet.)
- Tent or bivvy sack, depending on conditions. Think insects.
- Air mattress or pad

First Aid
- Iodine (for first aid and water purification if necessary)
- Moleskin (for foot blisters)
- Adhesive tape
- Gauze pads and bandages (several sizes)
- Comb, tweezers, and/or pliers (to comb-out or pull-out cactus thorns)
- Toiletries

Miscellaneous
- 50 feet of 1/8" nylon cord
- Duffle bag, backpack or knapsack. Travel with all gear in one bag.
- Spending money (works when nothing else does)
- Writing materials
- Sewing kit (needle, thread, buttons, safety pins)
- Camera, film, extra batteries
- Eating utensils (2 Sierra cups and a spoon are sufficient)
- Miscellaneous plastic bags
- Group cooking gear and food supplies

DESERT CITIZENSHIP AND COMMON SENSE (RULES AND REGULATIONS)

We the people, through our elected officials and public administrative systems, have developed laws and regulations for the purposes of: enhancing the quality of our outdoor experience; protecting the natural resources upon which those experiences depend; providing safety and security for all. Below is a general summary of good desert citizenship standards, not a detailed list of rules

Vegetation is damaged when approved routes are not followed

and regulations. Check with rangers for specifics in your area of interest. Again, these are *our* standards of good environmental and outdoor civility, not random rules dreamed up by inaccessible bureaucrats. You don't like something in our democratic system? Fine—write, phone, fax, debate, lobby, and vote. Our public land managers want to hear from you. Finally, they are we.

ABDSP standards follow, with BLM and OWSVRA comments where they differ. The lack of regulatory posts or signs is not an excuse for unethical behavior nor a defense for illegal acts. "You are responsible" say our signs, brochures, and courts.

Motor Vehicles
ABDSP
- Travel is permitted only on established state roadways, paved and dirt. No trail riding and no cross-country. Established roadways are posted and are shown on the ABDSP map and on maps in this guidebook.
- Vehicles must be street-legal, even on dirt roads.
- Operators must possess a valid driver's license.

OWSVRA
- Cross-country travel permitted unless posted closed.
- All vehicles must be registered and display a current license plate or "green sticker."
- Unlicensed minor operators must be under the immediate supervision of a licensed adult. ATVs have additional, specific rules.
- Speed limit 15 mph within 50 feet of a campsite or group of people.
- Any speed greater than reasonable or prudent is illegal.
- Lights required for operation between sunset and sunrise.

BLM
- Cross-country travel permitted in Superstition Mountain and Plaster City Open Areas unless posted closed.
- Travel is permitted on approved Routes of Travel in almost all other BLM areas, unless Wilderness (e.g., Coyote Mtns, Jacumba), Closed (e.g., San Sebastian ACEC, Crucifixion Thorn Natural Area) or posted closed route (e.g., old roads in Table Mountain area).
- An approved Route of Travel is a significantly used road or trail at least two feet wide and includes major washes unless posted closed. Recommended Routes of Travel are shown on BLM maps and on maps in this guidebook. An "open route" has a slightly larger definition. Check with a BLM ranger for specifics. Go with signage—you won't go wrong.
- All vehicles must be registered and display a current license plate or "green sticker." Green stickers may operate in Open Areas and on most Routes of Travel except paved roads and "maintained dirt roads" such as Wheeler Rd into Superstition Mountain or McCain Valley Rd.
- In summary, all BLM land is classified as Open (cross-country OK), Closed or Wilderness (no vehicles), or Limited Use, which is the most common (approved Routes of Travel, which may be dirt roads, trails, or washes).

- Organized Events, including competitive, commercial, or recreational gatherings of 50 or more off-road vehicles, require a permit.

Private and Military Property:
- Permission of the owner or range manager required.

Bicycles
- Same rules as motor vehicles—travel on established paved and dirt roads unless specifically allowed (e.g., Middle to Upper Willows in Coyote Canyon).

OWSVRA and BLM
- Same as motor vehicles although allowed on some posted Closed Routes (e.g., Table Mountain,) but not Wilderness or Closed Areas.

Fires
- Campfires only in fireproof metal containers that completely contain the fire. Flame or smoke must not discolor or damage any feature.
- Do not use live, down, or dead vegetation. Much apparently dead desert wood is only dormant, awaiting rain. Dead material helps rejuvenate soil and provides wildlife habitat.
- Fire debris, ashes and trash were packed in and must be packed out.
- Negligence incurs liability for cost of fire suppression and damages.
- Backpackers must use portable stoves for their cooking needs.

OWSVRA and BLM
- Use existing fire rings where available, bring own fuel: gathering firewood illegal.

Weapons
- Loaded firearms or weapons prohibited. Weapons must be temporarily incapable of discharge and be in a case.

Pets
- Under control in a tent or vehicle, or on a leash no longer than 6'feet.
- Dogs not allowed in the backcountry, on foot trails, or in the VC.

Fireworks including so-called "safe and sane" type
- Illegal on all public lands, period.

Horse Camp and Trail Riding
(Only Coyote Canyon has designated horse trails.)
- Campsites and corral must be cleaned after use.
- Park horse trailers on opposite side of camp from campsites.
- Vehicles must observe 15 mph speed limit in camp area.
- Ride single-file on horse trails, on primitive roads and in washes on routes designated by park management.
- No horses allowed at Sheep Canyon picnic tables or beyond parking lot.
- Horses not allowed in a natural preserve if the values of that preserve may be endangered.

Backcountry and Primitive Camping
- "The park's open camping policy works because visitors care for the land and work to keep it clean and pristine."
- Open camping is restricted around established campgrounds, the VC, day-use areas and where posted.
- Vehicle may be parked up to 25 feet from established roadways, assuming no damage to vegetation.
- Camp 100 feet from a stream and 200 feet from a spring or pond.
- Use of the some 500 previously established campsites in ABDSP is encouraged. Use of spur-roads leading to these is OK.
- Special-use permit required for groups of 25 or more.
- "Take nothing but pictures. Leave nothing but footprints."

BLM
- General CDCA rule for vehicle parking is 300-foot limit from most open vehicle routes except in the Yuha Desert ACEC, where it is 25 feet.
- Limiting visits to less than 30 minutes at wildlife water sources is encouraged.
- Camp 600 feet from any man-made wildlife water source.

PROTECTION OF OUR PRE- AND HISTORICAL HERITAGE

Plants, Animals, and Artifacts
All natural and historic material is fully protected by law, prohibiting disturbance or removal. This includes wildflowers, dead wood, reptiles, potsherds, rocks, fossils, shells, and historic artifacts.

Paleontological features are the records in stone of plant and/or animal species from past geologic ages. They represent the only source of knowledge concerning life on earth in the geological past. They are irreplaceable, and if destroyed through carelessness or greed, are lost forever.
—CDPR Operations Manual

No person shall excavate, or remove, destroy, injure, or deface, any vertebrate paleontological site, including fossilized footprints.
—California Public Resources Code

It is a violation of federal and state regulations and Public Resource Codes to disturb, collect, or destroy fossiliferous and geological resources on public lands under the jurisdiction of the California Park System (state) and the Bureau of Land Management (federal).
—SDAG Field Guide 1995

Archaeological sites are endangered by the greatly increased number of people who visit them. Thoughtless damage can occur from people casually collecting arrowheads or other objects. Vehicle travel off established routes can damage fragile archaeological sites, especially in desert areas. Historical and archaeological sites and artifacts are protected as public resources.

Destruction, possession or theft of these resources are in violation of both Federal and State law. Violators are subject to fines of up to $10,000 or imprisonment for not more than ten years upon conviction.

—BLM Desert Access Guide

Agave

CHAPTER 3
Land Navigation:
Map, Compass, And GPS

T
he following discussion relates the basic tools and techniques of land navigation to the Anza-Borrego and Western Colorado Desert region. It is not intended as an introduction to the subject in general, for which there are many good books and training opportunities. For starters, try the Yellow Pages under Book Stores, Map Dealers, Camping Equipment or Sporting Goods and peruse their shelves and brochure racks. Many of these same stores also sell topographic maps ("topos") and related equipment and can refer you to community colleges or other organizations to learn land nav. See Thomas Winnett's *Backpacking Basics* in Appendix 1 for a concise introduction to the subject.

MAPS IN GENERAL AND TOPOGRAPHIC MAPS IN PARTICULAR

The backpocket map of Anza-Borrego and the Yuha Desert is sufficiently detailed for many outdoor activities in the region. At a scale of about 1:160,000 or about 1"= 2.5 miles it works well for paved and 4WD road trips and short hikes. It also works well, in conjunction with the text, to follow road logs and interpretive notes. A more detailed map is needed, however, for long hikes, backpacks, or precise field research. USGS topographic maps at a scale of 1:24,000 or 1"= 2000' provide maximum detail and are readily available.

In addition to displaying horizontal distances like any map, topographics uniquely display vertical distances or elevation via brown contour lines, which join all points on the map that have a common elevation. Contour lines close together indicate steep terrain (high relief). Contour lines farther apart indicate gentler slopes (low relief).

The map in the backpocket of this guidebook is divided into a 7.5' grid, each quadrangle of which is a named USGS map which can be cross-referenced to the topographic map index (see Appendix 4). This lets you select the correct

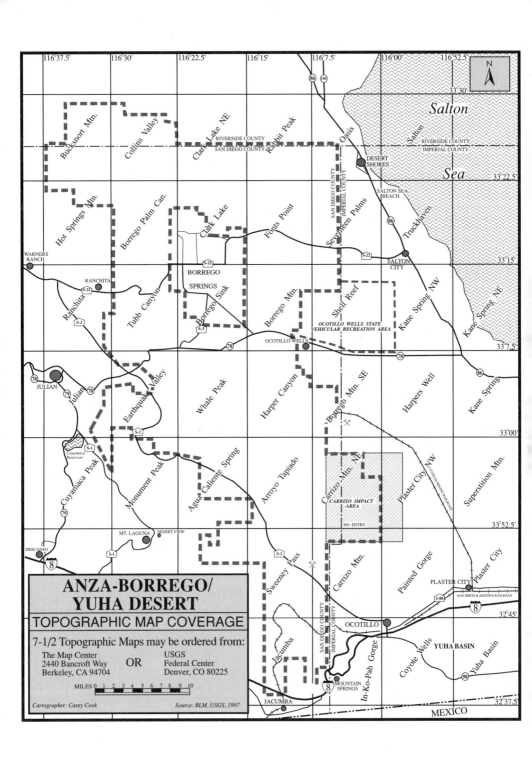

116°37.5'   116°30'   116°22.5'   116°15'   116°7.5'   116°00'   116°52.5'

N

33°30'

Salton

Bucksnort Mtn.   Collins Valley   Clark Lake NE   Rabbit Peak   Oasis

RIVERSIDE COUNTY
SAN DIEGO COUNTY

DESERT SHORES

RIVERSIDE COUNTY
IMPERIAL COUNTY

Sea   33°22.5'

Hot Springs Mtn.   Borrego Palm Can.   Clark Lake   Fonts Point

SALTON SEA BEACH

Seventeen Palms

86

Truckhaven

WARNERS RANCH

S-22

BORREGO
SPRINGS

S-22

SALTON CITY   33°15'

RANCHITA

S-22

Tubb Canyon

Borrego Sink

Borrego Mtn.

Shell Reef

Kane Spring NW

Kane Spring NE

Ranchita

S-2

S-3

OCOTILLO WELLS STATE VEHICULAR RECREATION AREA

78   OCOTILLO WELLS

78   33°7.5'

86

JULIAN

79   Julian   78

Earthquake Valley

Whale Peak

Harper Canyon

Borrego Mtn. SE

Harpers Well

Kane Spring

Kane Spring

S-2

33°00'

S-1   Cuyamaca Reservoir

Cuyamaca Peak

Monument Peak

Agua Caliente Spring

Arroyo Tapiado

Carrizo Mtn. NE

CARRIZO IMPACT AREA

NO ENTRY

Plaster City NW

SOUTHERN PACIFIC RAILROAD

Superstition Mtn.

79

MT. LAGUNA   DESERT VIEW

33°52.5'

DESCANSO

8

S-1

S-2

Sweeney Pass

Carrizo Mtn.

Painted Gorge

PLASTER CITY   Plaster City

32°45'

S-80

SAN DIEGO & ARIZONA RAILROAD

8

**ANZA-BORREGO/
YUHA DESERT**

TOPOGRAPHIC MAP COVERAGE

7-1/2 Topographic Maps may be ordered from:

The Map Center
2440 Bancroft Way
Berkeley, CA 94704

OR

USGS
Federal Center
Denver, CO 80225

MILES 0   1   2   3   4   5   6   7   8   9   10

Cartographer: Casey Cook   Source: BLM, USGS, 1997

Jacumba

SAN DIEGO COUNTY
IMPERIAL COUNTY

OCOTILLO

YUHA BASIN

Coyote Wells

Yuha Basin

98

MOUNTAIN SPRINGS

8

In-Ko-Pah Gorge

JACUMBA

MEXICO

32°37.5'

detailed maps for any area or point of interest shown on the large map or in the index on the back of the map. Each 7.5' topo is about the same size as the large map. In our area, each minute of longitude equals about a mile; therefore a 7.5' quadrangle map displays land about 7.5 miles in width and about 8.5 miles in height. It takes about 40 7.5' topos to cover the Anza-Borrego and Western Colorado Desert region.

Scale is the relationship between distance on a map and corresponding distance on the ground. For a 1:24,000 scale map, one inch on the map equals 24,000 inches or 2,000 feet, or about 3/8 mile on the ground. Similarly, one centimeter on the map equals 24,000 centimeters, or 0.24 kilometer, or about 1/4 kilometer on the ground. One kilometer is about 0.6 mile. One mile is about 1.6 kilometers.

One drawback to 7.5' quads is that a typical day's jeep trip will require two to four of them. Another disadvantage is that they are often outdated as to boundaries, road closures, and named points of interest. Commercial topographics which are more current than USGS maps are available at smaller scales, although at a sacrifice of some detail.

Another useful series of USGS maps is the newer 1:100,000 metric series where 1 cm on the map equals 1 km on the ground, or 1" on the map equals 100,000 inches or 1.6 miles on the ground. Like any topo they offer Latitude/Longitude and UTM ticks, and section lines, all of which are discussed below. Detail is good, and a typical day's jeep trip requires only one map. Four of these cover our region with a common-point reference of Lat 33°N Lon 116°W, as follows:

Northwest quadrant—Borrego Valley
Northeast quadrant—Salton Sea
Southwest quadrant—El Cajon
Southeast quadrant—El Centro

Other tools and techniques of safe and effective route-finding include the vehicle odometer, a written log of checkpoints passed, a compass to orient the map and take sightings from landmarks, and careful cross-checking with road and trail notes in this guidebook.

Magnetic declination in this area is 14° east of true or map north. This means that 14° must be subtracted from bearings measured on the map to find the magnetic or compass bearing. Conversely, 14° must be added to compass bearings to find the true bearing on the map. "Compass to True, Add East."

GPS AND UTM

The use of conventional map and compass work in field research and outdoor recreation is rapidly being enhanced by portable Global Positioning System (GPS) units, which are becoming more affordable and user-friendly. Current low-end price is under $200. Basic proficiency requires about a half-day study and on-going practice. The reward for this investment, however, is substantial in terms of position-fixing speed, precision and confidence.

The instrument, a specialized hand-held, battery-powered computer with a keypad and screen, utilizes a network of 24 satellites to fix its position via a line-of-sight lock-on to three or more satellites. Line-of-sight is about its only environmental limitation. It must be able to "see" three satellites; it can see them at night or through clouds. It is blind in such places as Cave Canyon in Arroyo Tapiado or under the canopy of Lower Willows. Because such blind spots are rare in our sparsely vegetated and big-sky desert, GPS is the bee's knees when used in conjunction with a topographic map. It is desirable to draw lines across the map connecting margin ticks of latitude-longitude (lat-lon) or Universal Transverse Mercator (UTM) with a pencil prior to using a topo in the field in conjunction with GPS.

UTM, like degrees and minutes of lat-lon, is a grid system by which any position on the map or the land can be referenced. Read-outs in GPS units can be selected in UTM or lat-lon. This guidebook heavily favors the use of UTM over lat-lon. The advantage of UTM over lat-lon is that the measuring marks, ticks, of UTM are closely spaced on the margin of topographic maps. Lat-lon ticks, lines, or crosses are placed too far apart for rapid and precise use under field conditions. Even on large-scale USGS 7.5' maps, the lat-lon ticks and crosses are separated by about 2 ½ miles whereas UTM ticks are shown in one kilometer (0.6 mile) increments. (Commercial map publishers are beginning to show ticks as close as one mile in lat-lon and one kilometer in UTM.) Another advantage of UTM is its metric simplicity: centimeters on the map are simply translated to meters and kilometers on the ground. (A genius decided that 100 centimeters equals a meter, 100 meters equals a kilometer. The Wicked Witch of the West decided that 12 inches equals a foot, 3 feet equal a yard, 5280 feet equal a mile—try to use all that for calculations in your head.)

UTM positions are described as "easting" and "northing" in a "zone." Our region, and all of eastern and southern California and northern Baja between longitudes 120° and 114°, is in UTM Zone 11. (Longitude 120° runs north and south through the middle of Lake Tahoe.) The numeral 11 is thus the first print-out on the GPS screen. A position is defined by two perpendicular metric distances. One distance is east of the western edge of the zone, equivalent to a measurement of longitude or meridian, with numerals followed by an "E" for east. The other distance is north of the equator, equivalent to a measurement of latitude or parallel, with numerals followed by an "N" for north. Here is a sample UTM position fix, that of Christmas Circle in Borrego Springs, as it appears on a typical GPS screen:

11 558.300E 3679.700N

This is read as Zone 11, 558.3 kilometers east of the western edge of Zone 11, 3679.7 kilometers north of the equator. Easy!

The actual presentation of the UTM numerals on the margin of the map and the GPS screen will vary according to the scale of the map or brand of the unit. A little practice will clarify the usage. Typically the initial 5 or 36 will be small numerals, followed by one or two larger numerals to bring the position fix to the nearest ten or one kilometer. Up to three smaller numerals may follow to bring the position fix up to the nearest meter. While this may sound complicated, it becomes readily clear after a brief study of the marginal data and the distance scale on a topo. Throughout this book we use the following UTM style of notation, again using Christmas Circle as an example:

11 5-58.3E 36-79.7N

This reads as "558.3 kilometers east of the western edge of Zone 11, 3679.7 kilometers north of the equator." We have chosen to use the hyphen to differentiate the leading numerals, which are common throughout most of the region, from the two, generally large, numerals, which define a position fix to the nearest kilometer. These two, generally large, numerals show up as such on GPS screens and detailed 7.5′ topographic maps. The numeral following the decimal point defines the position fix to the nearest tenth of a kilometer (i.e. 100 meters or approximate yards), which is sufficient for desert land navigation and the accuracy of the average GPS unit. (We don't repeat the "11" for Zone 11 because our whole region is in that zone.)

Christmas Circle in Borrego Springs is a good position to practice land nav because the major roads into the circle run true north-south/east-west and key high points are readily identifiable as follows:

Fonts Point bears 090°true (map), 076°magnetic (compass).
Toro Peak bears 352°true (map), 338°magnetic (compass).
Coyote Mtn bears 025°true (map), 011°magnetic (compass).

Cardinal directions from Christmas Circle are as follows: Fonts Point is true east, Toro Peak is about true north, and Coyote Mtn is about true north-northeast. Use the backpocket map to identify other directions or bearings. When your practice session is complete, proceed about 100 meters west-southwest or west-northwest for refreshments.

Throughout the book we give UTM and, less commonly, lat-lon positions at most historic markers to enable practice at known points before you venture into the wilderness, where accurate position fixes may be crucial to safety and efficient route-finding.

SECTIONS, RANGES, TOWNSHIPS

Users of topographic maps, especially in the desert areas of the western United States under the present or former jurisdiction of BLM, often encounter references to sections, ranges and townships. This is the U.S. Public Land Survey System (PLSS), which was established by the Land Ordinance of 1785. (This predates the U.S. Constitution!)

PLSS conveniently divides land parcels into rough squares which are rough square-mile sections, which can then be subdivided into quarter- or eighth-mile parcels. For land-nav purposes, used in conjunction with a map that displays sectional information, features can thus be called out within a quarter or eighth of a mile. Data in the margin supplies the township and range identification. In this book we do not use this system where it is confusing or non-existent on a 7.5′ topographic map. We do use the system to identify selected features in remote areas as a supplement to other methods.

In our region and for our purposes, it is sufficient to know the following general rules (there are exceptions):

- Sections are roughly a mile on each side and contain 640 acres.
- There are generally 36 mile-square sections in a township.
- Section numbers start with 1 in the upper right-hand corner of a township and wrap around to end with 36 in the lower right-hand corner.
- Townships are numbered south from the San Bernardino baseline.
- Ranges are numbered east from the San Bernardino meridian.

Here are some sample section, township, and range descriptions which define a location to within 440 yards, close enough for land nav in the desert:

ABDSP Visitor Center—SE qtr of SE qtr of Sec 36, T10S, R5E
Iron Door Saloon (Ocotillo Wells)—SE qtr of NE qtr of Sec 9, T12S, R8E
Pegleg Smith Monument—NW qtr of NW qtr of Sec 19, T10S, R7E.

The desert is an excellent place to develop your map, compass, and GPS skills because of long sight distances and open sky. These skills will payoff when you venture into remote areas or conduct field research.

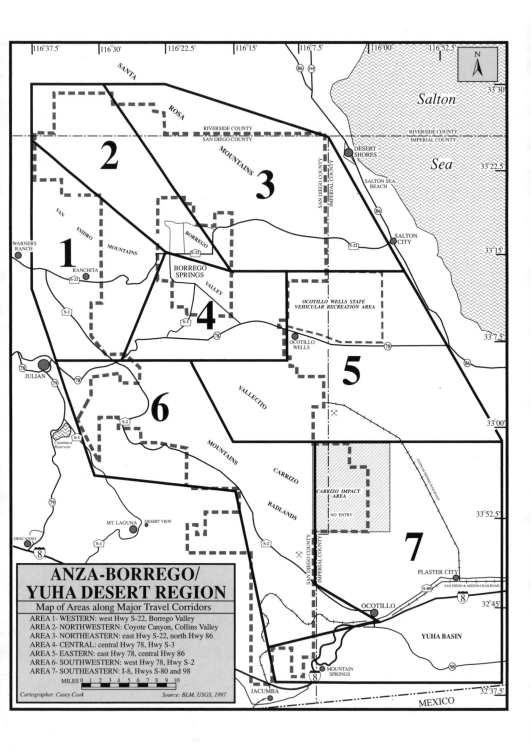

116°37.5'   116°30'   116°22.5'   116°15'   116°7.5'   116°00'   116°52.5'

N

SANTA

ROSA

Salton

33°30'

RIVERSIDE COUNTY
SAN DIEGO COUNTY

RIVERSIDE COUNTY
IMPERIAL COUNTY

MOUNTAINS

2

3

DESERT
SHORES

Sea

33°22.5'

SALTON SEA
BEACH

SAN DIEGO COUNTY
IMPERIAL COUNTY

SAN

YSIDRO

86

WARNERS
RANCH

1

MOUNTAINS

BORREGO

S-22

SALTON
CITY

33°15'

RANCHITA

S-22

S-22

BORREGO
SPRINGS

VALLEY

OCOTILLO WELLS STATE
VEHICULAR RECREATION AREA

S-2

4

33°7.5'

S-3

OCOTILLO
WELLS

78

78

78

86

JULIAN

79

78

5

VALLECITO

33°00'

S-2

6

MOUNTAINS

OPTISM MINING RAILROAD

Cuyamaca
Reservoir

S-1

CARRIZO

MT. LAGUNA

DESERT VIEW

BADLANDS

CARRIZO IMPACT
AREA

33°52.5'

79

NO ENTRY

DESCANSO

S-1

S-2

7

8

SAN DIEGO COUNTY
IMPERIAL COUNTY

PLASTER CITY

SAN DIEGO & ARIZONA RAILROAD

S-80

32°45'

OCOTILLO

8

**ANZA-BORREGO/
YUHA DESERT REGION**

Map of Areas along Major Travel Corridors

AREA 1- WESTERN: west Hwy S-22, Borrego Valley
AREA 2- NORTHWESTERN: Coyote Canyon, Collins Valley
AREA 3- NORTHEASTERN: east Hwy S-22, north Hwy 86
AREA 4- CENTRAL: central Hwy 78, Hwy S-3
AREA 5- EASTERN: east Hwy 78, central Hwy 86
AREA 6- SOUTHWESTERN: west Hwy 78, Hwy S-2
AREA 7- SOUTHEASTERN: I-8, Hwys S-80 and 98

YUHA BASIN

MOUNTAIN
SPRINGS

98

MILES 0 1 2 3 4 5 6 7 8 9 10

8

32°37.5'

Cartographer: Casey Cook   Source: BLM, USGS, 1997

JACUMBA

MEXICO

AREA 1-WESTERN:
west Hwy S-2 and Borrego Valley

There are four major gateways to the Anza-Borrego Desert area. The oldest, and still the most popular, is the historic Southern Emigrant Trail/Butterfield Overland Mail Route, today's Hwy S-2 and the Hwy S-22 branch through Borrego Valley. Most San Diegans and almost all Orange County and Los Angeles traffic come via this northwestern gateway at Warner Junction (Hwys 79 and S-2). The western gateway, through Julian via Hwy 78, is the next most popular access. The eastern gateway, from Hwy 86 with entry points at Hwy S-22 and Hwy 78, brings visitors from Riverside and Imperial counties. The southern gateway, Hwy S-2 from Ocotillo, brings visitors from San Diego and Imperial counties via Interstate 8 (I-8). The following roadlog starts at the first of the major gateways.

Note on terminology: this book uses the names used by native Americans to refer to themselves, primarily Cahuilla in the northern part of the region and Kumeyaay in the southern part of the region. The term "Indian" is retained, however, for place names and in some other contexts, to avoid confusion.

TRIP 1A:
Warner Ranch Junction to Earthquake Valley via Hwy S-2

From: Warner Ranch Junction (Hwys 79 and S-2)
To: Scissors Crossing (Junction of Hwys 78 and S-2)
Via: Hwy S-2 (paved)

Connecting Trips:
1B–Montezuma Junction to Borrego Springs via Hwy S-22
4A–Earthquake Valley to Ocotillo Wells via Hwy 78
6A–Earthquake Valley to Ocotillo (Imperial County) via Hwy S-2
6B–Julian to Earthquake Valley via Hwy 78

Points Of Interest:
Warner Ranch, Teofulio Pass, San Felipe Stage Station, Scissors Crossing, Sentenac Cienega.

Summary:
This route, coupled with Trip 6A, starts in oak and pine meadowland near Lake Henshaw in east San Diego County and descends slowly through the desert to near sea level at Ocotillo in Imperial County. Most of Hwy S-2 coincides with the historic Southern Overland Trail, the most important historic road to southern California and the only year-round historic route to California. It is no coincidence that it follows the great Elsinore fault zone, one of three major fault zones that slash southern California northwest to southeast, all of which are major historic routes of travel. (The San Jacinto fault zone contains the Coyote Canyon route of Anza and subsequent Spanish expeditions. The San Andreas fault zone contains the Southern Pacific Railroad and the I-10 corridor through San Gorgonio Pass).

Prominent county post mile markers appear almost every mile until the San Diego/Imperial County line and so odometer mileage is not necessary.

POST MILES FROM:
Warner Junction

0.0   Warner Junction—Hwys 79 and S-2 (elev. 2800′).
This junction in the historic Rancho Valle de San Jose, better known as the Warner or the Lake Henshaw Valley, is 3.3 miles southwest of Warner Springs at a SDG&E electrical substation. Drive east on Hwy S-2, San Felipe Road, in a gentle ascent through the oak meadowlands of Buena Vista Creek.

0.7   Warner Ranch (California Historical Landmark No. 311).
General Kearny's Army of the West passed here in the winter of 1846, followed by the Mormon Battalion a few weeks later in 1847, both bound south and west to San Diego. Gold Rush Argonauts streamed through commencing in the summer of 1849. The first Butterfield stage rumbled through in 1858, bound northwest through Temecula on its 2600-mile, 24-day trip from Tipton, Missouri, to San Francisco, California.

The old ranch house here, built in 1857 by the Carillos, was indeed the Butterfield stage stop but it was not Warner's home. His home, built in 1844 and burned in a Kumeyaay uprising in 1851, was just behind the present house, overlooking Buena Vista Creek.

2.2   Kimble-Wilson Store (site).
The tumble-down structure behind the hill to the north (on private property) was described in the 1868-69 diary of the Stanley Rogers family as "a very popular stopping place where supplies were purchased in a pleasant cottonwood grove."

4.7   Montezuma Junction of Hwys S-2 and S-22 (elev. 3200′).
This is mile 0.0 for Hwy S-22, the Montezuma Valley Road, Trip 1B.

5.5   Teofulio Summit (elev. 3636′).
This is the lowest crossing of the Peninsular Ranges between San Gorgonio Pass, fifty miles north in Riverside County, and San Matias Pass, two

hundred miles south in Baja California—hence the historical importance of Teofulio Summit as the major east-west gateway to southern California until the completion of the Southern Pacific Railroad through San Gorgonio in the 1870s. Teofulio Summit, like San Gorgonio Pass, is a watershed divide between easterly drainage into the below-sea-level Salton Basin versus west-flowing streams which reach the Pacific Ocean.

6.2   San Felipe Store (elev. 3477').

The route drops gently into San Felipe Valley, a linear fault-controlled feature of the right-lateral Agua Tibia/Earthquake Valley fault. Vegetation changes from pine and oak woodlands and meadows of the Transition life zone to the high-desert Upper Sonoran life zone. Volcan Mountain is to the southwest and the San Felipe Hills are to the northeast.

The deep canyon, which slices into Volcan Mountain to the west, is part of the Rutherford Ranch which is slated for public park land. The Kumeyaay name for Volcan is *Ha-ha-che-pahg*, "place where the water comes down." Observe the extensive tailings from a major tourmaline mine on the ridge to the right of the main canyon.

15.9   San Felipe Valley and Stage Station (BM elev. 2338').
(California Historical Landmark No.793)

Before this cottonwood-shaded grove became the site for a Butterfield stage station, it was an active seasonal Kumeyaay Indian village area, as indicated by the several morteros and slicks found on the granitic rocks near the creek. The Kumeyaay are a branch of Yuman-speaking Indians related to the Paipai and Kiliwa of Baja California, the Mojave, Quechan (Yuma Indians), and Cocopah along the Colorado River, and the Maricopa, Yavapai, Hualapai, and Havasupai of Arizona. They were the first of the historic Indian groups to enter the Anza-Borrego area 1000-1500 years ago, after the formation of ancient Lake Cahuilla. As the lake water became increasingly saline, most of the Kumeyaay dispersed to the mountain areas to the west, but a few stayed along the Colorado River. The Mountain Kumeyaay, who were traditional gatherers, were heavily influenced by the Spanish mission system, adopting western clothing and learning Spanish soon after contact. The Desert Kumeyaay, on the other hand, were growers who had a close association with the Quechan along the Colorado River, adopting basic agricultural techniques to cultivate melons, pumpkins, corn, beans, and peas. Here at San Felipe, the Mountain Kumeyaay (previously referred to as Southern Diegueños) and the Desert Kumeyaay (previously known as Kamia) came together to trade and share a common language, culture, and a long history of friendly relationships.

California-bound emigrants and members of the International Boundary Commission reported an active village site in the fall of 1849. Emigrant William R. Goulding described the village of "San Fellippi" as having "30 small rude constructed huts," several gardens with melons, beans, and onions, and women actively employed in sorting, drying and cleaning corn, acorns, pinyon nuts, and various berries.

By the time the stages were rolling, the lifestyle of these Indians had permanently changed. Waterman L. Ormsby, one of the first passengers riding the Butterfield Overland Stage, wrote in 1858 that "...in the Valley of San Felipe we saw a number of prosperous Indian ranches where they raise corn and melons and live much like white folks."

The San Felipe Station was located on a knoll next to a giant cottonwood tree, at the base of which was once a spring. It was an "L" shaped two-story wood-framed building that was reportedly the only wooden station on the western length of the Butterfield line.

17.0 Scissors Crossing (East) and Sentenac Cienega.

Hwy S-2 intersects Hwy 78 on the north edge of Sentenac Cienega. Earthquake Valley and San Felipe Valley merge at this marsh, which drains as San Felipe Creek through Sentenac Canyon, a water gap through the Grapevine Mountains. Desert naturalist Paul Johnson notes that, at some fifty miles, this is the longest watercourse in the Anza-Borrego region. The Sentenac Cienega is one of the largest undeveloped marshes remaining in California. The cienega and the canyon were part of the privately held San Felipe Ranch purchased by the Anza Borrego Foundation (ABF) in May 1998 for the state as an addition to the park. The Kumeyaay village site and the stage-station site are still part of the ranch and the focus of a future purchase.

TRIP 1B:
Montezuma Junction to Borrego Springs via Hwy S-22

From: Montezuma Junction (Hwys S-2 and S-22)
To: Christmas Circle, Borrego Springs
Via: Hwy S-22 (paved)

Connecting Trips:
1A–Warner Ranch Junction to Earthquake Valley via Hwy S-2
3A–Borrego Springs to Salton City via Hwy S-22
4A–Earthquake Valley to Ocotillo Wells via Hwy 78
4B–Tamarisk Grove to Ranchita via Grapevine Canyon

Points Of Interest and Side Trips:
Montezuma Valley, Ranchita, Jasper Trail, Culp Valley, Pena Spring, Hellhole Canyon Ridge Trail (CRHT), Old Culp Valley Road, Paroli Homesite, Wilson Trail, Pinyon Ridge, Montezuma Grade, Crawford Overlook.

Summary:
Prominent county post mile markers appear almost every half mile, so odometer mileage is not necessary. Roadside geology along this and many other regional routes is described in Paul Remeika's *Geology of Anza-Borrego* (see Appendix 1.)

POST MILES FROM:
S-2/S-22 Junction

0.0 Montezuma Junction (Hwys S-2 and S-22, elev. 3300').
This pleasant oak- and pine-shaded junction is just east of post mile marker 4.5 on Hwy S-2. Drive east on Hwy S-22, Montezuma Road, up Cañada

Verruga. Pine trees found along the highway were planted by the county highway department. Warner Pit #706 is operated by the county highway department as a source of "road metal"—road materials including boulders, cobbles, decomposed granite "DG", and sand. At the east end of the north side of the road cut just beyond, a gray fault-crush zone may be observed at the contact between reddish granitic and metamorphic bedrock in the Agua Caliente fault zone. The natural hot pools at Warner Springs several miles northwest are another feature of this fault zone.

The Pacific Crest Trail (PCT) crosses at mile 1.0, Barrel Spring, in a shady grove of coast live oaks. Gray-leaved Great Basin sagebrush is the dominant shrub from here to the beginning of the plunge down into the desert.

2.5 Hoover Canyon entrance to Grapevine Canyon (dirt road, seasonal 4WD).

This is signed as "Vista Irrigation Dist." Tamarisk Grove is about 14 miles southeast down a 4WD road. Be sure to close gates behind you. See Area 4 for route description coming from Tamarisk northwest via Grapevine to Hoover Canyon.

2.8 Old Mine Road (dirt road).

A dirt road north (left) enters U.S. Bureau of Land Management (BLM) land about a mile north and works up Buck Canyon past some oak-shaded campsites. After a couple more miles, it dead-ends high on the mountain at a caved-in gold mine workings, Montezuma Mine. California Dept. of Mines and Geology (CDMG) *Report* #3 offers this on the Montezuma (Rice) Mine district:

> *Gold-bearing deposits in the district consist of northeast-trending quartz veins in metamorphic rocks which consist mainly of schist, and hybrid rocks composed of schist and quartz diorite. The deposits probably were prospected first in the 1890s by the Rice brothers of Warner Springs.*

5.1 Ranchita store, elev. 3985'.

5.8 Wilson Ranch/W-W Ranch road, opposite Oak Grove Lane.

This double dirt road is another entrance south (right) into Grapevine Canyon. Camel Rock is about a mile south on the east side of the dirt road. Pass Chimney Rock Road on the north and enter...

6.3 Anza-Borrego Desert State Park (ABDSP).

The summit (elev. 4220') is marked with a painted cattle crossing and a warning of 8% down-grade. The clearing on the north side of the highway is the site of a 1950s ranger station. New state park signs here serve part of the purpose of the old stage—visitors are advised of park features ahead and applicable regulations.

6.7 Jasper Trail south (right)

The Jasper Trail, originally an old cattle trail, was named for cattleman Ralph E. Jasper of Montezuma Valley.

Former Park Manager (1972-1981) Maurice ("Bud") Getty on the Jasper Trail

Side Trip (4WD road)

0.0   Jasper Trail, and the paralleling California Riding and Hiking Trail
         (CRHT), winds through heavy chaparral growth of ceanothus,
Mojave yucca, cholla cactus, sagebrush, flat-top buckwheat, juniper, and
sugar bush. Bear west (right) and climb to a small summit at mile 1.1. The
view from here is a good orientation to the rest of the trip.

1.4   Cross old Culp Valley Road at "Four-way."

A turn west (right) crosses ABDSP boundary and leads 0.3 mile to
Camel Rock. It then goes another mile north (right) to Hwy S-22.

A turn east (left) descends about a mile to The Slab and Wilson Trail
junctions. (See details below on Old Culp Valley Road side trip, which
departs Hwy S-22 at post mile 10.4.)

The Jasper Trail continues south straight ahead, descends and then
climbs to a fork at mile 2.4. Although the left fork dead-ends immediately on a crest, the sweeping view of much of the northern Anza-Borrego
region is spectacular. The right fork drops steeply through a canyon,
climbs up the west bank to traverse a knife-edge ridge, and descends
steeply back into the same canyon. Great walls of pegmatite dikes course
the mountainsides. Vegetation sharply changes from chaparral to desert-
slope plants.

4.8   The road departs the canyon west over a small ridge. The W-W
         (Walt and Wanda Phillips) Ranch may be seen west and below in
Grapevine Canyon. The road drops into a small ravine and turns south.

5.5   Grapevine Canyon junction (elev. 2,900') at a phone pole. Stuart
         Spring is just downstream. Tamarisk Grove Campground is about

9 miles east (left); S-22 via Hoover Canyon is about 7 miles northwest (right). (See Trip 4B—Grapevine Canyon route.)
End Of Side Trip

6.7 Jasper Trail south (repeated from above).

9.3 Culp Valley campground (elev. 3360') turnoff north (left).
The dirt road forks just past the entrance kiosk and interpretive panel. Left fork goes to Pena Spring. Right fork goes to the campground, which is the highest in elevation in the park. The high elevation makes for cooler camping (10 to 15 degrees F. cooler than the floor of Borrego Valley) and later-flowering wildflowers. The old granitic mountains have weathered and exposed huge piles of boulders which are visible all about the valley and campground.

Chaparral & Fire Ecology (ABDSP Interpretive Panel)
UTM 5-50.5E 36-75.7N

Hike To Pena Spring
The left fork from the entrance kiosk leads about a half mile up to a roadhead, circling a desert plum, from which a hiking trail drops to the north. After a few hundred yards the California Riding and Hiking Trail (CRHT) crosses our route: If followed east for about a mile, the CRHT climbs to Lookout Point (see below). Ground water appears in the descending trail after a half-mile. Pena Spring, a year-round source of abundant water, is through thick bushes to the left. The excellent water source attracts a large number of birds and other wildlife. Deep morteros may be found in bedrock to the right. This area clearly has been attractive to people for a very long time. The spring is named for Pena Paroli. The old Paroli homestead was located off the Old Culp Valley Road (see below). Another mile down-canyon brings the hiker to a seasonal cascade of water, plunging into the depths of Hellhole Canyon below. An arc from the cascade around the north side of this bowl passes more morteros. Jerry Schad's *Afoot and Afield in San Diego County* (see Appendix 1) describes a hike from here north to Hellhole Flat.

A loop hike may be accomplished by departing from the bowl to the west, up the South Fork of Hellhole Canyon through stands of fluttering cottonwood trees. From the NW quarter of section 16 (UTM 5-47.5E 36-75.7N) climb south toward Jim and By-Jim Spring and then work back east along "Wee" ridge to the Pena roadhead. This loop totals about 5 miles.

Culp Valley Campground and Hellhole Canyon Ridge Trail (CRHT)
The dirt road right fork from the entrance kiosk leads into the primitive campground area, nestled in a boulder-studded valley. As there are no facilities, campers must be self-contained and practice "Pack It In, Pack It Out."

A trail from the north end of the campground leads about one-half mile north to Lookout Point, which overlooks Hellhole Canyon and much of Borrego Valley, backdropped by the mile-high Santa Rosas to the east.

Large, whitish pegmatite rock dikes appear as giant, man-made cement walls winding across the landscape. Also conspicuous are the number of dark-colored inclusions, or xenoliths (Greek for "foreign rock"), that appear like huge prunes in the oatmeal of light-colored granitic rocks. These xenoliths are fragments of an ancient sea bed that solidified into sedimentary rock bodies that were subsequently almost entirely consumed by molten granitic material rising from below. These pegmatites and xenoliths are common throughout the Peninsular Ranges and are evidence of major sea-floor subduction under the land mass of the Californias from a hundred to seventy million years ago.

Lookout Point is the beginning of the Hellhole Canyon ridge trail, which descends about 6 miles to a large parking lot at the bottom off Hwy S-22 at post mile 16.5. It is not unusual for fitness buffs to do this trail up and down in a day. Normal hikers arrange a car shuttle.

The trail, which is part of the California Riding and Hiking Trail (CRHT), generally follows the ridge to the east but gets sketchy at times. The trail was originally an Indian trail and was later used by cattlemen to move their stock down to the desert for winter grazing. The 2500' descent is a great way to experience the transition from chaparral to desert-slope to low-desert plants. Beginning at the Culp Valley Lookout Point, plants to note include juniper, sugar bush, mountain mahogany, nolina, Mojave yucca, and scrub oak. Santa Rosa sage, jojoba, barrel cactus, agave, and Mormon tea are found midway down. Plants at the lower elevations include desert lavender, indigo bush, brittlebush, creosote, ocotillo, and burrobush. Participants in an ABF-sponsored hike down Hellhole Canyon in April 1997 saw nine mountain sheep on this trail at the 3000' level.

Key UTM checkpoints are as follows:

> 5-51.1E 36-76.4N   Elev. 3400'. Double vertical pegmatite dikes.
> Trail turns southeast and climbs onto the ridgeline and then descends east to a saddle.
>
> 5-51.6E 36-76.3N   Elev. 3340'. Saddle with weathered CRHT post.
> Trail works along the north side of ridge and makes two major descents across benches to the northeast (left).
>
> 5-53.3E 36-77.0N   Elev. 2600'. Saddle with agave-roasting midden.
> Trail bears east to ridgeline and descends northeast (left).
>
> 5-54.4E 36-77.7N   Elev. 1877'. Survey point "Rass".
> Continue descent to the bottom of Hellhole Canyon.
>
> 5-55.2E 36-78.5N   Elev. 960'. Posted trail fork in wash.
> Parking lot at mile 16.5 on Hwy S-22 is several hundred yards east.

9.3 Culp Valley campground (elev. 3360') turnoff north (left).

The paved highway descends through a large S-turn. From here, west-bound travelers get an excellent view of The Thimble—the great pyramidal monolith on the western horizon which can be seen from miles out on the desert floor, a beacon to travelers for many years.

10.4 Old Culp Valley Road (elev. 3,040').

Side Trip (4WD road)

0.0 Turnoff west (right). A turnoff south (left) at 0.5 mile leads in less than 0.2 mile to the Paroli homesite. For a picnic, it just doesn't get any better than this—a couple of tables, shade, and a peaceful setting. A sign indicates that the site was a project of the Youth Conservation Corp in 1980.

0.6 Turnoff north (left) drops down to a turnaround after 0.2 miles. A short hike north from here, over a low, rocky ridge, leads down into an east-west drainage which contains Chimney Spring (elev. 3200'). The welcome sound of the trickling spring is heard from atop the rocky prominence. Nearby springs just north include Don, Johnnie, Rusty, and Lews. All of these, in a line with Pena Spring to the north and Bubbling Spring to the south, suggests a fault line through here.

Old Culp Valley Road bears south now, passing La Cienega Spring on the west (right).

1.3 Cottonwood Spring. Large, old cottonwoods in this beautiful glade shelter the cement tank that holds water piped from the year-round spring.

3.0 The trail heading south (left) is the Wilson Trail, named for Alfred Wilson, an early-day cattleman of Ranchita, who ran cattle in Borrego Valley before the turn of the century.

Hike To Wilson Peak Via Pinyon Ridge

The Wilson Trail may be followed on foot several winding miles east along Pinyon Ridge to survey point "Wilson" (BM elev. 4573'), i.e., Wilson Peak, from which the panorama of the desert may be viewed. The late Skip Ruland, founder of the San Diego Backpacking Club, was the first to recommended this hike as a moderate overnight backpack, in his 1981 series of backpacking guides to the county. Using Ruland's recommendation, hike 4.5 miles from the trailhead, beginning at 4,000 feet elevation, across a series of ridges and valleys to a meadow nestled between two peaks less than a mile below the peak summit. Save the peak climb for late afternoon to catch the shadows which bring the landscape into sharp contrast. From the top there are unobstructed views of Palomar Observatory, 30 miles to the northwest, Toro Peak, 25 miles to the north, Salton Sea, 30 miles to the east, Whale Peak, 12 miles to the southeast, and Cuyamaca Peak, 18 miles to the southwest. Vegetation en route includes chamise, mountain mahogany, pinyon pine, juniper, manzanita, and jojoba as well as yucca and cacti.

End Of Hike To Wilson Peak

Hike Extension From Wilson Peak (Pinyon Ridge) To Yaqui Pass

Ranger Mike Wells offers another possibility for those looking for a moderate-to-difficult one-way hike which would add five miles to the hike described just above, beginning from the end of the Wilson Trail road, following Pinyon Ridge down to Yaqui Pass Primitive Camp. This hike is for experienced hikers only as there is no trail, no water, and it requires boulder-hopping and scrambling. Ranger Wells considers this "one of the most beautiful hikes in the park."

Beginning where the Wilson Trail ends (see hike above), traverse uphill to the left, and continue hiking as necessary to stay on the ridge top. Do not follow any of the washes down. There is no trail. After slowly descending for about 3.5 miles, the ridge will broaden and then rise to a second summit just over 3000 feet in elevation. Beyond this second summit is the descent to Yaqui Pass. The descent is steep, requiring careful route selection. The ridge top offers spectacular views of Borrego Valley. Vegetation en route changes from pine and juniper to agave and cactus. Hike ends at the highway over Yaqui Pass.

End Of Hike Down To Yaqui Pass

3.4   Turnoff south (left) 0.3 mile to The Slab, a former foundation of a house that was made of white granite rocks and cement. It rests on a brushy knoll overlooking Grapevine Canyon.

4.4   "Four-way" crossing of Old Culp Valley Road and Jasper Trail.

See side trip from Hwy S-22 post mile 6.7 above for options from here. To access the highway, turn north (right).

5.8   Hwy S-22 at Jasper Trail turnoff.

End Of Side Trip

10.4 Old Culp Valley Road (repeated from above).

Hwy S-22 passes post mile marker 10.5 and descends through a rocky gorge into lower Culp Valley. A large turnout is on the north (left) at post mile

11.3. Two trails depart from this turnout.

A faint trail leads north a few hundred yards to an overlook into upper Dry Canyon. The trail to Big Spring departs from here to the south, crossing over a low divide into the middle fork of upper Tubb Canyon and over another low divide to the south fork of upper Tubb. (The *Borrego Sun* has recently dropped Tubb's second "b" in an attempt to restore the original spelling.) Big Spring is about a mile from the highway in the latter fork and is heavily overgrown with willow, catclaw, mesquite and cottonwood. The spring is one of the biggest water producers in the Anza-Borrego area, flowing on the shrub-choked surface for one-quarter mile, then going underground. The spring is a main watering hole for bighorn sheep.

11.5 Culp Canyon turnout south (right), elev. 2600'.

Gear down and commence the steep descent down Montezuma Grade to the desert floor. Note how the weathered, bouldery landscape of Culp Valley transitions to walls of banded gneiss and schist, evidence of regional metamorphism from extreme heat and pressure at depth.

12.4 Crawford Overlook (elev. 2300').

This overlook, named for park ranger Leo D. Crawford and memorialized in an ABDSP plaque as "A View Forever," offers magnificent vistas from this vantage point. Also visible from the overlook is an old trail across the canyon to the south, climbing up Tubb Canyon, that was used by Mrs. "Doc" Beaty in the 1920s to carry mail by foot or muleback from Borrego Valley to Culp Valley. Two interpretive panels are located at the overlook as well as a plaque saluting ABF land donors from 1967-1992 who collectively have added many thousands of acres of private in-holdings to the public park. It is not unusual to see bighorn sheep in this area. Keep an eye on the ridgelines to the west.

Borrego Valley Orientation (ABDSP Interpretive Panel)
UTM 36-74.8E 5-53.8N

The highway continues to descend, past the last of the junipers into the Upper Sonoran life zone, and crosses Dry Canyon at mile 13.4. Mile 15 commences the dramatic transition from the gray granitics of the Mesozoic 100-million-year-old Peninsular batholith to the dark brown, mottled, and layered metasediments of a far-more-ancient Paleozoic seabed. The transition is complete by mile 15.5. (Don't confuse the desert varnish on granitics with the dark metasediments.)

The highway crosses Church Spur at post mile marker 16, curves to the left, and rolls out into Borrego Valley.

16.5 Hellhole Canyon trailhead (elev. 880').

A large parking lot on the west side of the highway, with interpretive signs, affords hiking and equestrian access to the popular Hellhole Canyon area (see Trip 1C). The highway curves east, passes post mile marker 17, and exits ABDSP.

17.5 Palm Canyon Drive/Hoberg Rd/Palm Canyon Resort & RV Park.

Park headquarters is 0.2 mile west (left) with the visitor center just beyond. Borrego Palm Canyon Campground is 1.5 miles northwest. Downtown Borrego Springs is east (right) on Palm Canyon Drive, centered on Christmas Circle at mile 19.

Christmas Circle is the hub of the valley's highway network at the intersection of Palm Canyon Road (S-22) and Borrego Springs Road/Hwy S-3.

TRIP 1C:
Borrego Springs, Visitor Center, Borrego Palm Canyon

Connecting Trips:
1B–Montezuma Junction to Borrego Springs via Hwy S-22
3A–Borrego Springs to Salton City via Hwy S-22
4C–Tamarisk Grove to Borrego Springs via Hwy S-3

Points Of Interest and Side Trips:
Hellhole Canyon, Flat Cat Canyon, Indianhead, North Fork Borrego Palm Canyon Backpack.

BORREGO SPRINGS

The town of Borrego Springs sits snugly on the floor of Borrego Valley surrounded by the park's imposing mountain ranges. It is a quiet community offering a welcome slower pace for those seeking tranquility, clear air and sunshine. With its many luxury developments, it is worlds apart from that cold, snowy day in December 1775 when the second Anza expedition crossed Borrego Valley to its encampment at the mouth of Coyote Canyon.

For those who prefer non-camping accommodations, Borrego Springs offers motels, apartment houses and condominiums, almost all with pools and some with kitchen facilities, the prices ranging from $40 to $100+ per day. There are also trailer and RV parks available, but in a peak tourist season all accommodations fill up quickly.

Grocery stores, pharmacies, service stations, post office, small novelty and gift shops, art galleries, restaurants, sheriff's office and the chamber of commerce are found near Christmas Circle. The Northeast Rural Bus System, operated by the County Transit Authority, offers daily bus service to El Cajon (in San Diego's east county) and to Escondido (in San Diego's north county). The 19-passenger bus will carry bicycles with advance notification. Call number in Appendix 2 for schedules and more information. Three community golf courses and tennis courts are open to the public. Night life is quiet, centering around the few restaurants and cocktail lounges in the valley. For further information about the town and accommodations, see Desert Directory, Appendix 2.

Camping areas in the Borrego Valley vicinity include the developed campground at Borrego Palm Canyon, and primitive, no-facility camps in Coyote Canyon, in Glorietta Canyon, at Pegleg Smith Monument and around Borrego Sink. The latter two areas are privately owned but have been open to public camping. Backpack-only camping is permitted in the west-side canyons.

A 130-space RV park, called Palm Canyon Resort, is located at the junction of Palm Canyon Drive and Montezuma Grade (S-22), about a mile from the visitor center. This facility has full hookups, two jacuzzis, two pools, a store, laundry, and restaurant facilities in addition to a 60-room hotel.

Notice: Much of Borrego Valley is private property, requiring compliance with regulatory signs, fences, etc. Camp and travel only where obviously permitted or designated.

VISITOR CENTER

The architectural award-winning visitor center is 1.7 miles west of Christmas Circle on Palm Canyon Drive, just past the Anza-Borrego Park Headquarters. It was built in 1979 at a cost of $1 million, largely with the support of the Anza-Borrego Desert Natural History Association (ABDNHA), which was created to help fund and build the center. The visitor center was built literally into the desert to conserve energy and to be unobtrusive. Natural vegetation was carefully removed for construction of the center and then replaced, and it is now part of the center's roof and observation viewpoint. The unique design has been recognized by the American Institute of Architects.

Stop at the visitor center to obtain interpretive literature and information about the park and the desert in general. It is open 9-5 daily, except from June through September, when the center is open on Saturdays and Sundays only and is closed July Fourth and Labor Day. The visitor center has excellent slide programs and exhibits on desert geology, plants and wildlife. Park staff and volunteer naturalists do presentations or lead guided walks and hikes almost daily. School groups, senior centers, scouts, and other non-profit groups may also call the visitor center to arrange for special presentations. Profit from the sale of merchandise supports ABDSP. The center is operated by the state park with volunteer assistance.

The grounds surrounding the visitor center are planted with typical plant specimens found throughout the park. Check with the visitor center staff for the schedule for guided garden walks.

Several trails radiate from the visitor center. A short loop nature trail, advertised as "five blocks long," is marked by a sign located between the palm tree and the flag pole. Another trail, beginning on the north side of the visitor center

Award-winning visitor center

parking area, leads approximately one mile north to Borrego Palm Canyon Campground. A third trail, beginning on the southwest side of the parking lot near the lot's exit, leads southwest to join the Hellhole Canyon trail and the California Riding and Hiking Trail (CRHT, see below). The wash west of the parking lot is the drainage from Hellhole Canyon. It can also be followed southwest to the mouth of either Flat Cat Canyon or Hellhole Canyon. If hiking to one of these canyons from the visitor center, be sure to look for the visitor center flag pole on the return hike. The structure is not visible from the return hike, an intentional design feature that has been lament of some returning hikers.

A desert-pupfish pond is next to the palm tree on the north side of the visitor center entrance. The interpretive panel located there attributes the demise of the pupfish in Fish Creek to a flash flood, no doubt the January 1916 flood long associated with rainmaker Charles M. Hatfield (see Trip 5C below). Pupfish are unique fish that have survived since the end of the Pliocene Epoch because of their ability to adapt rapidly to changing conditions, be it extremes in temperatures, high salinity with occasional periods of salt-free water during spring floods, or limited fare.

Park Headquarters

Park headquarters is the administrative center and control point for the park. All ranger patrols are coordinated here by radio transmission. This is a business office. For general information and park orientation, go to the visitor center, not park headquarters.

Hellhole Canyon

This long, deep canyon curves southwest-west-northwest in a large arc to Hellhole Flat, and features superb stands of palms, sycamores and cottonwoods. There is no vehicular access into Hellhole Canyon. Hikers may enter Hellhole Canyon from either the visitor center (see above) or from the Hellhole Canyon/CRHT trailhead off Highway S-22 (see below).

Hellhole Canyon Hike
0.0   Hellhole Canyon/CRHT Trailhead (elev. 880').

This parking area for hikers and equestrians is mile 16.5 on Hwy S-22, right at the base of Montezuma Grade. This is the trailhead for both the CRHT and Hellhole Canyon. A bulletin board offers trail and nature information. This area has had several mountain-lion sightings and it is recommended that you not hike alone. This is a popular introductory backpack trip for many youth groups. Hike west up the alluvial fan.

Several hundred yards up the sandy trail is the CHRT turnoff south (left) up the ridge, which climbs 3000' in 6 miles to Culp Valley (see trail description above in Trip 1B). A trail to the north (right) leads across the alluvial fan to the visitor center parking lot. For Hellhole Canyon, continue following the trail west to the mouth of the canyon. Canyon walls close in where prominent bands of ancient metamorphosed sea beds are seen on the north wall. The vegetation in the lower canyon includes catclaw acacia ("wait-a-minute" bush), willow, mulefat, desert lavender, sugar bush, yerba santa, and ocotillo. Trees include palm, sycamore, and cottonwood.

2.2 Hellhole Canyon Grove (1500′).

This California Fan Palm grove offers a dozen or more of the Colorado Desert's signature tall tree. As the mouth of the canyon narrows, three palm trees will come in to view. About 150 yards ahead of this view is a large palm grove of about twenty trees. Some mortero holes are found above the large grove near some mesquite. The trail is difficult to follow with many boulders and thorny vegetation. Keep generally to the south side of the creek. Pass a series of single palms in the creekbed and listen for the waterfall, which is hidden in shrubbery beneath huge boulders. It is easy to miss. The waterfall is to the right of a very large boulder, above which are two palm trees.

2.4 Maidenhair Fall (elev. 1760′).

Seasonal water flow permitting, the 18-foot waterfall cascades into a pool. The face of the fall and its neighboring grotto are covered by a lacy curtain of maidenhair fern (*Adiantum capillus-veneris*), a rare sight in a desert canyon. Thick moisture-rich moss covers the grotto walls wherever fern is not attached. The falling water, the rich luxurious growth, and the sunlight dappling through the treetops create a very soothing setting, well worth the hike. From this point you will need to work along the canyon walls to the north, above the creekbed, to avoid the thick, thorny underbrush.

3.3 South Fork (elev. 2250′).

Hellhole Canyon forks above a sycamore grove. The South Fork climbs a very rugged, brush-choked mile southwest toward Pena Spring (elev. 3440′) and Culp Valley.

Main route continues west up-canyon, likewise in brushy rough stuff.

4.1 North Fork (elev. 2730).

Hellhole forks again. The North Fork branches right, climbing steeply northwest up the flank of San Ysidro Mountain. Work up the northeast (right) side of the canyon about one-half mile and then more northeast (right) at the 3400′ level over a saddle onto Hellhole Flat and eventually Flat Cat Flat. Once again, these are very, very rugged miles, where progress is measured in hours per mile, sometimes yards per hour. Be well prepared, well watered and in no hurry.

The main Hellhole Canyon continues west a couple more miles toward the Thimble, a symmetrical peak (elev. 5779′) at the head of Hellhole Canyon.

Flat Cat Canyon and Corral Canyon

The canyon immediately north of Hellhole Canyon is known as Flat Cat Canyon, thanks to ranger Frank Fairchild, who discovered the carcass of a bobcat in a sizable natural cave on the north side of the canyon at about the 2100′ level. Fairchild called the cave Flat Cat, and the canyon name followed.

Flat Cat Canyon, or "Surprise Canyon," is a very steep, boulder-strewn, vegetation-choked canyon that can be approached by following the trail toward Hellhole Canyon but diverting to the first canyon to the northwest at the mouth of Hellhole. It also can be reached by walking directly west south-west from the visitor center. The canyon contains both water and palm groves and eventually climbs to Flat Cat Flat. Flat Cat Flat, centering on survey point "Tuck" (elev. 3828") is northeast of Hellhole Flat, the flats being separated by a low divide at the 3980' level.

Corral Canyon is the canyon between Flat Cat Canyon and Borrego Palm Canyon. It was named for a state park horse corral that was located near the mouth of the canyon in the mid-1970s. The corral was moved when Horse Camp was built in Coyote Canyon.

BORREGO PALM CANYON
Main Campground

The main full-facility campground, originally constructed by the Civilian Conservation Corp in the mid-1930s, is located 1.2 miles northwest of the visitor center, at the mouth of Borrego Palm Canyon and at the base of the distinct Indianhead, "old rain-in-the-face," formation on the San Ysidro Mountain skyline. Visitors will find varied accommodations at the main campground. There are trailer sites with hook-ups, and tent sites with shade ramadas, tables and some fireplaces. Showers, laundry tubs and flush toilets are near the sites. Day-use picnic areas have shade ramadas, tables, water, gas stoves and flush toilets. Modest fees are charged according to the extent of services desired, with limits on the number of vehicles and people per site and on length of stay. Make reservations by referring to Appendix 2. Several group camp sites, with large shade ramadas, tables, fire rings, and wood-burning cookstoves, are also available. Each site can accommodate about 25 people or all five may be reserved for a single large group. A campfire center, featuring seasonal programs, is located near the upper parking area near the trailhead for Borrego Palm Canyon.

Swimming pool at Palm Canyon Campground (now gone)

A one-mile trail leads to the visitor center from the south side of the lower campground, just to the west of campsite #71. A second trail, beginning from the same location, leads one-half mile across the alluvial fan to the rocky hillside, where switchbacks lead some 300 feet up to the top of Panorama Overlook, from which one has a commanding view of the valley, the Santa Rosa Mountains, the Vallecito Mountains, the Borrego Badlands, and the Salton Sea beyond. The ridge can also be followed about another 5 miles to the top of the San Ysidros, but it is extremely rugged and not for the inexperienced.

THE BORREGO PALM CANYON NATURE TRAIL

The trail is accessible from the west end of the main campground near the campfire circle. This canyon, known as "Tala" by the Indians, was the first site sought for a desert state park, in the late 1920s. It receives more annual visitors than any other single section of the park. The reasons become obvious as the hiker walks up-canyon along the easy 1.5 mile self-guiding nature trail (3 miles round trip). What at first appears to be a dry, lifeless canyon turns out to have a variety of plant life, palm grottoes and a seasonal stream. The Borrego Palm Canyon Trail Guide is available at the trailhead or from a ranger.

Enhance the quality of your trail experience by studying the interpretive panels at the trailhead.

UTM 5-54.3E 36-81.2N   LAT 33°16.22'N LON 116°25.05'W.

The following comments supplement the 18 sites described in the Borrego Palm Canyon Trail Guide. Use of these interpretive materials along the Borrego Palm Canyon Nature Trail is a mini-course in Sonoran desert vegetation and the native American life style throughout the park area. Borrego Palm Canyon is a textbook example of similar stream-laced, palm-filled canyons along the east side of the Peninsular Ranges for 200 hundred miles from Palm Springs into Baja California.

The descriptions below emphasize the importance of this and similar canyons to the native Americans who called them home. It was more than just a place to live; it was the drug store, hardware store, and grocery store. Borrego Palm Canyon was an attractive resource area because of the combination of water, palm trees, harvestable plants, good grinding areas, rock shelters, and small and large game. A hike up Borrego Palm Canyon reveals the extent of Indian occupation by the number of slicks, morteros, and kitchen midden areas still visible along this trail.

The Cahuilla Indians who lived here had village sites up-canyon in the Borrego Palm Canyon Middle Fork and above the Borrego Palm Canyon North Fork at Palm Mesa. The Cahuilla are Shoshonean-speaking Indians who first arrived in southern California 1000-1500 years ago, attracted to the area by a large freshwater lake called Lake Cahuilla. This lake occupied the same basin as but was much larger than today's Salton Sea. When Lake Cahuilla dried up about 500 years ago, the various Cahuilla clans retreated into the surrounding mountains and canyons, most of the population settling in the Palm Springs, Banning, and Coachella Valley areas. Their most southern villages were found in Coyote Canyon and Borrego Palm Canyon. The village site at the head of the

Middle Fork of Borrego Palm Canyon was known as *Hokwitca*. *Pat-cha-wal*, at San Ignacio, was the most southerly village exclusively occupied by the Cahuilla. The Wiwaiistam people of Coyote Canyon moved to Pat-cha-wal in the 1870s after a smallpox epidemic ravaged their village at Middle Willows. To the south of this village was *Ho-la-kal*, today's San Ysidro, a mixed village consisting of Cahuillas, Cupeños, and Kumeyaay.

Like the Yuman-speaking Kumeyaay who lived to the south of the Cahuilla, these desert Indians followed a bi-polar village pattern, alternating between higher and lower elevations according to the harvest time of the main desert staples upon which they depended. In fall, the local Cahuilla harvested the acorns found at the higher elevations in the San Ysidros, in the area near today's Los Coyotes Indian Reservation. In winter and early spring they harvested desert agave. Spring was a time to gather all sorts of desert seeds. Mesquite was the main food source in summer, found abundantly in Borrego Palm Canyon.

0.0   Borrego Palm Canyon Trailhead (elev. 840').

The trail begins near the pupfish pond at the parking area of the upper campground. The narrative below uses the numbers and "labels" of the self-guiding markers as reference points.

Numbered Self-Guiding Trail Markers

  1. "Alluvial fan." To the right of the sign is a large lavender with a slick (metate) to the right of it. Staghorn cholla (*Opuntia acanthocarpa*) is common along the trail. The fruit was gathered in the spring and eaten fresh or dried for storage. Ashes from the stems were applied to heal wounds of cuts and burns.

  2. "Ocotillo." Directly across from the sign is a chuparosa (*Justicia californica*), staghorn cholla, and beavertail (*Opuntia basilaris*). The flower tips of the chuparosa were sucked for their nectar. It was also soaked in water for a sweet drink. The spines of both the fruit and joints of the beavertail were carefully brushed or burned off, and the fruit was eaten raw. The young and tender joints were boiled in water and eaten separately or with other food. It was a very desirable food, gathered March through June.

  3. "Dry Wash." The wash has creosote (*Larrea divaricata*), brittlebush, desert lavender (*Hyptis emoryi*), and indigo bush (*Psorothamnus schottii*). Creosote was called *atukul* by the Cahuilla. It was the "drugstore of the desert," used for treating colds, chest infections, stomach cramps, and runny noses, for inducing vomiting, healing wounds, drawing out poisons, preventing infections, aiding circulation, eradicating dandruff, eliminating body odor, and remedying constipation. Desert lavender seeds and leaves are edible. Boiled leaves and blossoms were given to patients as an infusion for stopping hemorrhages. The branches of the indigo bush were used as a foundation element in basket making. Indigo bush produces a brownish-yellow-to-orange dye when steeped in water. It also had an unspecified medicinal use.

4. "Ephemeral stream." Just to the right of the sign is an acacia, or catclaw (*Acacia greggii*), with mistletoe (*Phoradendron californicum*). The beanlike pods were collected May through August but were not a preferred food source because of their alkaloid nature. The wood was used for construction and fire. The blossoms were parboiled before eating if they were bitter. The mistletoe was toxic if not properly prepared. The sticky berries were mixed with ashes, then ground and boiled. Basket fibers were dyed black by boiling in a mixture made from mistletoe leaves. Behind the acacia is a dry willow, and to the left on the trail at the curve is another slick.

5. "Cheesebush" (*Hymenoclea salsola*). Although a common plant in the canyon, its use is not known. Ahead 25 paces as the trail curves is another slick and behind it small morteros. More morteros are found another 20 feet ahead, just before signpost #6, next to the trail by a large boulder. Before crossing the bridge, note the slick to the left on a boulder hidden behind the cheesebush.

6. "Animal Homes in the Rocks on the Right." Brittlebush (*Encelia farinosa*) is found along the trail. Resin from the plant was used as a healing salve—heated and applied to the chest for pain. The resin was also used as a glue for arrowheads. Blossoms, leaves and stems were boiled to make a decoction held in the mouth to relieve toothache.

7. "Morteros and Metates"—found on top of the large boulder.

8. "Brittlebush." Mormon or Indian tea (*Ephedra spp.*) is found to the right. Two large ocotillo (*Fouquieria splendens*) are on the right and left. Indian tea seeds were ground into meal and eaten as mush. Chewing stems relieved thirst. Dried and ground up stems were placed on open wounds to aid healing. A tea made from fresh or dried twigs was used for stomach and kidney ailments, to cure canker sores in the mouth, and to "cleanse the blood." Indian tea also may have been used as a remedy for syphilis and gonorrhea. Edible ocotillo blossoms were collected from March through summer. Blossoms could be soaked for a flavored, bitter-tasting drink. Seeds were ground into a flour for mush. Resinous ocotillo wood splinters were used for torches and later for fences. The ocotillo was also important as a firewood.

9. "Desert Varnish." After the sign, the trail swings around a rock ledge into the canyon. The first white sage (*Salvia apiana*) is on the right as well as a small rock shelter, and a slick at the point of the ledge. White sage seeds were gathered in July through September, parched and ground into a flour. It was used as a food flavoring and as a body deodorant, and was used to cure colds. The leaves were crushed and mixed with water to wash, dye, and straighten hair. It was used in sweat houses to eliminate body odor and to purify hunting equipment that had been touched by a menstruating woman.

10. "Flash Floods and Huge Boulders." The trail turns right and the first mesquite and willow are visible in the creek. Saltbush (*Atriplex spp.*) is also to the right. The seeds of the saltbush were harvested in July through September, parched and ground into a flour, and mixed with

water to form a mush. The leaves contain saponin, which was used as a soap. The leaves, flowers, and stems were crushed, steamed and inhaled for nasal congestion. Fresh leaves were chewed to relieve head colds.

11. "Midden and mesquite" (*Prosopis glandulosa*). Note the dark soil to the right of the trail. There are slicks on the boulders. This was a Cahuilla campsite. In spring, the mesquite blossoms were roasted in a pit and squeezed into balls and eaten. In summer, the green pods were pounded in wooden morteros into a pulpy juice and water was added. According to Cahuilla elder Katherine Siva Saubel, in her authoritative book *Temalpakh*, the beverage was kept available in a clay jar, or olla, and drunk whenever anyone was thirsty. As it sat, a light fermentation occurred, which enhanced its flavor. In fall, dried pods were eaten directly or were ground into a flour meal, pounded into cakes, and eaten dry or mixed with water to make a mush or beverage. Every part of the tree was used. The limbs were used for bows and arrows, corner posts for houses, and firewood; the trunk was used to make wooden mortars; the bark was used to make skirts for women, diapers for babies, and kindling for cooking; the leaves were boiled and made into a tea that was used to inhibit diarrhea; the sap was used as a glue, and when diluted with water, it was used as a wash for sores and wounds and an eye wash; and the thorns were used as needles for tattooing. Mesquite groves were also used as an indicator of the groundwater supply and as a locale to collect favored insects, such as cicadas.

12. "Layered Rocks." Behind the sign is another slick.

13. "Creosote." Across the creek is the first agave to be noted. By the boulders to the right is a rock shelter and to the left a slick.

14. "Acacia." The creek has willows.

15. "Chuparosa."

16. "Bighorn Sheep." Note the first palm in the creek. Sheep sightings have substantially increased in this area.

17. "Phainopeplas and Hummingbirds." Across the creek toward the canyon is a clump of agave (*Agave deserti*). In the creek note mulefat (*Baccharis salicifolia*), which looks similar to willow. Agave is called "amul" by the Cahuillas. It is the #1 cultivated plant in the world and was a basic staple for desert Indians. It was especially important because agave could always be counted upon even during periods of drought when other plants might not be available to harvest. Every part of the agave was used although its primary use was as a food. The blossoms were eaten as well as the leaves, and the stalk was roasted. Stored agave meal could be preserved for up to 60 years. Agave was used for making cordage, fiber sandals, skirts, and bowstring, for cleaning brushes and mats, and as a needle and thread. The stalks were used for firewood. A dye made from agave was used for tattooing. Mulefat was used as a preventative for baldness at the onset of baldness. The hair was washed in a solution made from the leaves. The leaves could be steeped and used as an eyewash. The limbs and branches were used in home construction.

Leaves and stems were boiled into a concoction for use as a female hygienic agent.

18. "First Clear View of the Palm Oasis." After the sign and to the right is the old trail and old #18, which marks an ironwood tree (*Olneya tesota*). Two other ironwood trees are nearby. Ironwood seeds were roasted and ground into flour. Throwing sticks and clubs were made from the dense hard wood. Ironwood was also used for firewood. Pods and seeds were gathered in May through June. Just past this last stop is an interpretive panel:

The Palm Oasis: A Rare Desert Treasure (ABDSP Interpretive Panel)
UTM 5-53.5E 36-82.0N   LAT 33°16.65'N LON 116°25.53'W.

After stop #18, the trail leads to a bridge that crosses the creek to the south side. From here the alternate trail heads back east to the trailhead. This alternate trail parallels the creek trail but is higher on the dry south side of the canyon, so that one obtains a different perspective of the desert biotic community. Barrel cactus (*Ferocactus cylindraceus*) is common on the return trail. Barrel-cactus buds were a source of food that could be eaten raw, but they were usually eaten roasted and steamed or after parboiling several times.

As the trail continues up-canyon on the south side of the creek, the mesquite becomes thick, as the canyon walls begin to narrow, and large boulders begin to dominate the floor of the canyon. Note the rock shelters with slicks on the boulders alongside the trail, across from the water gauge that sits visibly in the creek. The stair-step cuts in the granitic rock make it easy to negotiate the trail up-canyon to the beginning of the palm grove, where sycamores and alders are also found. Agave becomes visible on the steep hillsides with the increase in elevation. Note desert willow (*Chilopsis linearis*) growing beside the creek. Desert willow, although very pliable, was a source of structural wood. It was also used for bowmaking and to make granaries. Occasionally the blossoms and seed pods were eaten. The bark was shredded to make fiber for nets and clothing, and the long limbs were used to reach palm dates. Cross the creek to the north side, above the small waterfall, working your way around the palm fronds and boulders, and continue up-trail to the main palm grove. Arrow weed (*Pluchea sericea*) is found along the canyon hillside trail. The roots of these young plants were gathered for roasting and eaten. Long slender stems and leaves were used in house construction and were excellent as roofing material. Arrow weed could also be used for ramadas, windbreaks, fences and granaries. It was also used to make arrows. The trail drops down to the creek and the main grove, and the sound of falling water becomes very audible.

1.5   First Palm Oasis (elev. 1440').

At the shaded and cool palm-tree grotto, with cascading water falling from the top of massive boulders into the pool below, it is hard to believe that there is a desert "out there." Sycamores, cottonwoods, and desert willow help make this a refreshing desert oasis for both today's hiker and yesterday's Indian. This site is the reason why "Borego" Palms Desert State Park (forerunner of today's ABDSP) was first created. Park proponents called this cascading waterfall Abbott Falls, in honor of Clinton G. Abbott, a Fellow of the San Diego Society of Natural History, who was instrumental in the park's formation.

Oases were favorite habitat sites for the park Indians. The California fan palm (*Washingtonia filifera*) was called "maul" in Cahuilla. The Indians ate both the fruit and the seed, which were usually ground together. The moist, pithy center of the tree could be boiled and eaten as a famine food. Fronds were used to make sandals, baskets and ceremonial effigies, and as housing construction material. Palm trees were burned periodically to kill insects. A large sugar bush (*Rhus ovata*) is located against the canyon wall across from the creek. Its drupe-like fruit was gathered in June through August. Ripe berries were eaten or stirred into water to make a lemonadelike drink. Dried berries were ground into a flour for mush. Tea made from the leaves was used to cure coughs and colds. Note the interpretative panels found here and just above the grove.

> Restoring The Oasis (ABDSP Interpretive Panel)—Borrego Palm Canyon Grove
> UTM 5-52.9E 36-82.4N   LAT 33°16.8'N LON 116°25.93'W.

BORREGO PALM CANYON BEYOND THE NATURE TRAIL

1.5   First Palm Oasis (repeated from above).

Hiking is much more difficult up-canyon beyond the first palm grove, with dense undergrowth, thorny vegetation, and huge boulders to scramble over and around. Sturdy boots, long pants, and a long-sleeved shirt are recommended. Pick up the trail around the boulders on the right side of the

First grove of palms in Borrego Palm Canyon

waterfall and hike up-canyon. Twists and turns prevent seeing more than one-quarter mile ahead. This is the most difficult part of the canyon to traverse because of the huge boulder field. However, the effort is well worth it, as this is the most colorful section of the canyon. In one brightly hued area, the canyon walls close in and the stream tumbles over a rocky cataract of tan-colored schist rock. Most of the 800 or more palms in the canyon are in these upper reaches.

2.5 Indianhead turnoff (elev. 1800').

A dry tributary canyon branches off to the right. A large cairn marks the turnoff for the climb to the top of Indianhead. Climb to the top of the ridge and over the saddle, working your way around boulders to the southeast to reach the flat top of Indianhead at elevation 3960'. From this vantage point you can see the broad extent of the San Ysidros and Borrego Valley below.

3.2 South Fork Borrego Palm Canyon (elev. 2200').

After the fourth palm grove and a very large cottonwood at elev. 2160', the main (middle) fork trends west (right) while the South Fork trends southwest (straight ahead), leading toward the summit of the San Ysidro Mountains. A waterfall is about 0.7 mile up the South Fork past thick, almost impenetrable brush.

4.3 North Fork Borrego Palm Canyon (elev. 2680').

Backpack from Middle Fork Borrego Palm to Indian Canyon via North Fork.
The North Fork branches up a fairly prominent side canyon marked by a light-colored triangular peak at its head. Experienced backpackers can work up North Fork to Palm Mesa and descend to Indian Canyon in Collins Valley for a shuttle pickup or hitchhike return. Plan a minimum two-day, better three-day trip. Three-season water is fairly reliable from Borrego Palm Canyon until Palm Mesa. The traverse and descent to Indian Canyon is dry until Valley of the Thousand Springs at the bottom.

Several dry waterfalls on the ascent will require careful route selection and occasional backtracking. Bushwhacking and boulder scrambling slow progress to yards per hour at some points. At elev. 3750', about two miles or three hours from the Middle/North Fork junction, is an option. The left fork leads west and north to the 4610' saddle into Indian Canyon. The right fork leads another mile north onto Palm Mesa at elev. 4200', where pinyon pines welcome the climber into the "high lonely." Morteros evidence earlier Cahuilla occupation of this remote bowl. Sweeping views of Coyote Canyon and the Santa Rosas unfold from the north and east rim of Palm Mesa.

Hike over the west rim about a half mile from Palm Mesa to the edge of deep Indian Canyon at about the 4000' level and then pick a two-mile route north down the ridge to the bottom. It is about two more miles north to the Sheep Canyon roadhead.

Total distance from Borrego Palm Canyon roadhead to the Sheep Canyon roadhead is about twelve hard but unforgettable miles.
End of Backpack

4.3   North Fork Borrego Palm Canyon (repeated from above.)

The Middle Fork of Borrego Palm Canyon continues for about another 2.5 miles to the boundary of Los Coyotes Indian Reservation (LCIR), and eventually leads to the old Indian village of San Ignacio, or *Pat-cha-wal*. Permission is required to cross this boundary from the LCIR tribal spokesman (see Appendix 2). Schad (see Appendix 1) describes the descent down Borrego Palm Canyon from LCIR.

Silver cholla

AREA 2-NORTHWESTERN:
Coyote Canyon and Collins Valley

C oyote Canyon and its extensive tributary canyons account for about 100,000 acres, one-sixth of the park's entire acreage, and 23% of the total state wilderness area of California. These areas offer genuine wilderness retreats, a wealth of animal and plant life, unique riparian habitats, and extensive archaeological, cultural, and historical features. Trips here are always interesting, no matter how many times one travels the rocky road or hikes the palm-studded, boulder-strewn canyons.

Coyote Canyon is within the Peninsular Ranges geomorphic province of southern California and is controlled by the northwest-southeast trending San Jacinto fault zone, one of the major branches of the 600-mile-long San Andreas fault system. The canyon's creekbed, generally following the fractured rock of the fault zone, separates two mountain ranges, the San Ysidro on the southwest and the Santa Rosa on the northeast.

Three clusters of desert willows, known as Lower, Middle, and Upper Willows, are found along year-round Coyote Creek. The riparian woodlands along the creek include not only dense stands of willow, but also California fan palms, cottonwood trees, mesquite, acacia, mule fat, and arrow weed. Most types of plants and animals found anywhere in the Anza-Borrego area can be found in Coyote Canyon.

The land surrounding Coyote Canyon is protected through its designation as either state natural preserve or wilderness area. Such protection extends to all features that are representative of natural communities existing in California before the impact of civilization. Consequently, all vehicle entry into these protected areas is prohibited.

Caution: Most of this route is not passable by automobiles. Dangerous rocks, sand traps, and high road centers await the careless driver.

Note: **THE CANYON IS CLOSED** from June 1 to September 30 to protect bighorn sheep watering areas. The reopening each year often reveals a "new" canyon, for summer floods can dramatically alter the shape and route of the road through Coyote Canyon, especially near Lower Willows and over the rugged jeep trail into Collins Valley. Mileages listed for Coyote Canyon may vary somewhat from year to year because of flooding. Inquire at the visitor center for latest route conditions.

Northbound mileages are from Christmas Circle in Borrego Springs to Upper Willows and Fig Tree Valley. Southbound mileages are from Highway 371 near Anza in Riverside County to Fig Tree Valley and Upper Willows. Motor vehicles may not travel the 3.1 mile segment between Upper and Middle Willows although this segment is open to hikers, cyclists, and equestrians.

Hikers, mountain bikers, and horseback riders can traverse the entire canyon from end to end. The segment between Lower Willows and Terwilliger Valley is closed to all users from June 1 to September 30 annually to facilitate bighorn sheep access to water.

Total direct distance from the Highway 371 junction in Anza to Borrego Springs for hikers, bikers, and horseback riders is about 36 miles. Total distance from Anza to Borrego Springs via Warner Springs by auto road is about 72 miles.

Coyote Canyon is presented in three segments as follows:

> Trip 2A—Christmas Circle to Upper Willows (northbound)
> Trip 2B—Collins Valley West-Side Canyon Hikes
> Trip 2C—Anza (Hwy 371) to Upper Willows (southbound)

TRIP 2A:
Christmas Circle To Upper Willows (northbound)

From: Christmas Circle, Borrego Springs
To: Upper Willows, Fig Tree Valley
Via: Borrego Springs Road, Henderson Canyon Road, Di Giorgio Road (paved roads); Coyote Canyon (dirt road to Second Crossing, 4WD road to Middle Willows, hike/horse/mountain bike to Upper Willows.)

Connecting Trips:
1B–Montezuma Junction to Borrego Springs via Hwy S-22
3A–Borrego Springs to Salton City via Hwy S-22
2C–Anza (Hwy 371) to Upper Willows (southbound)
2B–Hiking Routes in the West-Side Canyons of Collins Valley

Points Of Interest and Side Trips:
Henderson Canyon, Horse Camp, Alcoholic Pass, Desert Gardens, Coyote Creek, Box Canyon, Lower Willows, Santa Catarina, Collins Valley, Middle Willows, First Child Monument, Upper Willows, Fig Tree Valley.

Summary:
Several paved roads may be taken to reach the southern Coyote Canyon dirt road. Mile zero starts over at the beginning of dirt at the north end of Di

Giorgio Road. RVs and heavy vehicles should not drive past Desert Gardens. Conventional vehicles should not drive through the ford at Second Crossing. 4WD is mandatory between Third Crossing and Collins Valley although a short, steep, one-mile pitch dooms many vehicles every year.

POST MILES FROM:
Christmas Circle

0.0   Christmas Circle (elev. 590'). Drive north on Borrego Springs Road.

3.1   Galleta Meadows Memorial Plaque.
This private monument, placed in 1994 with the assistance of the Squibob Chapter of E Clampus Vitus, commemorates both Anza expeditions, with particular recognition of Cochimi guide Sebastian Tarabal of the 1774-75 exploratory trek, and Lt. Jose Joaquin Moraga, of the 1775-76 colonizing trip.

3.4   Henderson Canyon turnoff (elev. 670').
Highway swings hard to the east (right) at this point.

Side Trip Up Henderson Canyon
This gated road is on private property with access subject to owner's permission. Drive northwest up the dirt road for a mile to the ABDSP boundary. Hike west from the roadhead up the alluvial fan across Galleta Meadows from the roadhead. Galleta Meadows was named for the galleta grass (*Pleuraphis rigida*), or bluestem, found here. It is a coarse, stiff grass that grows in clumps from two to four feet high, and is an excellent forage plant for browsing animals.

This canyon, unlike most west-side canyons, contains no palm trees. It is a steep, rough, dry scramble, rising rapidly to the ridge line about five miles from the roadhead.

The luxury homes around De Anza Desert Country Club, built on the flood plain of Henderson Canyon, suffered extensive damage from flash flooding during Hurricane Doreen in August 1977. This was termed a "50-year flood," meaning that this volume of water has a two-percent probability of occurring in any given year. The same 50-year-flood volume had occurred the previous year (September 1976) when Hurricane Kathleen roared through, and also three years later in 1980. So much for statistics.

End Side Trip

3.4   Henderson Canyon turnoff (repeated from above).
Drive due east, passing Indianhead Ranch, to...

3.6   Horse Camp turnoff north (left)

Side Trip to Horse Camp
0.0   Turn north (left) onto a good dirt road (no through traffic). A welcome aroma exudes from citrus groves on the northwest corner.
Drive north and enter ABDSP through a gate at mile 2.2.
3.1   EL VADO (California Historical Landmark No. 634)
        UTM 5-56.5E 36-89.3N LAT 33°20.6'N LON 116°23.6'W

Juan Bautista de Anza was presidio captain at Tubac, the most northern outpost of Mexico outside of California, when he received orders to find an overland route to California to colonize San Francisco. Some historians view this 1774 expedition as the third most important event in California history after the discovery of California by Juan Cabrillo and the settlement of San Diego and Monterey by Captain Gaspar de Portol and Father Junipero Serra.

The successful completion of this expedition allowed the newly promoted Lt. Col. Anza to recruit 240 colonists for a second expedition that would reinforce Monterey and establish the presidio of San Francisco. The success of this second expedition proved the feasibility of bringing large groups of people and herds of animals over the desert. In the first five years after the opening of the Anza trail, over 300 colonists came to California. A census taken in 1790 shows that 35-50% of all colonists in California at that time came by way of the Anza trail.

El Vado, "The Ford," was the campsite on December 20, 1775.

3.5   Vernon F. Whitaker Horse Camp (elev. 960'). Foot and horse trails go a mile north from the camp to rejoin the main Coyote Canyon route at First Crossing and another El Vado monument. The Horse Camp has 10 campsites, 40 corrals, and solar-heated showers. Campsites are restricted to campers with horses. Each site holds up to eight people and four horses. Sites are available on a first-come basis or via reservations through Destinet (see Appendix 2).

Largely through the efforts of park volunteer Vern Whitaker, funds were raised to establish the Horse Camp in 1977. A park leaflet entitled "Riding Trails of Coyote Canyon" describes the 30 miles of signed horse trails within the canyon. A memorial plaque at the Horse Camp reads: *In Memory of Vernon Whitaker, 1911-1987, A Horseman's Friend.*

End Of Side Trip

3.6   **Horse Camp turnoff north (repeated from above).**

Continue east on Henderson Canyon Road to Di Giorgio Road, mile 4.6, and turn north (left). End of pavement is mile 6.2. If you've come from Christmas Circle direct via Di Giorgio Road this would be mile 5.2.

"Anza's Angel" is the light-colored metasedimentary marble outcropping on rust-red Coyote Mountain ahead. The legendary angel is said to have appeared in 1775 to point the way to San Gabriel Mission when Anza's second expedition was struggling through Borrego Valley during one of the bitterest winters on record.

Reset Odometer To Zero.

0.0   **Coyote Canyon dirt road at the 760' level.**

Check with the visitor center for road conditions, especially during wet spring weather. Cross Coyote Creek and enter ABDSP at mile 0.5. Ranger Jim Meier calls this "the bog" during rainy seasons. If boggy, go carefully.

Coyote Creek in Lower Coyote Canyon

You Are Entering Lower Coyote Canyon
(ABDSP Interpretive Panel)

To protect natural and cultural resources along Coyote Creek, the jeep trail from Middle Willows to Upper Willows is closed to motor vehicles. There is a locked gate (11.4 miles) ahead at Middle Willows. Collins Valley, Sheep Canyon, Cougar Canyon trailhead, and Salvador Canyon are accessible to vehicles. The jeep trail is rough, rocky and challenging. Coyote Canyon is open to mountain bikes, equestrians and hikers. Bikes must follow the jeep trail around Lower Willows into Collins Valley, but are allowed on the horse/foot trail though Middle and Upper Willows. All trail routes are signed for appropriate uses.

Prominent perennials here include ocotillo, mesquite, creosote, brittle-bush, cheese bush, smoke tree, and burro bush. Swing northwest at the base of Coyote Mountain at mile 1.4, where the horse Desert Trail turns off to Horse Camp. A large ocotillo forest commences here, with abundant beavertail and barrel cactus and teddybear and staghorn cholla successively joining in the botanical chorus.

2.5 Alcoholic Pass trail is northeast (right).

Hike Up Alcoholic Pass

The trail commences at elev. 920′ and works up the rocky ridge, twisting to the east (right) and crossing the saddle at elev. 1550′ after about a mile. En route to the top of the pass is a register, where you have sweeping views of the Santa Rosas to the northeast and the San Ysidros to the southwest. It is about 2.5 miles from the saddle to Rockhouse Canyon road (see Area 3).

This route was part of a Cahuilla trail from Los Coyotes Indian Reservation to Clark Dry Lake. Early cattlemen Fred and Frank Clark used this route as a short cut between Clark Valley and Coyote Canyon rather than go six miles farther southeast around the end of Coyote Mountain. One accounting claims that the name "Alcoholic Pass" derived from some dry Clark Valleyites using the short cut to wet their whistles in Borrego Springs. Lester Reed, in his *Old Time Cattlemen and Other Pioneers of the Anza-Borrego Area*, reported that the two large boulders near the top of the ridge, between which the old Cahuilla trail passed, are "so close together that the short-legged burros had to be unpacked before leading them through."

Coyote Mountain is composed of complex crystalline rocks, metavolcanics, and late Tertiary sediments that have been uplifted between the Coyote Creek and the Clark strands of the San Jacinto fault zone. An extensive sedimentary deposit, containing prehistoric land-mammal fossils, overlies the Mesozoic bedrock of Coyote Mountain north of Alcoholic Pass.

End of Hike

3.0   A plaque at this pullout identifies this stop as Desert Gardens:

Desert Gardens
UTM 5-56.6E 36-91.0N   LAT 33°21.5'N LON 116°23.5'W

The Anza-Borrego Committee of the Desert Protective Council established this Desert Garden as an example of a privately owned inholding within the park boundaries that was purchased for the benefit of the public through private donations. ABC has since become the independent, nonprofit foundation Anza-Borrego Foundation (ABF), but its goal remains the same—to eliminate private inholdings within the ultimate boundaries of Anza-Borrego Desert State Park. When the park was formed, almost 50,000 acres of privately owned land were scattered throughout it. In the 30 years that ABF has worked diligently to buy out these private parcels from willing sellers, almost 25,000 acres have been converted to state ownership, including such critical parcels as the entrance to Fonts Point, Hawk Canyon, the entrance to Coyote Canyon, and Clark Dry Lake.

ABF actively seeks private donations to help purchase other properties as they become available in order to assure the integrity of this fragile desert environment under the state's management. To support ABF through membership and/or a tax deductible donation, write or call as noted in Appendix 2. ABF also sponsors an annual Desert Walk each spring, led by an expert guide in the field of geology, archaeology, botany, zoology or history. Check with the visitor center for the exact date each year.

A path from the sign here leads to two stone-and-slab tables, a peaceful and relaxing place for a picnic. Overlooking these tables is a trail to a low hill where a stone bench is found, and one can sit and enjoy the view of the ocotillo forest that surrounds this slope of Coyote Mountain. A park interpretive panel is also at this location.

Desert Gardens & Plants (ABDSP Interpretive Panel)
UTM 5-56.6E 36-91.4N   LAT 33°21.5N LON 116°23.5W

RVs and heavy vehicles should consider Desert Gardens the end of travel. Others continue northwest, dropping abruptly into Coyote Creek wash.

3.6   First Crossing (elev. 980').

The creek usually runs this far in spring. The Ocotillo Trail (horse and hiking trail) departs north from here and arcs west for a couple of miles around Ocotillo Flat to rejoin the main route at Second Crossing. The Coyote Badlands backdrop the flats to the north.

Scattered at intervals over the flat are spots of black dirt indicative of ancient fires, and at the base of the confining north ridge badlands, one may see mortar holes and the chips of arrow makers. This area and the vicinity of Lower Willows were heavily populated by Cahuillas because of the presence of agave, water and mesquite.

Across the creek on the southwest side is...

3.9   Anza's Overland Expedition (ABDSP Interpretive Panel)
UTM 5-55.7E 36-91.0N   LAT 33°21.5'N LON 116°24.1'W

This panel gives further details about the profound significance of this epic journey in the Hispanic history of the Californias.

4.0   The Horse Camp Trail, in part a self-guiding nature trail, goes a mile south to camp from here, following an abandoned acequia (Spanish for "irrigation ditch") up against the mountainside. The ditch brought Coyote Creek water from Second Crossing to the old de Anza Ranch, now Horse Camp. Make note of the interpretive panel found here:

Sensitive Resource Area (ABDSP Interpretive Panel)

Coyote Canyon provides an exceptional opportunity for a desert experience that can be found few other places in the world. The cultural and natural resources of the canyon are among the richest of any area in Southern California. The main trail passes through three precious desert wetlands. Birds, mammals, reptiles, amphibians and insects abound. The canyon is one of the last remaining homes to several rare species including the Peninsular bighorn sheep and the least Bell's vireo. Bighorn live among the steep, rocky slopes and rely on the creek for water. Bell's vireo is one of over 100 bird species that require this canyon for nesting, food and water. Enjoy your visit, but please observe the following:

- *Motor vehicles must remain on established roads*
- *Horseback riders must remain on designated trails*
- *Bicycles must remain on designated routes of travel*
- *Camping is not permitted in Lower, Middle, or Upper Willows*
- *Please help us safeguard this valuable canyon.*

Turn northwest (right) up the canyon between the creek and the acequia past BM 1008'. The state park sign at mile 4.0 describes the abundant vegetation and wildlife value of lower Coyote Canyon and warns of the vehicle closure at Middle Willows.

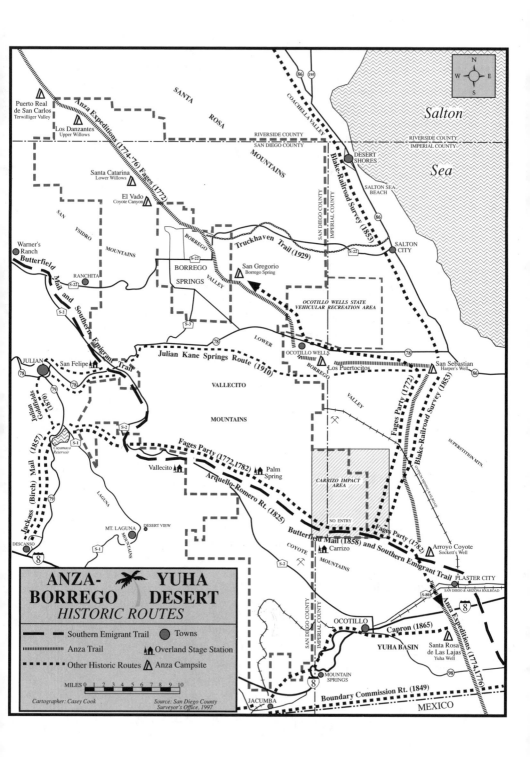

ANZA-BORREGO / YUHA DESERT
HISTORIC ROUTES

4.6   Second Crossing (elev. 1085').

An automated gaging station is located on the southwest side of the creek. For many years a jeep pickup truck, victim of Coyote Creek in a raging flood mood, was buried here. (If it's still here, it's really buried.) Common plants alongside the creek include arrow weed, bladderpod, acacia, tamarisk, mesquite, and mulefat.

𝟙   An excellent riparian nature walk along the southwest side of the creek leads a half-mile to remnants of the rock dam and pond in the northeast quarter of Section 26. This dam and pond managed water from the large drainage to the southwest and Coyote Creek into the de Anza Ranch acequia. Pipe scraps can still be seen along the route.

The stream crossing itself is fun to watch. Novice off-roaders wait and ponder; macho men blast through it and often drown out, stalled in mid-stream; the rest gently enjoy the aquatic ride. Go deliberately without spinning your wheels.

The Ocotillo Trail for riders and hikers rejoins on the north side of the creek. On the left side of the road is a long, straight row of 15-foot-high ocotillos about 75 yards long. At the west end of the row another line of ocotillos runs perpendicularly south for about 50 yards. The south and east sides of the rectangle are not so well defined, but one can readily see that this was a man-made enclosure and a very effective living corral, once protecting a Cahuilla's garden. It was a common practice in the west to use armed ocotillo staves as fencing. Such living ocotillo fences are frequently seen in rural Mexico today. Given a little water, a living plant usually results.

Old Tractor Camp, so named for the big mechanical carcass still there, is about one-quarter mile upstream from Second Crossing in the creekbed. Vehicle access is no longer permitted (unless it's already there, like the dead tractor or the buried pickup. Who knows what else may be buried in the wild and shifting creekbed of that trickster Coyote?)

Continue northwest, paralleling the Ocotillo Trail on the right.

5.1   Entrance to Lower Willows.

Access is prohibited beyond here from June 1 to September 30.

Lower Willows & Riparian Habitat (ABDSP Interpretive Panel)
UTM 5-53.9E 36-92.3N   LAT 33°22.1'N LON 116°25.2'W

5.3   Third Crossing (elev. 1150').

The Lower Willows bypass route is southwest (left) across the creek. The route in the creekbed beyond this point is for hiking and horseback only. The bypass was completed in 1988 to protect the sensitive and invaluable desert treasure of Lower Willows from adverse vehicular impact. This habitat of rare and endangered species and summer watering hole for bighorn sheep is unmatched in the vast expanses of the Colorado Desert.

𝟙   **Hike Through Lower Willows**
Mile 0.0 is the Third Crossing parking area. Hike northwest along the creek. Box Canyon joins Coyote Canyon from the north at mile 0.2.

Side Hike Up Box Canyon
0.0   Third Crossing parking area (repeated from above).
0.2   Box Canyon joins Coyote Canyon from the north (right).
1.5   Fork. The main branch goes north (right) through a deep, narrow gorge. This fork of Box Canyon can be followed about five more miles to Jackass Flat and on to Hidden Spring in Rockhouse Canyon. This is an old Cahuilla trail connecting Rockhouse Canyon with Coyote Canyon described by Lester Reed (see Appendix 1).

The northwest (left) branch rises gradually for another mile through a low saddle, from the top of which can be seen the entrance to Salvador Canyon on the opposite side (west) of Coyote Creek.

2.5   From this saddle the top of the ridge can be followed southeast (right) to a small dry pond, or playa. The playa is approximately five acres in extent and has one outlet—a steep gulch coming out of its south side and ending in Coyote Creek at Lower Willows. The gravelly bottom of the playa contains creosote, ocotillo, burrobush, and wild buckwheat, and buckhorn and barrel cactus. The descent down the gully passes through a wildly mixed and colorful suite of heavily banded metamorphics and solid granitics. A round-trip hike from Box Canyon to the playa, down the drainage to Coyote Creek and back down to the entrance of Box Canyon, is about 6.5 miles.

End Of Side Hike

Cooling off in Coyote Creek

Mile 0.3 is marked by an old gaging station (elev. 1189') at the entrance to Lower Willows/Santa Catarina. A hiking/horseback trail on the north side skirts this unique wild and jungle-like growth of willows, vines and tamarisks. Exit the dense willow growth at mile 1.7. Water from Indian and Salvador canyons joins the main creek here from the west. Hike the main route northwest up the creek through a final dense willow grove.

New Spring is on the southwest (left) side of the creek at mile 1.8. This high-volume spring erupted unexpectedly in the El Niño winter of 1983-84. Water from it is crystal clear, in contrast to the muddier water of the main creek. The creek opens up into the broad expanse of Collins Valley. Middle Willows, always a guaranteed water supply, is about a four-mile hike northwest.
End Of Hike

5.3   Third Crossing (repeated from above).
The Lower Willows bypass route crosses the creek to the southwest (left). It parallels the old Collins Valley cattle trail, which is still visible, and is used by hikers and riders. The challenging vehicle route is absolutely 4WD-only for a one-mile pitch AND requires a highly skilled and experienced driver. Whether you are climbing or descending, a scout should be deployed afoot to restrain opposing traffic from the gully until your vehicle is clear. There may be more brutal jeep traverses somewhere out in that great desert, but the authors know of none. (This approach to Sheep Canyon separates them from the goats.)

6.1   Drive across the divide and then descend a rollercoaster route into Collins Valley.

6.5   Turnoff to Santa Catarina State Historical Monument.
The monument is on a knoll about a quarter mile east overlooking the Santa Catarina marsh, named by Anza on the first, 1774, expedition. A lone eucalyptus tree in the valley below marks the cabin site of early-day home-steader Joel Reed. Although Reed homesteaded there beginning in 1887, it was another homesteader, John Collins, who moved into the area 10 years later, whose name is so well associated with this valley.

The plaque was placed in 1967 by Squibob (San Diego-Imperial County) chapter of E Clampus Vitus, an historical fraternity which flourished in mid-19th century gold camps of California's Mother Lode country. The group now perpetuates the rich trove of Californiana and related folk lore. The monument is located at:
    UTM 5-52.2E 36-92.4N   LAT 33°22.28'N LON 116°26.38'W

7.1   Turnoffs to Santa Catarina Spring and Sheep Canyon horse trail.
Horse trail forks to the southwest (left).

Hikers may follow the Santa Catarina Spring trail which forks to the northeast (right) and goes about one-half mile into an impassable bog. This is a major source of Coyote Canyon's permanent water supply, which is of prime importance to Borrego Valley. Santa Catarina Spring covers an area of

Spring in Coyote Canyon

several acres and is the largest single natural emergence of water in San Diego County. The great amount of water and the resultant growth of vegetation make Santa Catarina Spring very attractive to wildlife. Small animals and their predators abound, and the area has a year-round population of a variety of birds. A wild growth of willows, young palms, vines and tamarisks enmeshes the spring area.

The largest Cahuilla site in the park is at the spring, where heavy midden deposits cover a large area. Cahuillas inhabited this area until about four generations ago. These were Mountain Cahuilla who called themselves "Coyote People" and were known as Los Coyotes.

7.3   Anza/Sheep Canyon junction (elev. 1345′).

North fork (right) is the main Coyote Canyon route, which continues northwest toward Salvador Canyon and the Middle Willows roadhead.

West fork (left) leads to the important Sheep and Indian canyons complex, also known as the Collins Valley west-side canyons. This west fork also offers a clockwise loop trip around Collins Valley, to rejoin the main Coyote Canyon route at survey marker "Wash".

Side Trip to Sheep And Indian Canyons and Clockwise Loop Trip

Drive west (left), climbing the alluvial fan to the Collins Valley loop junction (elev. 1600′) at mile 9.0.

Turn southwest (left), past the Indian and Cougar canyons trailhead, another mile to Sheep Canyon Primitive Campground, which offers several shade ramadas. Lone palms on the canyon walls to the north welcome one to this secluded camp area, which is reached by a gurgling stream in the winter and spring. This is an excellent base from which to explore the canyon treasures beyond. See Trip 2B below for hikes and backpacks in this area.

A northeast (right) turn from the loop junction continues the clockwise Collins Valley loop trip, leading down the fan about a mile and a half to survey point "Wash" (BM 1402') in the center of the valley. This is the main Coyote Canyon jeep road.

A horse trail proceeds directly north from the loop junction to Salvador Canyon junction, bypassing "Wash" and the jeep road.
End of Side Trip and Loop Trip

7.3 Anza/Sheep Canyon junction (elev. 1345', repeated from above).

North fork (right) is the main Coyote Canyon route, which continues northwest toward Salvador Canyon and the Middle Willows roadhead. Hikers, bikers, and horses may eventually reach Anza, hence the name of the junction.

8.5 Fork at survey point "Wash" (BM 1402') in the center of Collins Valley.

Northwest fork (right) is the main Coyote Canyon route, which continues northwest toward Salvador Canyon and the Middle Willows roadhead.

Southwest fork (left) is the Collins Valley loop trip noted just above but, if taken, do the loop counter-clockwise.

9.7 Salvador Canyon junction (elev. 1560').

The Monkey Hill horse trail crosses from southwest to northeast at this point. Vehicles may travel another one-quarter mile up-wash from this junction toward the entrance of Salvador Canyon. This canyon, known to the Cahuilla as "Mowal," is named for the youngest member of the second Anza expedition. Within its steep, narrow, verdant gorge are the many palms that once earned it the name of Thousand Palms Canyon, so referenced by Randall Henderson, desert explorer and founder of *Desert Magazine*. Henderson once counted 360 palms within the main canyon and its forks. See Trip 2B below for the hike up Salvador. See below after Middle Willows for a loop hike via Yucca Valley and the mouth of Salvador Canyon.

The main jeep road turns northeast (right) into a braided-stream (multiple channel) flat area of Coyote Creek. Monkey Hill is the granitic outcrop on the east side of Coyote Creek. According to Lester Reed (see Appendix 1), Monkey Hill was named by vaquero Carlos Moreno (known to cattlemen as Charlie Brown) because it resembled a like-named outcrop near Lake Henshaw.

11.9 Middle Willows closure.

The fence is just south of BM 1837'. The route for 3.1 miles northwest from here is horse, hike, or mountain bike only to the roadhead of the 4WD road, which continues to Anza via Turkey Track. Hike along the stream, deep at times, into the Yucca Valley area.

13.2 Entrance to Yucca Valley to the south (left).
Hike Up Yucca Valley

This elongated little valley, known for its thick cover of stubby Mojave yucca, extends due south from the west upstream entrance to Middle Willows. It offers an up-and-back hike or a loop hike.

The old cattle trail climbs 400 feet in 1.6 miles to Canyon View, through creosote, juniper, yucca and joint fir. This is recognized as a major

The longest year-round stream in San Diego County—Coyote Creek

route for bighorn sheep descending from the west-side mountains to water at Middle Willows. Canyon View (elev. 2250') provides a superb overlook of the dense palm groves of Salvador Canyon and its South Fork directly south, opposite. Hikers may descend 0.5 mile into Salvador and turn southeast (left) one mile to join the main Coyote Canyon road. It is 2.2 miles northwest (left) from here back up to the roadhead at Middle Willows. Total loop hike is about 6.6 miles.
End of Hike

13.2 Entrance to Yucca Valley to the south (repeated from above).

13.5   Riverside/San Diego County line (elev. 2000').
        An ancient barbed-wire fence still marks the county line. The canyon walls narrow into Cleveland Gorge, so named for the rare Cleveland penstemon (*Penstemon clevelandii*) which grows in these rocky clefts. The red blossoms on long stems make this plant easy to recognize when in bloom.

14.7 The First Child Monument at BM 2207' and an old corral just west (left) of the route are found here. Salvador Ygnacio Linares was long thought to have been the first child of European descent born in California, until a search of baptismal records proved otherwise. Juan Joseph Garcia, born in a field near Mission San Luis Obispo on November 11, 1774, preceded Linares by some 13 months. The location of the monument is:

        UTM 5-45.9E 37-00.2N   LAT 33°26.41'N LON 116°30.35'W

        The trail swings west into the tree-lined tunnel of...

14.8 Upper Willows and exit into the bright sun of Fig Tree Valley.

15.0 Upper closure fence.
        Bailey's Cabin is just west of the fence and a sharp turn south (left) out of the creekbed. The 10' x 14' concrete-floored shack, a former cattle line shack or

outpost which belonged to early-day cattleman Howard Bailey, offers storm shelter to hikers and a corral for riders.

The main village of Los Coyotes Cahuilla, called *Wiliya*, was also located in Fig Tree Valley and possibly spread to the mouth of Alder Canyon. Other villages were extensions or "colonies" of *Wiliya*. One was to the south in Alder Canyon. Others were located at Middle Willows (Santa Catarina), Salvador Canyon, and Mangalar Spring. Anza's second expedition camped at or near *Wiliya* on Christmas Eve, 1775. He called the Indians and their village *Los Danzantes* (The Dancers) because of the way they moved and gestured.

There are several condescending descriptions found in the Spanish diaries that refer to the Cahuillas either running away or gesturing to the Spaniards to stay away. The Spaniards interpreted these reactions as a sign of inferiority. But what of the Cahuillas? What were their thoughts about the intruding Spaniards? Katherine Siva Saubel, Cahuilla elder whose people lived in Coyote Canyon, describes their prophetic view of the Spaniards:

> *When the first Spaniards landed in the territory, the Cahuilla people were look-ing at them and were afraid of them. They thought they were ghosts. They thought the Spanish were dead people because they looked so white; they needed blood, they were dying people. Here they were the conquerors, you know, they were coming in and the Cahuilla didn't want to go near them because they thought they had some kind of disease, see? That's what the Cahuillas said when they were looking at them. But it wasn't that way at all. The Spanish were here to get what they were going to get from us—and they did....They (the Anglos) were just as bad as the Spanish. They were just there to destroy the Cahuillas.*

End Of Trip 2A—Hikers, bikers, and horses can see trip 2C for the continuation (in reverse) of this trip from the town of Anza (Hwy 371) to this point.

TRIP 2B:
Collins Valley West-Side Canyon Hikes

With the exception of Borrego Palm Canyon, the west-side canyons of Collins Valley are the most popular hiking and backpacking areas in the park, and with good reason. Here, probably more than anywhere else in the park, the visitor can stand amid the mystery, majesty, and solitude of this desert wilderness. Mountain plateaus and peaks overlook arid bajadas and wet lowlands in stream-laced canyon tongues. Whether by short walk, overnight hike, or challenging inter-canyon traverse, these gorges beckon to all who would encounter the essential spirit of this land.

The water and the vegetation, along with the isolation, make the area attractive to bighorn sheep and mule deer. Near palm trees and along boulder-formed caves at the bottom of various canyons, evidence of Cahuilla use can be found—bedrock grinding spots, shards, flaking, and kitchen middens.

Collins Valley's west-side canyons are best explored from a base at Sheep Canyon Primitive Campground. *Caution*: Although stated mileages in these mountain-desert canyons may appear short, these are extremely rugged miles due to rapid ascents and descents, lack of defined trails, dense brush and shrubbery, repeated stream crossings, often waterless conditions, steep canyon walls, dry waterfalls, and challenging map-and-compass work. A rough guide to time planning is that these miles take three times as long as miles on trail or across open desert. The best cross-reference to use in planning extensive hikes in this area is Schad (see Appendix 1).

Indian Canyon

0.0 **Elevation 1620'. Trailhead is 0.2 mile east of Sheep Canyon Campground.**

0.8 Cross Cougar Canyon stream bed—access to Cougar Canyon (see below)—and follow the trail which hugs the hillside to the west and then opens up to the entrance of the Valley of a Thousand Springs.

2.0 The draw to the west (right) leads one-quarter mile into Bennis Bowl, named for Karl V. Bennis, one of the earliest recreational visitors to the Anza-Borrego Desert, who began his desert excursions around 1910.

2.2 Old Tin Mine tunnel on west (right) side of trail.

2.3 Elevation 2180'. Deering Canyon enters from the west (right). This canyon ascends rapidly for about a mile. It is typical of the several named and unnamed canyons that are tributary to Indian Canyon, most of which contain palm trees and seasonal streams. Although these side canyons are rugged and remote, it is well worth the extra physical effort to enjoy the peaceful isolation among the palm fronds and the sounds of water trickling over the boulders.

3.1 Elevation 2560'. The canyon forks. At the confluence of the two canyons a spring supports a grove of California fan palms and several sycamore trees in the heart of the area known as the Valley of the Thousand Springs. An old Cahuilla trail turns southwest (right) and climbs steeply via switchbacks along the ridge between the canyon branches. This trail swings west, keeping south of the creekbed for about another mile to a saddle at about 4160' feet on the boundary of Los Coyotes Reservation. Permission to enter must be obtained in advance from the Los Coyotes tribal council (see Appendix 2).

The main canyon continues due south from the fork. Experienced backpackers may work up the steep, exposed ridge to the east of the main canyon, heading toward Palm Mesa at the 4500' level. (See Trip 1C above for a description of the backpack from Borrego Palm Canyon to Indian Canyon via Palm Mesa.)

Cougar Canyon

Cougar Canyon, a fork of Indian Canyon 0.8 mile south of the vehicle route, is known for its cool running stream, its massive jumble of granite

Temescal (sweathouse) at entrance to Cougar Canyon

boulders, its high waterfalls, its shady sycamore, cottonwood, and palm trees, and its Cahuilla *temescal*, or sweat house, found on the north side of the canyon's mouth. The very rugged canyon has a wide opening but it narrows suddenly and rises in a series of rock steps. The lowest pools, near the mouth of the canyon hugging its south wall, are tree-shaded and easily accessible as a day hike from Sheep Canyon. Going up-canyon becomes more challenging. A rope may be needed for security in scaling some of the near-vertical canyon walls and boulders. A waterfall cascading down a grotto system and pools deep enough to swim in await adventurous souls about two miles up-canyon from Indian Canyon.

Sheep Canyon

Sheep Canyon, centrally located in the Coyote Canyon west-side canyon system, offers good inter-canyon traverses. Its stream, like those in most west-side canyons, is seasonal. In late summer it is completely dry and only a few seeps, mud holes and small springs high up in the canyon provide water for bighorn sheep and other animals. When the fall rains come, the stream starts running, and at the height of the winter rains, it runs well past the Sheep Canyon campground toward Coyote Creek. As summer approaches, the streams become smaller, receding farther and farther up-canyon until the cycle is complete in late summer.

0.0   Elevation 1640'. The trailhead is at the west end of Sheep Canyon Primitive Campground. Slicks and morteros on boulders near the trailhead attest to Cahuilla presence in this canyon. In 1993, Boy Scouts discovered the skeletal remains of an Indian in the stream bed near the trailhead, which were removed for reburial by area Cahuillas.

0.2   South Fork of Sheep Canyon joins from the west (left). This fork is very steep and rugged although its palm grove is visible from camp. A peak (elev. 4649') near the head of the canyon, separating the South Fork from main fork to the north, is locally called Square Top for its obvious aspect. Continue up-canyon, following a footpath that occasionally disappears, winding up, over, and around sometimes enormous boulders, past shady cottonwoods and sycamores, watching out for thick brush, downed tree limbs, and occasional thorny plants as you cross and recross the creek several times, working your way up to...

0.5   First palm grove and spring grotto, with a 20-foot waterfall and a 30-foot-long tree-shaded pool. Because this is such a picturesque setting, hikers should take particular care to leave only footprints. *Do not* burn your toilet paper. Two fires have occurred in this canyon due to campers accidentally starting fires while attempting to burn their toilet paper—pack it out! The last fire, in spring 1996, scorched 1350 acres beginning at the 2000' elevation and burning west and north for 2.5 miles before it was contained at the 5000' level. Many of the canyon's palms, cottonwoods and sycamores were burned.

1.1   Elevation 2250'. A small tributary canyon climbs steeply north (right) about a mile to a saddle at elev. 2900'. On the other side of this saddle, the south fork of Salvador Canyon leads north to enter the main Salvador Canyon about two miles from the saddle.

The main Sheep Canyon continues ascending through palm and sycamore groves within steep canyon walls. Large boulders and dense shrubbery make passage difficult, with progress measured in hours per mile.

1.9   Elevation 2450'. Past a narrow portal in the canyon between a small ridge ascending right and a steep wall to the left, the canyon opens up into a large bowl surrounded by distinct peaks. This beautiful bowl may be the place called "Panoquk" by the Cahuilla, and "Hellhole" by early cattlemen, as reported by Jack Welch. From a vantage point on the hillside north of the brush-choked stream bed, two westward routes can be studied. The one to the southwest (left) is a loop trip back to Sheep Canyon campground via Square Top peak and South Fork canyon. The one to the northwest is the main route continuing up Sheep Canyon.

Loop Trip Back to Campground Via South Fork

Southwest of the bowl a canyon rises abruptly above a thick grove of trees. This grove can be followed about a mile to a point from where one can climb south (left) up to the saddle west of Square Top (peak

4649'). By traveling another mile over this saddle, the hiker can reach the South Fork of Sheep Canyon. About 3 miles east (left) is Sheep Canyon Primitive Campground (see above).
End of Loop Trip

1.9 Elevation 2450' (repeated from above).

From the bowl, main Sheep Canyon continues northwest, and it requires very careful route selection and map work. From mile 1.9, just inside the bowl west of its entrance, continue along the hillside north of the creekbed, go through the prominent gully that runs north (right) past "Knob" and "Collins" survey points, continue to the west edge of the bowl, and identify the point at which the canyon swings north (right) around a prominent ridge line. This point is about mile 2.9.

2.9 Elevation 2840'.

The best guide is to follow the main watercourse of Sheep Canyon. Continue to swing right as the canyon abruptly climbs. You will view cliffs at the 3200' level. After climbing these cliffs, either left or right of the stream bed, you will be in a small bowl. Now keeping to the east and north, (right) side of the stream bed, negotiate another set of cliffs, from atop which, at about mile 3.8, one can view the upper reaches of Sheep Canyon.

3.8 Elevation 3800'.

Continue west from these cliff tops, working along the hillside just north (right) of the stream bed.

4.8 Elevation 4050'.

Directly north (right) of this point, at the low point of the ridge, is the saddle between Sheep and Salvador canyons and also a tributary of the south fork of Alder Canyon. From this point (elev. 4050'), there are two choices: a side trip continuing west up-canyon to the head of Sheep Canyon

Fairy Grotto in Sheep Canyon

(described just below); or a climb one-quarter mile north (right) to the Sheep/Alder/Salvador saddle for an excellent view and more route possibilities. "Sage Flat" is just on the other side (north) of the saddle (described after the side trip below).

Side Trip West to Head Of Sheep Canyon and Lost Valley

A large grove of pine and oak trees, known as "The Grapevine," is visible about a half-mile southwest from mile 4.8 (elev. 4050'). This grove is a spring (elev. 4550') near the head of Sheep Canyon. From here an old Cahuilla trail can be followed about two miles southwest up-canyon and over an easy saddle at 4900' into Shingle Spring and Lost Valley. This important trail connected villages in the Warner Springs area with those in middle and upper Coyote Canyon via Lost Valley and Agua Caliente Creek. An old, now-closed jeep trail followed part of it.

End of Side Trip

From mile 4.8 (elev. 4050') in Sheep Canyon, climb one-quarter mile north (right) of the stream bed to...

5.1 Sheep-Salvador-Alder Saddle (elev. 4400').

From this saddle one can see the often-snow-capped summit of Mt. San Jacinto, 35 miles north. Sage Flat (elev. 4200') is the large flat area just north of the saddle. It is a welcome respite from the rigors of canyon and cliff climbing.

There are three possible northerly routes down from the saddle and Sage Flat into Coyote Canyon: 1) northwest (left) via a tributary to the south fork of Alder Canyon; 2) north (straight ahead) via the old Cahuilla trail; and 3) northeast (right) via Salvador Canyon. Each of these routes leaves "Sage Flat" about a half mile north from the saddle. Mileage is continuous from the saddle.

Route 1—Sage Flat to Fig Tree Valley Via South Fork, Alder Canyon

5.1 Saddle at 4400'. Bear northwest (left) when descending through Sage Flat, into the head of a small canyon. This canyon deepens, and some rock scrambling is required.

7.2 Join the south fork of Alder Canyon near a very large alder tree, and turn north (right). Vines, down trees, stream crossings, and thorny catclaw thickets make travel difficult. A series of springs here generally provide year-round water for wildlife.

9.7 Junction of North and South forks, Alder Canyon near an old cabin site and a huge cottonwood. Continue east downstream into...

11.6 Fig Tree Valley, just northwest of Bailey's Cabin.

Route 2—Sage Flat to Fig Tree Valley Via Cahuilla Ridge Trail

5.1 Saddle at 4400'. Cross Sage Flat and ascend a small hill north of the flat. Work down the ridge to the north.

8.1 Fig Tree Valley near Bailey's Cabin.

Route 3—Sage Flat to Coyote Canyon Via Salvador Canyon

5.1 Saddle at 4400'. Bear northeast (right) when descending through Sage Flat, into a small canyon. This is the head of Salvador Canyon.

See below for a description of hiking up Salvador to this point.

11.0 Vehicle junction in Collins Valley. About 2.5 miles southwest is Sheep Canyon Campground, making this Sheep-to-Salvador Canyon traverse an excellent one-or two-night backpack. Water is generally available for this loop trip.

Salvador Canyon

Salvador debouches into northwest Collins Valley, just over a mile northwest of survey point "Wash" (elev. 1402'). The Salvador/main Coyote Canyon junction is mile 9.7 Trip 2A at elev. 1560'.

0.0   Salvador Canyon junction (elev. 1560').

A short 4WD road leads northwest up the canyon to dead-end at about mile 0.3. Northwest is a prominent hilltop, elev. 2490' on a topo map.

1.2   South Fork of Salvador Canyon (elev. 1850'). Side hikes are available both south and north from here:

Side Hike South to Saddle into Sheep Canyon

A steep canyon leads south about one-quarter mile to a little palm oasis with a seasonal waterfall. About two miles farther south is a saddle (elev. 2900'). The canyon down the other side of this saddle leads about another mile into Sheep Canyon, a mile west of Sheep Canyon Campground.

Side Hike North Into Yucca Valley

To the west of the prominent hilltop 2490', mentioned above, is a saddle. Climb up the gully for about a half-mile to Canyon View at the head of Yucca Valley, from where a loop hike via Middle Willows is possible (see Trip 2A, mile 13.2).

Main trail continues west up-canyon. From here on, it is apparent why Salvador was named "Thousand Palms Canyon" by Randall Henderson. A fire on July 4, 1980, totally engulfed the canyon, with smoke visible from Palomar Mountain, and destroyed all visible growth. Just four years later, Skip Ruland, author of the now out-of-print *Backpacking Guide to San Diego County*, reported that the palms had three- to four-foot green fronds sprouting from the crowns of the fire-blackened trunks, which attests to the resiliency of these trees. Today, the brush-choked canyon floor, the tangle of palm fronds, the thorny mesquite, the long reedy grasses, and the continual stream crossings combine to make passage difficult.

After another mile the canyon forks at elevation 2200'. The southwest fork is better watered but is very brush-choked. The drier west (right) fork is the main Salvador Canyon. Bear southwest (left) at a fork at mile 3.2 (elev 2750').

4.4   Elevation 3500'. Main canyon turns decisively south and goes another mile to about elev. 4100'. From here, take any route west a few hundred yards onto Sage Flat.

5.5   Sage Flat (elev. 4200') and Sheep/Alder/Salvador Saddle (elev. 4400'). See Sheep Canyon hike above for description of Sage Flat.

TRIP 2C:
Anza to Fig Tree Valley, Upper Willows Via Coyote Canyon

From: Anza (Hwy 371)
To: Fig Tree Valley, Upper Willows
Via: Terwilliger Valley (paved roads), Coyote Canyon Road (dirt road until Turkey Track grade), Coyote Canyon (marginal 4WD road)

Points Of Interest and Side Trips:
Nance Canyon, Turkey Track, Tule Canyon, Horse Canyon/White Wash, Parks Canyon, Alder Canyon, Fig Tree Valley, Bailey's Cabin.

Connecting Trips:
   2A– Borrego Springs to Upper Willows, Fig Tree Valley
   2B– Collins Valley west-side canyon hikes (Alder Canyon)

Summary:
It is about 75 miles from Borrego Springs to the town of Anza via Hwys S-22, 79, and 371. The route as described here guides motor vehicles from Anza south to the road closure at Upper Willows. Hikers, mountain bikers, and horseback riders can continue through the 3.1-mile closed segment to Middle Willows and on to Borrego Valley, 36 miles from Anza to Christmas Circle. This entire northern Coyote Canyon area is closed to all from June 1 to September 30 annually to facilitate bighorn-sheep access to water. With the termination of through motor-vehicle traffic, this area has become the most lonely, remote, and wild area of the park that still has a road.

   To even call the half-mile pitch down Turkey Track a 4WD road is being generous. Look up "bad" in a thesaurus. There aren't enough synonyms there to do justice to this bad boy. After "bad" try "nasty" or "treacherous" or "terrifying." Better yet, don't drive down at all. This is a great place to start backpacking, dayhiking, mountain biking, or giddyup. (By the way, the unmaintained, so-called "road" gets worse every year.)

POST MILES FROM:
Anza

0.0   Anza (elev. 3918'), junction of Kirby Road and Hwy 371.
   This junction is 1.5 miles east of the center of town via Hwy 371. Go south (right) one mile to Wellman Road, east (left) one mile to Terwilliger Road, south (right) into Terwilliger Valley. Kamp Anza RV park, a couple of miles down the road, offers full services and a fish pond. It's a great base camp from which to explore the entire area described below.

4.4   Terwilliger/Coyote Canyon Road junction.

Side Trip To Tule Springs And The PCT
   From the Terwilliger/Coyote Road junction, continue south 2.5 miles to the Tule Canyon dirt road. Drive east (left) another couple of

𝕏   miles through the high chapparal to the ABDSP boundary. Walk east from here, crossing the Pacific Crest Trail (PCT), to the spring (elev. 3560'). Schaffer et al (see Appendix 1) offer this:

Year-round Tule Spring is the only reliable water hole on the PCT for miles. It emerges from a dry, brushy hillside to feed a stand of large cottonwoods that in turn shade a sandy, grassy creekside terrace—a fine campsite.

It is a pleasant 2.9-mile stroll from here to the Coyote Canyon Road northwest along the PCT, offering hikers an option to be dropped off near Tule Spring and be picked up in Coyote Canyon just southeast of the summer closure gate.

End Of Side Trip

4.4   Terwilliger/Coyote Canyon Road junction (repeated from above). Turn east (left) onto Coyote Canyon Road.

6.0   Private road to south (left) leads one-quarter mile to the Art Carey Ranch. A monument on the ranch, erected by the Native Sons of the Golden West in 1924, marks "La Puerta Real de San Carlos." San Carlos Pass itself drops between the two high points across the ranch into Nance Canyon, noted below. This pass (elev. 3800') is of major significance and elation in the Anza chronicles. The Spanish leaders knew it to be the dividing point between the hardships and the rigors of the desert crossing, now behind them, and pastoral, coastal California ahead. San Carlos Pass is analogous to Teofulio Pass (elev. 3636') on the Southern Emigrant Trail (Hwy S-2) in that they both mark the watershed divide on a major historic route between desert and green California. San Carlos Pass hosted most of southern California's immigrants during the Spanish period (late 18th century) while Teofulio hosted those of the Mexican period (early 19th century) and the American imperial period (middle 19th century).

6.2   Road turns south and climbs a small rise at BM 3937'. "High Country Estates" development is the complex of roads to the east, straight ahead, of this junction.

8.0   Nance Canyon.

The small valley at the headwaters of Nance Canyon assumes major historical significance, with the arroyo from San Carlos Pass entering its far northwest edge from Terwilliger Valley. A narrow finger of ABDSP runs from the road one mile west along the north side of the valley to San Carlos arroyo which was the Anza second-expedition campsite on December 26, 1775. With the sudden arrival that afternoon of almost three hundred colonists and eight hundred cattle, it is little surprise that the quiet Cahuilla village here was "hastily abandoned" per Padre Pedro Font's report. Of additional portent that evening was an earthquake which Font noted and Anza recorded as lasting four minutes.

This was the first documentation of seismic activity on what is now known as southern California's most active fault zone, the San Jacinto. It is ironic that the most feared portion of that fault zone, because of its inactivity

Lower Nance Canyon

and strain buildup, is a twenty-mile segment called the "Anza Gap." It is in this now-dormant "gap" that Anza and Font recorded the major quake noted above.

Private property is on either side of the ABDSP finger, so tread responsibly should you explore this historic little valley.

The road crosses Nance Creek and climbs left, entering...

8.7   ABDSP, summer closure gate, closed from June 1 to September 30.

9.2   PCT crossing (elev. 3500').

Tule Spring is 2.9 miles southwest (right) on the PCT (see description above). Nance Creek, just a half-mile down the PCT on the left, offers a seasonal creek and campsites. Nance may be hiked down into Coyote Canyon but it's a rugged bushwhacker.

The road undulates southeast with the vistas into Coyote and its tributaries opening up. The Santa Rosas, topped by 8716' Toro Peak, massively dominate the eastern skyline. There is a sense that, beyond this mountain rampart, lies *the abyss*.

10.7   Top o' Turkey Track (elev. 3300').

Shift into compound low, put passengers out, cinch your seat belt, tighten other loose stuff, and commence the descent down a steep half-mile of rocky, rutted, rough track featuring overhangs, hairpin curves, and huge potholes. (This must be the original E-ticket ride.)

This is "Anza Ridge" which CCC road builders punched through in 1933. In terms of restoring wilderness, it's inspiring to see what sixty subsequent years of neglect can do to a road. Joseph Wood Krutch would be proud—he

who celebrated "how much bad roads can do for a country. Bad roads act as fil-
ters...the rougher the road, the finer the filter."

11.3 Turkey Track—Tule and Nance Canyons (BM 2696').

A spring and seasonal stream are about a mile north up Nance Canyon,
named for an old homesteader. A jeep trail extends about a mile west up
Tule canyon past CDF water tanks to a cottonwood grove and spring. The
name "Turkey Track" derives from the vertical plan view of these two canyons
and Horse Canyon joining to form Coyote Canyon proper in a giant print, worthy of a *T. rex*. Question—which way was *Turkey rex* walking?

11.7 Horse Canyon.

This, the largest of the Turkey Track canyons, supports a seasonal creek,
sometimes a river, which rises high on Toro Peak, where it is called Coyote
Creek. There are several groves of cottonwoods within the ABDSP reaches of
Horse Canyon. Old-time cattleman Carlos Morena (Charlie Brown) referred to
Coyote Canyon as "The Ranch," and the wild horses of the canyon as "The
Ranch Remuda." Wild horses are still very much a part of this canyon.

Side Trip Up Horse Canyon (hike or backpack)

About a mile north of Turkey Track is a shaded area, just before the
turnoff to White Wash, which is an old cattle camp that provides a
good campsite (elev. 2850). We have seen huge lion-paw prints and wild-
horse hoof prints in the sand here. In this area, near the entrance to White
Wash was the Mountain Cahuilla Indian village of *Nacuta*.

Hike up White Wash

Broad White Wash to the east (right) offers a fine four-mile
hike to the saddle overlooking Dry Wash. From cottonwoods in
Horse Canyon, the hike passes through groves of large nolina yucca
and staghorn cholla, then juniper, redshank and agave, and finally a
thick pinyon-juniper forest at the saddle at elev. 4150'. Abundant
dark-green amphibolite intermixes with the classic salt-and-pepper
granitics of the Peninsular Ranges. The erosive detritus from the latter gives White Wash its name. The view from the saddle, overlooking Dry Wash, Jackass Flat, Butler Canyon, and Clark Valley far to
the southeast, is superb.

End of Hike

Backpackers can continue due north from the cottonwood grove up
Horse Canyon, passing Medicine Canyon (right) just north of White
Wash. At about mile two, Horse Canyon turns northwest (left). The
canyon narrows as the route crosses and re-crosses the stream several
times through thickets of arrow weed and tamarisk. Box Canyon joins
from the northeast (right) just north of here.

At about mile three from Turkey Track, select the most likely-look-
ing route climbing northwest (left) up onto Table Mountain. Any route
will do—any will be a steep climb onto the flat mesa where the Table
Mountain dirt road or the PCT will be intersected, still in the northern-

Backpackers in upper reaches of Horse Canyon

most extension of ABDSP. From the Table Mountain viewpoint, one may select a route which works west into Terwilliger Valley through the High Country Estates area. The objective is the junction of Terwilliger and Coyote Canyon roads, 4.4 miles south of Anza.
End Of Side Trip

11.6 Horse Canyon (repeated from above).

12.6 Parks Canyon.
A hike goes west into the broad mouth of Parks Canyon, named for the Parks brothers who lived in Anza Valley and had a cattle camp in Parks Canyon. Oak trees and a seasonal stream are located about two miles in (approximately elev. 3000').

Our road continues southeast downstream, past a narrows at BM 2415', into Fig Tree Valley. The name "Fig Tree" was the original name for Upper Willows when it was used by early-day cattlemen of Anza-Borrego.

14.1 Alder Canyon southwest (right).

Hike up Alder Canyon

At mile 0.9 a hiking trail turnoff left leads east and south around the hillside to Mangalar Spring. The spring lies on the east slope of the bottom of a small canyon, a few feet above the wash. The sumacs by the spring, known by the Cahuilla name of *Mangalar*, are not tall but very old, gnarled, and heavily trunked. Mangalar Flat, which slopes gently down from the spring toward Coyote Creek, is covered with creosote bush, Mojave yucca, buckhorn cholla, catclaw, cheese bush and burro weed. Desert apricot, sumac and beavertail are found on the hillside above the spring.

Mile 1.9 is the old jeep roadhead (elev. 2650'). Seasonal streams ripple down both forks of Alder to join in the tree-shaded grove where old cottonwoods are found, with alders upstream. The diameters of some of these trees are about three feet. A few remains in the clearing mark the location of an old cabin belonging to cattleman O. Valentine "Val" Bixby, who took up an 80-acre homestead here in 1921.

Just south of the cabin site, where the trail starts up South Fork Alder Canyon, was a spring that Howard Bailey developed in later years. An old pipe still sticks out of the hill, marking the site. This was also the site for the Mountain Cahuilla Indian village called *Tepana*, an outlying village for Wiliya in Fig Tree Valley.

An old Cahuilla trail leads up the South Fork and over a saddle into Lost Valley. Cupeño and Cahuilla from Los Coyotes Indian Reservation continued to use this trail to Coyote Canyon well into the 1910s. Its lower reaches involve serious bushwhacking. Up-canyon vegetation is indicative of higher elevation and changing life zone—juniper, scrub oak, white sage, Mojave yucca, Mangalar sumac, buckhorn cholla, desert apricot, goatnut and catclaw. (The descent from Sheep Canyon and Sage Flat down the South Fork is described above in Trip 2B.)
End Of Side Trip

14.1 Alder Canyon (repeated from above).

14.5 Bailey's Cabin and the Cahuilla village site of Wiliya. (See description above at the end of Trip 2A.)

15.0 Upper Willows, motor-vehicle-closure fence.

It is 3.1 miles afoot downstream, past First Child Monument, past the Riverside/San Diego County line, through Middle Willows to the lower Coyote Canyon 4WD roadhead in northwest Collins Valley (see Trip 2A above). Southbound hikers, bikers, and horses will travel another 18 miles southeast to Christmas Circle, making the Anza-to-Borrego Springs distance a total of 36 miles.

AREA 3-NORTHEASTERN:
east Hwy S-22, north Hwy 86

The Santa Rosa Mountains and the Borrego Badlands are the main geographic features of this area. The Santa Rosas, part of the Peninsular Ranges geomorphic province, are fault-block mountains which have been uplifted on their west side and tilted eastward, with a distinct west-facing escarpment.

The sere Santa Rosas are the loftiest and the loneliest area in the Anza-Borrego region. From the 8716' summit at Toro Peak, the Santa Rosa massif runs 30 miles southeast, splitting desert from desert, until even this great range is swallowed up in its own outwash of sand flats and mud hills 200 feet below sea level. Much of this area is within the boundaries of Anza-Borrego Desert State Park and is a state wilderness area. This is a rough, rocky, little-visited wilderness, where one of the last remaining herds of desert bighorn sheep survives. The lower desert slopes, dotted with ocotillo, cholla, yucca, and barrel cactus, give way to juniper and pinyon pine at higher elevations.

The presence of long-departed ones can still be sensed in burial grounds of prehistoric man, traces of ancient Indian trails and cairns of early prospectors. There is little evidence of modern man in the Santa Rosas save for the Borrego-Salton Seaway, which slices across the southern flank, and its associated 4WD routes.

Standing in stark contrast to the Santa Rosa Mountains are the highly eroded badlands to the south and east. The Borrego Badlands consist of fairly recent stream, lake and plain deposits that were uplifted through fault action and then carved and eroded by running water and wind, creating a labyrinth of V-shaped gorges within these clay hills.

This vast, undulating badlands area is rich in Pliocene and Pleistocene fossils which show that mastodons, camels, sabertooth cats, and horses lived here one to two million years ago. The basin-margin area of the badlands was once part of a grassland with wooded areas and streams.

TRIP 3A:
Borrego Springs To Salton City Via HWY S-22

From: Christmas Circle, Borrego Springs
To: Salton City (Hwy 86)
Via: Hwy S-22 (paved road)

Connecting Trips:
   1B–Montezuma Junction to Borrego Springs via Hwy S-22
   2A–Christmas Circle to Upper Willows (northbound)
   3B–Clark Valley and Rockhouse Canyon
   3C–Fonts Point—Central Borrego Badlands
   3D–Seventeen Palms—Eastern Borrego Badlands
   3E–Calcite Mine Area to Salton City via Palm Wash
   3F–Salton City to Travertine Rock via Hwy 86
   3G–Travertine Palms to Palo Verde Canyon (backpack)
   5F–Trifolium (Hwy 78) to Salton City via Hwy 86

Points Of Interest and Side Trips:
Pegleg Smith Monument, Coyote Mountain, Clark Valley, Beckman Wash, Inspiration Point/Western Borrego Badlands, Thimble Trail, Rattlesnake Canyon, Palo Verde Wash, Smoke Tree Wash, Coachwhip Canyon/Ella Wash, Arroyo Salado, Truckhaven Rocks.

Summary:
Prominent county post mile markers appear almost every mile until the San Diego/Imperial County line, so odometer mileage is not necessary. Between the county line and Salton City, two way odometer mileage is given. Although the main route is paved, any driving off it may encounter deep sand traps. Check with the visitor center for current conditions.

POST MILES FROM:
Junction of Hwys S-2/S-22

0.0   Montezuma Junction (Hwys S-2 and S-22).

19.0 East exit from Christmas Circle, Borrego Springs.
   Drive east on Hwy S-22 Palm Canyon Drive toward Fonts Point, passing the airport at mile 21.5. Hwy S-22 swings to the north at Old Springs Road (mile 23) and becomes Pegleg Road. The largest sand-dune field in the Borrego Valley is just east of mile 23.
   Old Springs Road (aka Palm Canyon Drive East) curves south, reaches the dump, and becomes a very sandy 4WD road which leads several miles southeast to the original "Borego Spring" and the site of Anza's San Gregorio campsite.

24.8 West Beckman Wash.
   This 4WD road to the east (right) penetrates the western edge of the Borrego Badlands and loops north to rejoin Hwy S-22 near post mile marker 27 after about five miles (see description below of North Beckman Wash).
   Just north of this turnoff, the old Truckhaven Trail strikes east through tamarisk groves that are popular RV campsites.

25.7 Pegleg Monument Junction.

This is the junction of Pegleg Road and Henderson Canyon Road. Henderson Canyon leads west (left), crossing Coyote Creek wash at one of the valley's most likely wildflower displays in the month of March. Ranger Jim Meier reports acorns sprouting here in the wet spring of '93, possibly washed down from the Turkey Track area.

A rock mound, a desert mail box, a hand painted sign, and a California historical landmark mark the site of the Pegleg Smith Monument and the place to begin the search for the elusive black-coated golden pebbles found on or near the legendary "three buttes" in the Anza-Borrego area.

Peg Leg Smith Monument (California Historical Landmark No. 750)
UTM 5-65.4E 36-84.1N   LAT 33°17.75'N LON 116°17.87'W

Smith's tales of lost gold evolved into one of the best-known legends of the Southwest. The sign at the monument reads, "Let him who seeks Pegleg Smith's gold add ten rocks to this monument." The monument and sign were created by Harry Oliver, Borrego homesteader and self-proclaimed press agent for Pegleg Smith. This is the site of the annual Pegleg Smith Liar's Contest, held the first Saturday night in April. (Call the Borrego Springs Chamber of Commerce to confirm the date.) The contest, a revival of those held in the late 1940s and early 1950s, began in 1975 and continues to this day under the tutelage of CACTI Southwest, an unorganized non-group that befits the decorum of desert yarn-spinning. The contest starts at sundown on the first Saturday on or after April Fools Day except when the next day is the first Sunday after the first full moon on or after the Spring Equinox, when said contest goes to the second Saturday in April. (This sounds preposterous but is no lie.) The desert mailbox was erected by Desert Steve Ragsdale in 1949 so that prospectors could leave clues to Pegleg's gold. Today, comments and observations written by park visitors can be found in the mailbox.

🚶 A steep trail up Coyote Mountain begins northeast of the Pegleg Smith Monument. Vegetation is scarce—a few ocotillos, some brittlebush and creosote. The rocky surface of the mountain is deeply impregnated with dark red-brown desert varnish. It continues another couple of miles up the mountain toward peak 2589'. The actual summit of Coyote Mountain, at elev. 3192', is a mile further north, but the best and shortest approach to the summit is from the east side, just west of Clark Dry Lake. See Schad's *Afoot and Afield in San Diego County* for a description of this east-side approach.

Hwy S-22 curves to the east.

Jack Calvert, first full-time Supervisor of Anza-Borrego in his "recommendation" for desert uniforms

26.2 Paved road turnoff to the northeast (left) goes into Clark Valley and Rockhouse Canyon (see trip 3B below).

26.7 North Beckman Wash, south (right).

This 4WD route loops about five miles southeast into the Borrego Badlands and west back to Hwy S-22.

Drive up an unmarked wash into ABDSP. At mile 2.5 is an overlook of Mammoth Cove. The edge of the Borrego Badlands, which starts near here at Inspiration Point and winds east past Fonts Point and Vista del Malpais, is locally known as the Ocotillo Rim. The road turns west over a low saddle into West Beckman Wash. Just north of this point is a thick layer of three-quarter-million-year-old Bishop tuff—a whitish volcanic ash fall from Long Valley near Mammoth Lakes, hundreds of miles to the north. This ash bed was discovered by ranger Paul Remeika in August 1992. West Beckman reaches S-22 near post mile marker 25 about five miles from the beginning of the loop.

27.9 ABDSP Boundary—Truckhaven Trail crosses from southwest to northeast.

The dirt track straight ahead (where the paved road angles slightly right) is the old Truckhaven Trail, built in 1929 by pioneer Borrego homesteader A.A. "Doc" Beaty, using mule-drawn Fresno scrapers. One of these Fresnos was donated to the park and can be seen today at Horse Camp. The Truckhaven Trail was used by Borrego residents as a major route to Coachella Valley until 1968, when the paved Borrego-Salton Seaway was completed. The trail was named for the Truckhaven Cafe, which was at the trail's east end at Hwy 86. This segment of the Truckhaven Trail may be followed by 4WD for about 5 miles, paralleling the paved road to the Thimble Trail turnoff.

28.2 Inspiration Wash south (right).

A 4WD road southeast (right) leads up Inspiration Point Wash about three miles to Inspiration Point saddle (elev. 1050'). The last half winds through narrow sandstone passages. This is the ragged western edge of the Borrego Badlands, which overlooks Mammoth Cove to the south and west, named for the largest Pleistocene fossils to be found here.

Inspiration Point (elev. 1211') is the high point southeast (left). Fonts Point (elev. 1294' until the next big quake) is on the skyline beyond Inspiration. People can sometimes be seen standing on Fonts Point, a crow's mile away.

The road drops into Mammoth Cove, and proceeds about four miles to the county dump. Turn north here onto paved Old Springs Road 0.7 mile to Hwy S-22 at mile 23. Total loop trip from S-22 to the dump via Inspiration Point is about nine miles.

29.4 Fonts Point Wash south (right).

See Trip 3C for routes in the central Borrego Badlands.

30.0 Santa Rosa Overlook south (right).

Earthquakes! sculpting the face of the desert (ABDSP Interpretive Panel)
UTM 5-72.1E 36-84.9N   LAT 33°18.16'N LON 116°13'W

31.7 Thimble Trail turnoff south (right).

Short Wash is a couple of miles south down this 4WD road. Sandy areas along S-22 here produce fine displays of annual wildflowers, especially sand verbena and evening primrose, after winters of sufficient rainfall. Rattlesnake Canyon and Villager Peak/Rabbit Peak hiking routes depart north from here.

Hike Up Rattlesnake Canyon (day hike or overnight climb)

0.0 Thimble Trail turnoff (elev. 970'). Hike north on a trail, lined with rock cairns.

0.4 Lute Fault Scarp is marked by the steep ridge and narrow gully to the west (left).

1.4 Base of ridge. The route to Villager and Rabbit peaks climbs left up the ridge (see below). For Rattlesnake Canyon, hike ahead up the canyon, which is dotted with palo verde trees.

2.6 The arroyo joining from the northeast (right) at elev. 1700' is the best access to Rattlesnake Spring. The following side hike is straight north up main Rattlesnake Canyon.

Side Hike Up Main Canyon

Day hikers may continue north from here another mile to another fork at elev. 2240'. Then a sharp right (east) turn leads quickly to a large, dry waterfall and the end of the day hike.

End Of Side Hike

2.6 An arroyo joins from the northeast (right) (repeated from above). The climb around "The Wall" from here is considered difficult, suitable for experienced hikers only. Novice hikers should be roped to their more seasoned leaders. Carefully work up the steep, agave-covered north side of the arroyo known as "The Wall" to bypass a series of dry waterfalls. When comfortably above the falls, drop back into the arroyo. The bad stuff is behind.

3.2 Elev. 2400'. Once back in the arroyo, take the first obvious northwest (left) gully. A large white boulder and inclined white strata mark the point. Hike north up the gully, bearing generally left and over a saddle at elev. 2970' into the Rattlesnake Spring area.

3.7 Rattlesnake Spring is located in a bushy amphitheater, backdropped by white marble cliffs on the eastern ridge line. Reliable water may be found in the draw below a solitary tree. Return via the same route, again being very careful on the descent of "The Wall".

End Of Hike

Hike Up Sierra Ridge To Villager Peak and Rabbit Peak (one- or two-night backpack—no water available)

0.0 Parking turnout 5.6 miles east of Pegleg Smith Monument at Thimble Trail turnoff (elev. 970'). Hike north on the Rattlesnake trail noted above and head toward the ridge west of Rattlesnake Canyon.

1.4 Base of ridge. The route climbs left up the ridge, following an old Indian trail which is marked by rock cairns.

3.4 This small plateau, elev. 3800', on the ridge is a good base camp. The time from here to Rabbit Peak and back to the highway is about 15 hours. The climb is somewhat steep, and there are several places where there are vertical drop-offs on the west side. Keep well back from the edges, which are unstable and constantly eroding. The route lies generally west of the ridgeline.

6.6 Villager Peak, elev. 5756'. A rock cairn and register are on the summit on a rocky outcrop on the west side of the peak. Pinyon pine and juniper predominate, and good campsites are near the top of Villager Peak for those who prefer a higher base camp from which to climb Rabbit Peak. The climb to Rabbit Peak is strenuous. It takes almost two hours to travel the 3.6 miles, following the undulating ridgeline generally north-northeast to Rabbit Peak's summit flat, which is covered with pinyon pine.

10.2 Rabbit Peak, elev. 6666', just yards north of the ABDSP boundary in Riverside County. The register is on top of the large boulder near the middle of the summit flat. (An ascent up the east ridge from the Coachella Valley is described in John Robinson's *San Bernardino Mountain Trails.*)
End Of Hike

31.7 Thimble Trail turnoff south (repeated from above).

This sandy 4WD road climbs and goes south to join the Short Wash route described in Trip 3C below off Fonts Point Wash. In its 2.2 undulating miles, Thimble Trail crosses several small, faulted ridges and a small basin, all of which are local responses to the strain of major vertical and right-lateral faulting along the nearby Clark and Coyote Creek strands of the giant San Jacinto fault zone. This was the site for scenes in the Marlon Brando movie "The Young Lions" as well as in the sci-fi movie "Damnation Alley."

32.9 Palo Verde Wash turnoff south.

The wash is named for the fine growth of palo verde (Spanish for "green stick") trees which line its sandy course. The distinct chlorophyll-filled, green-barked trees are leafless throughout much of the year until June or July, when the bright yellow blossoms of this member of the pea family are produced. This was the site of a 1950s ranger station.

Somewhere in these badlands is the surveying equipment for 60 men that was buried by a flash flood while the survey was being conducted. Patrol ranger Jack P. Welch recorded this information in his patrol notes of April 8, 1955, after a conversation with Charley Lewis of Ocotillo Wells.

Side Trip down Palo Verde Wash (4WD route)

Mile 0.0 is the junction of Palo Verde and S-22 (elev. 880'). Turn southeast (right). Short Wash joins from the west (right) at mile 2.6. (See Trip 3C below for Short Wash from Fonts Point Wash to this point in Palo Verde Wash.) Ella Wash joins from the northeast (left) at mile 2.7. (See Ella Wash side trip from Hwy S-22 to this point.)

Cut Across Trail intersection is at mile 6.3, which marks the entry to Ocotillo Wells State Vehicular Recreation Area (OWSVRA). You reach Hwy 78 at Ocotillo Wells at about mile 12.

End Of Side Trip

33.0 Palo Verde Canyon.

 Hike Up Palo Verde Canyon

Mile 0.0 is Hwy S-22 (elev. 880'). Hike north, through palo verde and smoke trees, and enter the canyon. At about mile 1.5 is an old mining campsite. A trail leads from this campsite east over a small ridge to an abandoned molybdenum ("Moly") mine. One report states that this was "Molly's Mine," not a molybdenum mine. This "Moly" Mine Trail can be followed over a ridge another 1.5 miles to the canyon bottom and then northeast to the three Natural Rock Tanks in Smoke Tree Canyon.

At mile 2.5, upper Palo Verde becomes a narrow, twisting canyon, which opens up into a small valley at mile 3.8. This is a steep, rock-strewn bowl, above which is Palo Verde Spring (elev. 2400').

End Of Hike

34.4 Borrego Badlands Overlook or Smoke Tree Overlook, south (right).

The ABDSP "Erosion Road" brochure of 1989 uses the former name, ABDNHA's *Weekender's Guide* uses the latter. Both are aptly descriptive.

34.5 Smoke Tree Canyon Wash.

Like the palo verde, the smoke tree grows only in areas that are periodically visited by flash floods. The hard outer coatings of the seeds of these plants must be scratched by the action of water and sand before they will germinate. Desert naturalist-photographer Paul Johnson describes an excellent walk south down this wash in his *Weekender's Guide*.

 A three-mile hike north (left) leads to the Natural Rock Tanks. Follow the wash up as canyon walls narrow and boulders need to be negotiated around and over. After a climb up a dry waterfall the canyon will open up and then narrow again as it turns northeast. Look for the large, deep natural depressions in the bedrock, called *tinajas*, which catch rain water after desert storms. These natural rock tanks can hold water for several weeks or longer and are an important source of water for bighorn sheep. Hikers can take a loop trip back to the highway via the Moly Mine and Palo Verde Canyon by climbing the sloping ridge to the west soon after leaving the tinajas (see Palo Verde Canyon hike above).

34.7 Ella Wash is south (right), Coachwhip Canyon is north (left).

Ella Wash was named for Ella Calvert, the wife of the first Anza-Borrego Desert State Park supervisor. It was one of her favorite washes. It is a 1.6 mile drive down Ella Wash via 4WD road to Palo Verde Wash. About halfway on the west (right), a hummock at the 800' level has rocks coated with travertine or tufa, evidence of an earlier fresh-water lake, according to park ranger Paul Remeika.

Coachwhip Canyon, a dirt road to the north, forks after one-half mile, the left fork going to the "Swiss Cheese Rocks," yellowish-red sandstone formations, pocked with holes and shaped in varied patterns. The right fork passes east of these rocks and soon dead-ends.

34.8 Arroyo Salado Primitive Camp turnoff, southeast (right).
See Trip 3D below for the Seventeen Palms area.

An Indian trail east of Arroyo Salado

35.5 Arroyo Salado and the Truckhaven Rocks, north (left).

𝕏   A one-mile hike north up Arroyo Salado leads to the fascinating Truckhaven Rocks. These are massive reddish-brown sandstones, derived from the Canebrake Formation, which were eroded from the rising Santa Rosa Mountains behind, solidified, and uplifted to tilt nearly 45 degrees from horizontal.

36.2 North Fork Arroyo Salado overlook, north (left).

This dramatic overlook of the North Fork of Arroyo Salado to the northeast has had a variety of names in various park and ABDNHA publications, all of which are aptly descriptive: Earth Movements, Sediments in Motion, Faults, Water and Wind, and Calcite Scenic Area. Confusion is eliminated by referring to it per the USGS topographic feature "North Fork...".

The isolated 2700' peak rising immediately north of this area is Travelers Peak, per former ranger Art Morley, and is so named in Remeika's *Geology of Anza-Borrego*. It is prominently seen from throughout Borrego Valley. It is not the same as "Pyramid Peak" (elev. 3500'), much farther north up the slope and unremarkable from Borrego Valley. Some recent literature has confused these high points. Both Trip 3G below and Schad (see Appendix 1) make clear the locations and relative positions of these peaks, which are very important to route-finding for backpackers along these rugged ridges.

The road crosses North Fork Arroyo Salado and five more bridge/culverts in the next two miles. The bridge east of mile 37 is Cannonball Wash, so named in the 1950s for its hundreds of cannonball-sized sandstone concretions. This is part of the "Blake's Ravines" section described by Horace Parker (see Appendix 1). Geologist William Blake and the U.S. Railroad Survey party, waterless and exhausted, passed through the Salton City area in 1853 while en route from the Coachella Valley to San Sebastian Marsh. Artwork in the official report strongly resembles these ravines, suggesting that at least one of the party detoured this far west into the Borrego region.

𝕏   Volunteer naturalist Roger Guernsey describes an interesting hike from the east side of the Cannonball Wash culvert. Hike north about 0.5 mile into the upper reaches of South Fork Palm Wash. Points of interest include wind caves, dry waterfalls, and imaginative sandstone outcrops.

38.0 Salton View Turnout (Calcite Mine Area), north (left).

This turnout too has had a variety of aptly descriptive names through the years, including Calcite Mine Overlook, Salton View, and The Inland Sea. The 1970 "Erosion Road" name, Salton View, seems most appropriate.

Today's Salton Sea is the latest edition of six major lakes to occupy this basin since about 300 A.D. All were born of the rampaging Colorado River. All, except the irrigation-fed Salton Sea, died of evaporation. The longest-lived, Lake Cahuilla, reached a high stand of 58' and lasted until about 1600 A.D., per SDSU geologist Eric Frost in a 1996 report. Cahuilla oral history is rich in stories of this great lake, as noted in Choral Pepper's *Desert Lore*. Other Salton basin lakes are reported in 1618, 1849, 1861, and 1891.

The Salton Sea was formed in 1905-07 after poorly built irrigation head gates failed on the flooding Colorado River near Yuma at about 100' above sea level. Almost the entire flow of that mighty river was diverted into the -279' below-sea-level Salton Basin, inundating farms, communities and the main line of the Southern Pacific Railroad. The Southwest's largest railroad battled her largest river for two years, dumping untold tons of material into the gap. The "Espee" finally triumphed after an outlay of millions of dollars, guaranteed for repayment by the federal government-which reneged on the deal.

A short stroll toward the mountains affords a view of Palm Wash. This is one of the main washes that drain the Santa Rosa Mountains to the Salton Basin. The microwave relay tower, located on the east boundary of ABDSP at the San Diego/Imperial county line, is about the only artificial object to mar the otherwise unspoiled view of thousands of acres of desert wilderness.

38.2 Turnoff to Calcite Mine (north) and Truckhaven Trail (south).

4WD roads depart on both sides. The route north leads 1.9 miles to the Calcite Mine (see Trip 3E below). An ABDSP interpretive panel tells the history of the mine.

> The Calcite Mine...and its role in World War II
> UTM 5-84.2E 36-82.6N   LAT 33°16.85'N LON 116°05.7'W

The 4WD route southwest is the Truckhaven Trail, which can be followed 2.7 miles, into and out of Cannonball Wash, into and out of North Fork Arroyo Salado, and into Arroyo Salado at the former location of Beaty's Icebox.

> Truckhaven Trail History (ABDSP Interpretive Panel)
> UTM 5-84.2E 36-82.6N   LAT 33°16.86'N LON 116°05.70'W

38.9 Microwave Tower, ABDSP boundary, San Diego/Imperial County line.

County post mile markers end. Continuing odometer mileage follows.

POST MILES FROM:

Hwy Salton
 79   City

39.1 8.4 San Diego/Imperial County line (elev. 500').

The mesa to the northeast, a popular RV camping area, offers serene views of the Santa Rosa Badlands, the latter term as used in the 1993 San Bernardino County Museum *Ashes, Faults, and Basins*. Four miles ahead a dirt track, known variously as the old Truckhaven Trail, North Marina Drive, and Anza Ditch, drops off the mesa to the north (left), down to Four Palms Spring. This is good campsite that was an important water hole for desert prospectors, albeit small and brackish. The highway veers right to drop off the mesa onto the flatlands. Coves west of here provide excellent sheltered campsites among the three buttes at the mouth of Gettysburg Wash. (Three buttes? Should ring a bell for Pegleg Lost Mine buffs.)

44.6 2.9 The dirt road to the south (right) leads about one mile to the site of Oh-My-God Hot Springs. This was an oil-test well from the 1920s which struck a thermal water layer, later to be designated a water reserve by the U.S.

Dept. of the Interior. This former popular camping area, surrounded by tamarisk trees and featuring stone-walled hot tubs, was bulldozed into oblivion by Imperial County authorities on June 6, 1993, allegedly for health reasons. (The life style of the long-term campers there probably led to the ultimate bulldozer solution.)

45.4 2.1 Clay Point is the concretionary mesa to the north (left). This is the final eroding alluvial whimper of the mighty Santa Rosas to the northwest. J. Smeaton Chase depicts rounding this point in the early 1900s, en route via horseback to Borrego Valley, in his classic *California Desert Trails*.

47.5 0.0 Salton City (elev. -87').
Junction with Hwy 86. A loop trip back to Borrego Valley follows Hwy 86 (Trip 5F) south about thirteen miles to Trifolium (Hwy 78), and then goes west about thirty miles via Ocotillo Wells to Borrego Springs (Trip 5A).

TRIP 3B:
Clark Valley and Rockhouse Canyon

From: Hwy S-22 east of Pegleg Smith Monument
To: Rockhouse Valley
Via: Clark Dry Lake (dirt road), Rockhouse Wash (4WD route), Rockhouse Canyon (hiking route).

Connecting Trips:
3A–Borrego Springs to Salton City via Hwy S-22

Points Of Interest and Side Trips:
Clark Dry Lake, Alcoholic Pass, Butler Canyon, Jackass Flat, Hidden Spring, Rockhouse Valley, Nicholias Canyon.

POST MILES FROM:
Hwy S-22

0.0   Clark Dry Lake turnoff (elev. 800').
The turnoff (aka Burnand Pit, CLRO Road) is just east of Pegleg Smith Monument and post mile marker 26 on Hwy S-22. Drive north and east on pavement which soon ends to enter ABDSP at mile 2.5. The park boundary has progressed southward by several miles in Clark Valley in recent years as more land has been acquired. The entire bed of Clark Dry Lake is now park land and is closed to vehicular traffic. Ranger Remeika observed canoes on Clark Suddenly-Not-Dry Lake in January 1993 in a month of 9" rainfall! (Normal annual average is 6.7".)

Clark Dry Lake hosted the University of Maryland's Clark Lake Radio Observatory (CLRO) from 1963 to the mid 1980s when it fell victim to Reagan-era budget cuts for scientific research. CLRO operated the most powerful and versatile low frequency radio telescope in the world. In 1986, CLRO lost its

Clark Dry Lake and Santa Rosa Mountains

grant support from the National Science Foundation. It had been fully opera-
tional only since 1984 and had cost several millions of dollars of public funds to
construct.

The road running along the west side of Clark Dry Lake was built by the
U.S. Army during the early 1940s when it used the area for desert maneuvers
and the dry lake bed for an airport. The dry lake was also the site of a U.S. Navy
aerial gunnery range during World War II.

Several large mesquite and tamarisk thickets, providing sun and wind
shelter, are popular campsites along this west side. These are a good answer to
the visitor center question, "Where can I camp nearby but away from people?"
They are far more wind-sheltered than the popular Pegleg area.

5.7   Survey Station "Noll".

On the hillside to the left is a seismographic sensing instrument that
relays data via a station on Toro Peak. One can visually trace the lines of the
Clark fault along the Santa Rosas across the valley to the east. The Cahuilla had
a winter camp in the low but sheltering mesquite sand dunes on the north side
of the dry lake. Nearby survey points named "Camp", "Shack", "Dare", and
"Corp(se)" evoke the sense of this remote area.

Clark Valley once supported a number of homesteaders. The remnants of
cabins can be found on the north side of the lake near Clark Well at UTM 5-
68.5E 36-90.8N. Straggling rows of tamarisk, brown and stunted from lack of
water, old fences and wells, broken glass and rusted auto parts, tin cans and
weathered boards could be seen as late as the 1980s. This is mixed private and
state park land so heed posted signs.

In the early 1980s, resource ecologist Mark Jorgenson discovered a
stand of rare elephant trees northeast of Clark Well, toward Barton Canyon.

Although they are abundant in Baja, this is the farthest north known stand of these peculiar trees in the U.S.

8.7   Alcoholic Pass Trail hiking route departs to the southwest (left) and leads
ㅅ   up a sandy wash several miles, over the rocky Coyote Mountain spur, to
    emerge just south of Desert Gardens in Coyote Canyon. This old Indian trail was one of the short cuts between water sources and habitations in Rockhouse Canyon and in lower Coyote Canyon (see Area 2 above).

  After the Alcoholic Pass trailhead, the road becomes 4WD with deep sand traps.

9.6   Butler Canyon and Dry Wash junction north (left). Hikers can go about
    four miles northwest up Dry Wash in Butler Canyon to Jackass Flat and drop down to Hidden Spring as described below. From the junction, the Rockhouse route turns sharply right up onto the stream bank, and S-turns back left up the wash, directly along the active Clark fault. Thanks to a large watershed and fierce summer storms, this can deteriorate to absurdity as a road. Take your choice between hard road building and easy hiking.

12.9 Roadhead (elev. 2000').
ㅅ   Hike toward the green thicket up the canyon.

14.1   Hidden Spring is at the entrance to Rockhouse Canyon narrows. This
    perennial spring is at the north bank below the large bench of Jackass Flat. A deeply worn switchback trail climbs up the steep bank from the spring to the flat, where a large Cahuilla village was located. Mortar holes dot most of the large boulders. The Nicholas Swartz mine is reported about four miles west of here across Jackass Flat.

  The route up Rockhouse Canyon to Rockhouse Valley is about 3.5 miles long, winding around the southeast end of Buck Ridge . This is a narrow, winding canyon with near-vertical walls. Somewhere in this canyon are reportedly the remains of an emerald mine that was worked from earliest times by desert Indians who traded the gems as far south as beyond Mexico.

14.9 Just below the Riverside County line, vertical fault lines and dikes are
    visible on the granite and gneiss rock walls at a prominent dry waterfall. Exit ABDSP into BLM land at the Riverside County line.

16.1 Mojave Valley, or "Flat of Yucca" per 1950s park ranger Jack Welch.
  From here a broad fork leads east (right) to where the remains of rock art and a Cahuilla camp have been reported.

17.5 Entrance to broad, juniper-covered Rockhouse Valley.
  Vegetation in the area includes juniper, Mojave yucca and rabbitbrush. The three lower rockhouse ruins are about one-half mile into the valley. Seek them on a rocky bench between the main northwesterly wash and a smaller northerly wash (elev. 3000'). The remaining walls are about 2-3 feet high.

  Lester Reed reported that one of the houses belonged to the Manual Tortes family. Tortes was one of the last chiefs of the Rockhouse Valley Cahuilla. Another house belonged to the Andreas family. They reportedly obtained their water by digging a shallow hole about one-half mile east of the Tortes rockhouse. (After much rainfall animals will also dig in this area for water.) The third rockhouse may have been built by miner Nicholas Swartz, who was reputed to have taken $18,000 worth of gold nuggets out of his mine.

Directly across the valley to the northeast is Nicholias Canyon, back-dropped by the towering visage of Toro Peak. This canyon is named for either Nicholas Swartz or Mountain Cahuilla Indian Nicholas Guanche and is mis-spelled on maps. Alder trees grow where springs are found in the canyon. Metates are found in the granite rocks in a small flat area in the west bank of the canyon. The ruins of Guanche's rockhouse are found on a ridge just east of the canyon near one of the springs. A row of cottonwoods is located in a basin to the north and east of the site of the rockhouse.

The locale of Old Santa Rosa is on the north side of the valley, in the low point across from the valley entrance where a reddish-brown hill is seen. It is about a two-hour hike from the valley entrance to the Old Santa Rosa ruins, fol-lowing an Indian trail across the valley. About five sites are here. A BLM sign is posted next to the largest ruin, which is circular in shape with a diameter of about 17 feet:

> *Ancient Indian ruins and artifacts in the vicinity of this notice are fragile and irreplaceable. The Antiquities Act of 1906 protects them for the benefit of all Americans. Enjoy but do not destroy your American Heritage. A dry seep is found behind the large ruin on the hillside, where slick mortars are also visible.*

An old Indian trail from Rockhouse Valley climbs the saddle into Martinez Canyon to the northeast. Martinez is today's Cactus Springs Trail. The AAA names Lorenzens Peak as the high point (elev. 6582') southeast of the saddle on the ridge between Rockhouse and Martinez. Lester Reed reports that this used to be a main route but "no doubt this trail would be found very rough at the present time, for it is seldom used any more." The Cactus Springs Trail is now the main access into BLM's Santa Rosa Mountains National Scenic Area as reported by the Coachella Valley Trail Council.

J.W. Robinson, in *San Bernardino Mountain Trails*, reports that an old Indian Trail went from the Santa Rosa Indian village up the mountainside to Alta Seca bench and thence down to Horsethief Canyon. Jerry Schad (see Appendix 1) also describes trails in Rockhouse Valley.

TRIP 3C:
Fonts Point—Central Borrego Badlands

From: Junction of Fonts Point Wash and Hwy S-22
To: Junction of Palo Verde Wash and Hwy S-22
Via: Short Wash (4WD roads)

Points of Interest and Side Trips:
Fonts Point, Short Wash, Thimble Trail, Vista del Malpais, Fault Wash, Ella Wash.

Borrego Badlands from Fonts Point—two views

Summary:

This trip covers the central section of the Borrego Badlands. The Inspiration Point side trip from Hwy S-22 (above) traverses the western section of the badlands, and the Seventeen Palms trip (following) covers the eastern section. It is wise to consider all roads 4WD although, conventional autos frequently attempt to reach Fonts Point. Check with ABDSP visitor center for current conditions.

0.0   Junction of Fonts Point Wash and Hwy S-22 (elev. 725′).

This turnoff is between post mile markers 29 and 30. Christmas Circle in Borrego Springs is about 10 miles west. Fonts Point was named for Pedro Font, Spanish priest and diarist on the second Anza expedition to California.

Drive up-wash to the south. This is one of the most popular places in the park to get stuck in the sand, real stuck, real up-to-the-hubs-long-time stuck. Plan ahead. Use 4WD and stay in well-traveled wheel tracks.

The bluffs to the left are the Ocotillo Formation, deposited less than one million years ago as floodplain outwash from the rising Santa Rosa Mountains. The central Borrego Badlands, now fully protected under state and federal law, are a rich trove of vertebrate fossils, including the last of the Ice Age megafauna. Paul Remeika's updated list of the Borrego Local (Paleo) Fauna in the 1997 NAGT guidebook contains these highlights: ground sloth, short-faced bear, dire wolf, sabertooth cat, mastodon, mammoth, giant zebra, half ass (*Equus hemionus*), camel, yesterday's camel, llama, giant camel, pronghorn, elk, deer, shrub oxen, and Bautista horse. (The latter is for those who think that Anza-Borrego had to wait a million years or so for Juan Bautista de Anza to bring in the first horses.)

1.9   Junction of Short Wash Road and Fonts Point Wash.

Side Trip to Fonts Point (mileage continuous).

19   Drive southwest (right) to climb out of the main wash.

ﾒ   **2.6**   A three-quarters mile walk northwest from mile 2.6 leads to a surprising discovery—a bench atop a knoll about midway between Fonts Point Wash to the east and Inspiration Wash to the west that commemorates the 1974 gift of 1600 surrounding acres to the park from the Burks family.

   UTM 5-71.5E 36-82.3N   LAT 33°16.7N′ LON 116°13.9′W.

4.8   Fonts Point loop (elev. 1294′).

A series of interpretive panels are found here:

Geological History of Fonts Point
    ...from ancient sediments to eroded badlands
Orientation of South View From Fonts Point
    ...across the badlands to Mexico
Orientation of West View From Fonts Point
    ...Borrego Valley and the Peninsular Ranges

   UTM 5-71.5E 36-79.9N LAT 33°15.9′N LON 116°14′W

End of Side Trip

1.9   Junction of Short Wash Road and Fonts Point Wash (repeated from above).

Drive east (left) out of Fonts Point Wash. Thimble Trail joins at mile 2.9. It is 2.2 miles north to Hwy S-22 on Thimble. This is a very subtle but an interesting watershed divide. Waters to the west flow north into the enclosed Clark basin. Waters to the east flow into the San Felipe drainage and the Salton basin. The Borrego Badlands, responding to the titanic forces acting in the San Jacinto fault zone, are a rapidly rising, deforming highland separating these two basins.

Continue east (straight) into Short Wash, named for Orville G. Short, ABDSP ranger in the 1950s.

4.3   Turnoff to Vista del Malpais (elev. 913') south (right).

11 miles up this wash is an excellent view of the chromatic badlands, named by Kenyon after seeing the view from this overlook. The name is Spanish for "View of the Badlands." Although it's not as high as Fonts Point, the scope of its view is much greater, with views of Borrego Sink, Borrego Mountain, San Felipe Wash, the Superstition Mountains, Mexico, the Salton Sea, and the Santa Rosa Mountains. To the north is the site discovered by volunteer paleontologist Vern Waters that yielded an almost-whole skeleton of a mammoth. The skull was so large that it had to be hauled out by helicopter.

Vista del Malpais is part of the Ocotillo Rim, connecting the high points of the badlands from here west through Fonts Point to Inspiration Point. (More than one marriage has been performed at Vista del Malpais. Don't know what the bride wore but the limos were 4WD.)

5.2   Fault Wash.

The Fault Wash road runs about 4.4 miles south (right) to San Felipe Wash and on a few more miles to Hwy 78 at Ocotillo Wells.

This Short Wash trip continues east (straight).

5.8   Palo Verde Wash. There are three options: Ella Wash is 0.1 mile southeast (right). It is 1.6 miles northeast up Ella to Hwy S-22 near post mile marker 35. Cut Across Trail at the OWSVRA boundary is another 3.5 miles southeast down Palo Verde and then it's several more miles into Ocotillo Wells and Burro Bend for some refreshments. A northwest (left) turn leads 2.6 miles up Palo Verde to...

8.4   Hwy S-22 near post mile marker 33.

END OF TRIP

TRIP 3D:
Seventeen Palms—Eastern Borrego Badlands

From: Hwy S-22 at Arroyo Salado Campground
To: Hwy 86 near Salton City
Via: Arroyo Salado, Tule Wash (4WD roads)

Connecting Trips:

3A–Borrego Springs to Salton City via Hwy S-22
4D–Ocotillo Wells to Borrego Valley via San Felipe Wash
5F–Trifolium (Hwy 78) to Salton City via Hwy 86

Points Of Interest and Side Trips:

Arroyo Salado Camp, Five Palms, Una Palma, Cut Across Trail, Basin Wash, Pumpkin Patch.

MILES FROM:
S-22

0.0   Turnoff to Arroyo Salado Primitive Campground.

2.2   Old Truckhaven Trail junction from northeast (left).
Main route continues southeast (straight) down Arroyo Salado. The side trip mileages from this junction describe some of the easterly track of the Old Truckhaven Trail, on which the off-road explorer can relive the early-day challenges of desert travel by Model A's and such.

Side Trip East on Truckhaven Trail (rough 4WD road).
0.0   Arroyo Salado/Truckhaven junction at "Beaty's Icebox." It was here that "Doc" Beaty made a permanent camp for himself and the men who constructed the Truckhaven Trail. They stowed perishable foodstuffs in a small mud cave, located at the foot of the grade, which came to be known as "Beaty's Icebox." The cave has since collapsed but the hill still carries the original name. Climb northeast through a narrow wash out of Arroyo Salado and into the north fork of Arroyo Salado. A sharp turn down-wash leads to...
1.2   A junction from which Truckhaven climbs steeply northeast (left) up and over another ridge. (One may travel down North Fork about eight miles to the confluence with main Arroyo Salado at sea level, just north of which is the Oh-My-God Hot Springs site.)
1.6   The Truckhaven Trail now traverses Cannonball Wash, so named because of its concretion formations similar to those at Pumpkin Patch. Cannonball Wash may be traveled 0.7 mile down-wash to the north fork of Arroyo Salado. Truckhaven climbs northeast (left).
2.7   Truckhaven/S-22 junction, 0.7 mile west of the microwave tower.
End of Side Trip

2.2   Old Truckhaven Trail junction (repeated from above).

3.6   Seventeen Palms turnoff to the west (right).
The main route continues down-wash.

Side Trip to Seventeen Palms
Two-tenths of a mile west from the turnoff lies this well-known watering place of the Borrego Badlands (elev. 410'). There are currently more than 30 palms. Wild animals in this area are extremely dependent on this water, it being the only year-round drinking hole for many miles.

A windy day at Seventeen Palms

Desert post office at Seventeen Palms

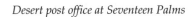

Because most animals come at night to drink, no overnight camping is allowed near the oasis. During the year, over 100 species of birds stop to rest and refresh themselves here.

Seventeen Palms Oasis & Pioneer Mailbox (ABDSP Interpretive Panel)
UTM 5-83.0E 36-79.6N   LAT 33°15.2N LON 116°06.5'W

End of Side Trip

3.6　Seventeen Palms turnoff (repeated from above).

3.9　Tule Wash/Arroyo Salado crossover, south (right).
Arroyo Salado continues down-wash southeast from here via a less interesting route than that via Five Palms and Tule Wash described below. For those who do it all, here it is:

Side Trip to Hwy 86 Via Arroyo Salado (mileage continuous).
3.9　Tule Wash/Arroyo Salado crossover. Continue southeast via survey point "Sugar" to the county line and...
5.9　Depart ABDSP into BLM land.
　　　See Trip 5F below for details from here to ...
16.9　Hwy 86.
End of Side Trip

Trip 3D route turns south (right), climbing out of Arroyo Salado to...

4.3　Five Palms Spring.
Only two of the palms remain standing. The others may have been temblor-toppled. Continue south over the mudhills and drop into...

5.2　Tule Wash (east) and Cut Across Trail (west).

Side Trip Up Cut Across Trail
Cut Across leads west up-wash (right) 1.4 miles west to Una Palma. Except for some mesquite near this lonely palm tree, the area appears void of vegetation and resembles a moonscape. From Una Palma, the Cut Across Trail turns south to the upper entrance of Basin Wash at mile 7.0. From here there are two options:
A. Turn east (left) down Basin Wash 2.3 miles to Tule Wash.
B. Continue straight ahead southwest into OWSVRA, cutting across several routes (see map and Trip 4D). Ocotillo Wells is about eight miles south from the Basin Wash/Cut Across Trail junction.
End of Side Trip

5.2　Tule Wash and Cut Across Trail (repeated from above).
Turn east (left) down Tule Wash to...

6.1　Basin Wash.
Basin offers mud caves and shady banks for mid-day lunch stops. It is 2.3 miles west (right) up Basin Wash to Cut Across Trail. The Tule Wash route continues east down-wash.

Co-author Lowell Lindsay in the Pumpkin Patch

6.5   ABDSP/OWSVRA boundary at the county line.

7.5   Pumpkin Patch Trail southwest (right) into OWSVRA can be followed
            about three miles to Bank Wash. The Pumpkin Patch is southeast of this
7.5-mile junction. It is a fascinating geologic feature—a field of concretions that
cover an area the size of a city block. Collecting is illegal.

9.6   Cross Over Trail south and west to Shell Reef.
            The Tule Wash route continues east down-wash.

12.6   Pole Line Road, BLM Rt SF131.

13.0   Giant Sand Dune (site). A huge moving sand dune once stood promi-
            nently alone here in the 1950s and was visible from miles away. Former
ranger Jack Welch reported that it reminded him of a "giant manta ray inching
its way across the desert, probing and feeling a tentative course across the gul-
lied plain with its two feeler-like horns." Dunes like this are common just to the
east, across Hwy 86 on the Navy Base road. In time, Giant Dune may build up
again.

14.3   Tule Spring. Year-round source of brackish water. A white alkaline moat
            surrounds the spring. Rangers Meier and Remeika recount finding a
newly-wed couple, en route from nuptials at La Casa del Zorro to their
Brawley honeymoon, majorly stuck in the middle of Tule Spring in 1994 whilst
searching for a shortcut.

14.4   South Fork of Tule Wash joins from the southwest (right).

16.8   Hwy 86 near Salton City at bridge #58-14. Salton City is about three miles
            north.

TRIP 3E:
Calcite Mine Area to Salton City Via Palm Wash

From: Calcite Mine Area, Hwy S-22
To: Salton City (Hwy 86)
Via: Palm Wash (4WD road)

Connecting Trips:
3A–Borrego Springs to Salton City via Hwy S-22
3F–Salton City to Travertine Rock via Hwy 86

Points of Interest and Side Trips:
Sheep Tanks, Four Palms Spring

MILES FROM: •
S-22

0.0   Calcite Mine Road (elev. 596').
Turnoff is located on Hwy S-22 (Trip 3A above) just east of Salton View turnout (mile 38) and west of the microwave tower (mile 39). Drop steeply down the sandstone cliffs into...

0.1   South Fork Palm Canyon. There are three options here.

Northwest (left) 4WD route up-wash goes about a half-mile and then becomes a hike into an interesting slot canyon which ends at a dry waterfall after another half-mile. East (right) is the main route down-wash to Salton City (see below). North (straight ahead) is a side trip to Calcite Mine. Calcite occurs in pockets and vertical fissures in sandstone and conglomerate of this area.

Calcite was mined during World War II to provide optical quality calcite for the Polaroid Company, which processed the crystals for the manufacture of optical ringsights for gunsights and rocket launchers.

Side Trip to Calcite Mine
The road climbs steeply, crosses a small mesa, and descends into main Palm Wash at mile 0.7. (A right turn here would join South Fork after two miles.) This is the best place to park and hike into Calcite Mine instead of risking a very rough 4WD trail. Ranger Jack Welch reported an abandoned miners' camp here in the mid-1950s.

The Calcite Mine trail continues north along main Palm Wash, winding in and out above the chasm.

Schad (see Appendix 1) describes an interesting slot wash at mile 1.4 from Hwy S-22 which may be hiked in either direction to rejoin the 4WD road/trail.

The Calcite Mine 4WD road pitches across this wash, often a washout, and then climbs steeply up and to the left. The long, narrow slots of the mining operation are now seen along the road, together with bizarre shapes of wind-carved sandstone heads.

The roadhead is about two miles from Hwy S-22 on a steep sandstone ledge where Jack Welch reported a "sturdy little shack" and also noted Locomotive Rock, which "looks like a modern streamliner forging its way up a steep hill." The streamliner has been climbing for three million years. The shack has come and gone in somewhat less time. The view forever from here is one of the finest and most sweeping in the Anza-Borrego region.

Hikers may climb wind-cave-pocked Locomotive Rock, which is Canebrake Conglomerate and, like the Truckhaven Rocks, is composed of erosive sediments from the rising Santa Rosas which uplifted and tilted their solidified ruins into the present formations. The mine trenches and their lodes of sparkling calcite crystals may be explored for hours. (Collecting is prohibited, of course.) Hikers may take an old mining trail west a few hundred yards from the mine area, affording different views down-dip of the faulted Canebrake Conglomerate cliffs.

End of Side Trip

In Sheep Tank Wash near Calcite Mine

0.1 South Fork Palm Canyon (repeated from above).

East (right) is the main route down-wash to Salton City. These banded cliffs are Diablo formation sandstone, derived from the ancestral Colorado River. See Remeika (Appendix 1) for a detailed description of the geology here. Cross the county line and exit ABDSP at about a mile.

2.4 Junction of main Palm Canyon and South Fork.

Side Trip Northwest to Sheep Tanks

Turn hard northwest (left) and drive up main Palm Canyon to the county line (again) and enter ABDSP at the junction with North Fork Palm Canyon. This point, at UTM 5-85.3E 36-83.5N, is 0.8 mile west of the junction noted above and 1.1 miles east of the Calcite Mine trail . Drive northwest (right) up North Fork. The Sheep Tanks are about 1.7 miles in from the main Palm Wash junction. Storm debris will vary the location of the roadhead.

The Sheep Tanks are in a small arroyo entering from the west (left) into a small circular bay in the wash just beyond a fairly deep sandstone cut. About 100 yards beyond the boulder-choked entrance is the first of three tanks, sparkling like a deep green jewel under the 50-foot cliffs. Access to view the other two tanks is by scaling the near-vertical south wall onto a wide sandstone shelf. They lie in the bottom of a deep, inaccessible cleft. The capacity of the three tanks is about 20,000 gallons, enough to fill a backyard swimming pool. These are typical *tinajas*, desert basins that collect and hold rain water, which support animals.

Schad (see Appendix 1) describes a hike west from here into main Palm Wash near Calcite Mine.

End of Side Trip

2.4 Junction of main Palm Canyon and South Fork (repeated from above).

Continue east down-wash. Some 29 palms have been reported in the Palm Wash system. Various field logs over the last 25 years note the following sites using the present mileage: palms and a spring 0.3 mile south of Palm Wash from mile 2.8; one palm in the wash at mile 4.5; two palms in the wash at mile 5.2.

6.0 Survey Point "Tipy" (BM 137').

A burnt palm trunk and vegetation mark the site of this spring. Four Palms Spring (now three palms) is about one-half mile south, beyond a low ridge. After another mile, North Marina Drive drops down from Clay Point mesa and parallels Palm Wash on the south side into...

9.1 Salton City, Hwy 86 at bridge #58-46, post mile 58.2 (elev. -60').

TRIP 3F:
Salton City to Travertine Rock Via Hwy 86

From: Salton City, Hwy S-22
To: Travertine Rock, Imperial/Riverside County line
Via: Hwy 86 (paved)

Connecting Trips:
    3A–Borrego Springs to Salton City via Hwy S-22
    3G–Travertine Palms to Palo Verde Canyon (backpack)
    5F–Trifolium (Hwy 78) to Salton City via Hwy 86

Points of Interest and Side Trips:
Wonderstone Wash, Salton Sea west-side beaches.

MILES FROM:
Salton City

0.0   Salton City (elev. -87'). Post mile marker 56.1.
    Post miles start at 0 in Heber, east of Brawley, and increase to the north-west, which is an exception to the general rule.
    This is the junction of Hwys S-22 and 86 at South Marina Drive. Borrego Springs is 28 miles west on Hwy S-22. This was the site of the old Holly (Sugar) House, and later the Sundowner Motel, which was the only hostelry between Indio and Brawley on State Hwy 86 (formerly U.S. Hwy 99 in the pre-interstate era). The abandoned motel was burned to the ground in 1998.
    Sunrise Drive at mile 0.9 is the access to the old Truckhaven Trail, which was the only direct route from this area to Borrego Valley from the 1920s to the 60s. The Truckhaven 4WD route goes west along Amerosa Wash about three miles, climbing onto Clay Point mesa and to Hwy S-22.

1.4   Truckhaven (site).
    The tamarisk trees around the slab on the east (left) mark the site of the Truckhaven Cafe and service station, an important stop on the old Hwy 99 route. The site is unmarked but the name persists prominently in historic lore, map names, and the memory of many an old trucker.

1.7   Anza Ditch Bridge #59-45 (BM -56'). Post mile marker 57.8.
    North Marina Drive is just beyond at mile 1.8. Marina leads east (right) down to the Salton City lake front area. As a dirt road it goes west (left) about three miles to Hwy S-22 on Clay Point mesa.

2.1   Palm Wash Bridge #58-46. Post mile marker 58.2.
    This 4WD route leads about nine miles west into the ABDSP Calcite Mine area. See Trip 3E above for detailed route description east down-wash from Hwy S-22 to this point on Hwy 86.

3.1   Coral Wash Bridge #58-47. Post mile marker 59.18.
    This wash, marked by tamarisk trees, is named for the fresh-water "coral," actually the mineral tufa or travertine, found in the terraces to the west.

3.7 Grave Wash Bridge #58-48. Post mile marker 59.8.

This is also Coombs Drive, Treadwell Blvd, and a powerline crossing. A dirt road heads west.

Side Trip to Ancient Beach Line and Fish Traps

About one-half mile west of the bridge is the ancient shoreline of Lake Cahuilla at about elev. 38'. The Cahuilla were first attracted to this area about 2000 years ago because of freshwater Lake Cahuilla. While this lake was existent, the Cahuilla fished along the shoreline, setting rock fish traps. Their fish camps were nearby at higher elevations.

These muleshoe-shaped rock alignments are visible here as well as all along this ancient beach line from I-10 in Indio down to Mexicali. Further south, Kumeyaay Indians, like the Cahuilla, also fished along the ancient shores.

Bernardo Segundo, chief of the San Ignacio band of Kumeyaay Indians, had told early Coyote Canyon homesteader John Collins and prospector Henry E.W. Wilson how the traps worked. The oblong rock traps had an opening at one end, on the land side. Segundo said that "the fish were stranded in these enclosures when the level of the sea dropped, as it often did." Archaeologists also conjecture that the fish traps functioned by having a person use a capstone to trap a fish that had swum into the enclosure.

Observe, but do not disturb, these fish traps, which are fragile and irreplaceable. They are protected under the U.S. Antiquities Act of 1906.
End of Side Trip

4.3 Big Wash Bridge #58-50. Post mile marker 60.5.

Also known as Tesla Wash, aptly named Big Wash slices deep and high into the Santa Rosa Mountains, reaching "Pyramid Peak" on the shared ridgeline with Smoke Tree Canyon. It can be traveled via 4WD about seven miles west into the mud hills past survey stations graphically named Hot (elev. 469'), Cool (elev. 857'), and High (elev. 1833'). Vegetation is smoke trees, cheesebush, indigo, ocotillo, tamarisk, galleta grass, catclaw, burroweed, and desert aster.

Next to the north is Gravel Wash, marked by a namesake pit on the southwest side of the highway. Unnamed Wash follows at mile 6.1. This wash may be followed via 4WD about five miles west to a group of palo verde trees near the boundary of ABDSP.

7.5 Salton Sea Beach (elev. -165'). Post mile 63.6.

Brawley Ave leads right down to a marina. The rising Salton Sea has flooded several structures along this waterfront.

Side Trip to Wonderstone Wash And Rainbow Rock (4WD road).

0.0 Hwy 86/Brawley Ave at Salton Sea Beach. Cross the highway to the west into Aggregate Quarry. The Rainbow Rock area can be seen from here as orange and red formations about three miles west.

0.7 Quarry Office. Stop here for permission to cross private property. Work south along the fence line about a half-mile and then turn west, passing under a powerline and climbing the alluvial fan into Wonderstone Wash. Enter the wash at mile 2.6 and bear left, southwest.

3.0 Rainbow Rock is prominent on the hill to the north (right) and may be explored afoot. San Dieguito Indians, ca. 11,000-12,000 years ago, used this wonderstone to make stone implements. At 80 acres, this is one of the oldest and largest known prehistoric stone quarries in the U.S.

A complex of 4WD trails fans out to the north and west onto privately owned mining lands or Torres Martinez Indian Reservation. Respect signs, proceed with permission, and don't disturb anything in this valuable archaeological site.

The wonderstone of Rainbow Rock, formerly and incorrectly called Truckhaven rhyolite, is a beautiful cream- and red-banded hot-spring "sinter" deposit of silicates with trace gold and embedded fossil reed casts. It was deposited by geothermal fluids percolating to the surface along the Truckhaven fault. This feature, known as the Modoc Fossil Hot Spring Deposit, is described by geologists from the University of California at Riverside in the 1993 SBCMA guide (see Appendix 1).
End of Side Trip

7.5   Salton Sea Beach/Brawley Ave (repeated).

8.9   Coolidge Springs (site).
The original route of Hwy 86 (then Hwy 99), via the defunct Coolidge Springs service station, diverges slightly left to rejoin Hwy 86 about two miles north. This slight detour is an excellent opportunity to study the high water line of prehistoric Lake Cahuilla at the 42' level on the mountain front to the west. The view, and the feature itself, is quite similar to that along the gypsum railroad in the Fish Creek Mountains described below in Area 5.

11.4 Travertine Rock (BM-100').
This historic point was described and illustrated in 1853 by the U.S. Railroad Survey which included geologist William Phipps Blake. The coating on the granitic rocks is calcareous tufa, a light and porous calcium carbonate from fresh water that coats solid objects along the shore. Remeika and Reynolds (see Appendix 1) record radiocarbon dates which begin the tufa deposition at about 17,590 years ago and extend to about 7,205 years ago. Petroglyphs are found in layers that date to approximately 9,000 years ago. Carvings on multiple tufa layers suggest that as the lake surface fluctuated, the artists would return again and again. Sometimes this was an island, sometimes a peninsula, and now a headland standing high and dry, for awhile.

The following monument was erected in 1968 by the Roads to Romance Association in cooperation with the Coachella Valley Historical Society. The authors photographed the plaque before it disappeared sometime in the 1970s:

THE SALTON SEA (Ancient Lake Cahuilla)

Where you are standing is at an elevation of 99 feet below sea level. But when the ancient 150-mile-long Lake Cahuilla existed, which was about 500 years ago, you would be 139 feet under water.

Travertine Rock

Geologically this area was once a part of a larger body of water extending north through the San Joaquin Valley. A great upthrust lifted the land and formed mountains. The down-folding created Salton Sink and the Imperial and Coachella Valleys.

Lake Cahuilla's ancient shore line is visible on the mountains to the west. The remains of the lake, today known as Salton Sea, cover that portion of the sink which was filled by "Old Red," Colorado River, when it carved out Grand Canyon. The silt, found to a depth of 12,000 feet, also formed the delta which rises 40 feet above sea level and cuts off Salton Sea from the Gulf of California.

The sink was dry for many years and salt was mined from it. In 1901 water was diverted from Old Red near Yuma and carried in canals through the Republic of Mexico to irrigate lands in Imperial Valley. In 1905 Old Red broke through and rushed into Salton Sink for two years, filling it to the elevation of 195 feet below sea level. Salton Sea's surface elevation in 1968 was 233 feet below-sea-level. The Boulder Canyon project resulted in the construction of Hoover Dam and the taming of the Colorado River.

Postscript: A BLM report from the late 1970s, referring to the apparent control of the great river, dryly remarks that "technology has merely introduced a temporary hiatus in the normal course of events."

11.7 Riverside/Imperial County Line and Travertine Palms.
Post mile marker 67.8.

A dirt road leads west (left) along a powerline. Follow this about a mile to a trailhead and hike southwest along Travertine Palms Wash. (The pole line turns north just beyond this wash at elev. -20'.) Head toward the third bay into the face of the mountains and cross into ABDSP. It is about 2.5 miles from the trailhead to the oasis at elev. 350'.

There are about 70 trees in the grove, the tallest being about 30'. An earlier name for the oasis was Stein's (or Steen's) Rest.

Immediately west of the palms, on the far side of the saddle, is a high cliff of red clay and gray mudstone. There is a small cave at the base of this cliff and bedrock mortars nearby. The cave is undoubtedly an Indian shelter with its roof blackened by the smoke of campfires. Farther south in this wash is a deep arroyo described in the following trip.

TRIP 3G:
Travertine Palms to Palo Verde Canyon backpack

This rugged, waterless, lonely, two- or three-day traverse across the south-eastern Santa Rosas offers the backpacker a challenging and intimate desert wilderness experience. Other than the Indian trails along the route, there is virtually no evidence of human presence to mar the awesome stillness and desolate grandeur of this remote desert mountain fastness. These canyons and slopes, lonely but far from lifeless, are the haunt of the desert bighorn sheep, while typical desert and arid-area vegetation abounds—palo verde and creosote at lower elevations, agave, ocotillo and some juniper in the higher reaches.

This difficult route, done by author Lowell in 1977, requires careful cross-country navigation and an ample supply of water—at least one gallon per person per day. There are two key landmarks with reference to topo maps: the pinyon-covered peak "Rosa" (survey station elev. 5038') and an unnamed peak herein referred to as "Pyramid" (elev. 3400'). Pyramid Peak is clearly visible from Hwy 86 at the Riverside/Imperial County line, resembling a pyramid on the southwest horizon atop the main ridge line.

Mile 0.0 is the San Diego/Riverside County and Hwy 86 junction, just north of Travertine Rock. Drive west about one mile along a good dirt road to Travertine Palms Wash. Hike southwest, climbing a rocky bajada toward Travertine Palms. Mile 2.5 is the entrance to Travertine Palms bay. The palms are about one-half mile in. Continue southwest in the wash around the north side of the ridge line, always toward Pyramid Peak on the horizon.

At mile 5.2 enter a narrow gully where walls squeeze in to shoulder width in some places, blocking out the sky overhead. At about mile 5.5 bypass a wash entering from the west. Continue southwest up-wash. A gully opens up at about mile 5.7. At mile 6.2 another wash enters from the west at the center of the west boundary of section 23. Bear south, toward Pyramid, keeping Rosa on the right side.

At mile 7.4 depart Travertine Wash, which turns west up onto Rosa mountain. Hike southwest up a small arroyo. A small Indian "sleeping circle" (possibly an agave roasting ring) on the right bank marks the entrance to this arroyo.

At mile 7.9 cross a saddle at the head of the arroyo (elev. 2000') and enter the Wonderstone Wash drainage area. Contour southwest (left) across a relatively flat but broken bench, crossing three arroyos and heading for a saddle just northwest of Pyramid. At approximately mile 8.9, atop a small knoll, are ruins of a stone structure, 10 feet square, with walls 1-2 feet high and a door opening to the south-southwest.

At mile 10.5 cross a saddle (elev. 3200') northwest of Pyramid into the Smoke Tree Canyon drainage. A lone juniper amid ocotillo and agave marks the saddle. Contour west (right) above arroyos at the head of Smoke Tree Canyon, cross a divide to the west and descend northwest to...

Mile 11.7 in Palo Verde Canyon. Hike down-wash about one-half mile to the great, dry waterfall, just above Palo Verde Spring, which drops far below to the canyon floor. Don't try it. Backtrack several hundred feet up-wash to the most feasible looking gully joining from the southwest. Ascend this gully to the ridge line just west of Palo Verde Canyon and descend the ridge line into Palo Verde Wash.

Mile 15.7 is the welcome junction with paved Hwy S-22.

Travertine Palms (Salton Sea in distance). Note the Arabian date palm in foreground, not native to the area.

AREA 4-CENTRAL:
central Hwy 78, Hwy S-3

The Highway 78 "San Felipe Corridor" forms the broad midriff of the Anza-Borrego region, extending east from pine-covered uplands and mile-high peaks to below-sea-level desert plains. Highway 78, from Julian to the Salton Sea, traversing the watershed of San Felipe Wash and its tributaries, has been a major corridor of travel since the late 1800s. As an east-west corridor, it is a notable exception to historic routes of travel in the Anza-Borrego region, which generally follow NW/SE-trending earthquake faults.

Highway 78 slices across the following faults: Elsinore fault at Banner, Earthquake Valley fault at Scissors Crossing, San Felipe fault at The Narrows, Yaqui Ridge detachment fault at Nude Wash, Coyote Creek fault at Ocotillo Wells, and Superstition Hills fault near Trifolium (junction of Hwys 78 and 86). Highway 78 generally follows the path of Banner and San Felipe creeks, which are antecedent streams, present before tectonic uplift. Subsequent uplift was slow enough to permit the flowing water to cut downward as fast as the rock barriers arose. Consequently, Highway 78 is never more than a couple of miles from San Felipe Creek except for the creek's northward loop around Borrego Mountain, which is influenced by the Coyote Creek fault.

As a recreational corridor, Highway 78 is the central entrance to the Anza-Borrego area. The park's second largest campground, Tamarisk Grove, is located on this corridor as is Ocotillo Wells, in Lower Borrego Valley, which is a popular recreational focal point for off-roaders and desert explorers. Ocotillo Wells features Borrego Mountain to the northwest, the Ocotillo Wells State Vehicular Recreation Area (OWSVRA) to the north and the Split Mountain/Fish Creek area to the south. Farther east the R9/R10 poleline road (BLM Rd SF131) offers access to the San Felipe Hills and the San Sebastian Marsh. Highway 86 forms the eastern boundary of the region, connecting Hwys S-22 and 78.

Sentenac Cienega and canyon, at the western gate to ABDSP, deserve particular attention because of the special effort that the Anza-Borrego Foundation

(ABF) spearheaded to preserve this unique riparian area, one of the last undeveloped wetlands in California and an area that park visionaries had hoped to include as a 220-acre "scenic easement" in the original boundaries in 1933. Preserving this area for future generations was a cooperative effort by several major agencies and groups including the California Departments of Parks and Recreation, Fish and Game, and Transportation (CALTRANS).

The abundance of water in the marsh and canyon supports a lush plant growth, including two rare and threatened plant communities, the Mesquite Bosque and the Sonoran Cottonwood Willow Riparian Forest. The cienega and canyon have long been a favorite haunt for students of botany. As early as 1832 English botanist Thomas Coulter collected screwbean mesquite and noted the variety of plants in and near the cienega. Many animals, including the endangered Least Bell's vireo, the three-spined stickleback warm-water fish, the willow flycatcher, and the Peninsular bighorn sheep depend on this permanent water supply. Over 33 sensitive species have been identified in this area. Bird life in Sentenac Cienega and Sentenac Canyon is outstanding in spring and fall due to its location on the migration flyway. The marsh is also a premiere area for butterflies, including the Eunus skipper, the Sonoran blue, the striated queen, and the migratory monarch.

In the early 1990s, preliminary discussions began between the current owners of the property and ABF about the possibility of acquiring this unique wetlands area as an addition to the state park. The actual acquisition will become a reality in 1998, realizing the dreams of park visionaries Guy L. Fleming and Newton B. Drury, some 65 years earlier.

TRIP 4A:
Earthquake (Shelter) Valley to Ocotillo Wells Via Hwy 78

From: Scissors Crossing in Earthquake (Shelter) Valley
To: Ocotillo Wells
Via: Central Hwy 78 (paved road)

Connecting Trips:
1A–Warner Ranch Junction to Earthquake Valley via Hwy S-2
4B–Tamarisk Grove to Ranchita (S-22) via Grapevine Canyon
4C–Tamarisk Grove to Borrego Springs via Hwy S-3
4D–Ocotillo Wells to Borrego Valley via San Felipe Wash
5A–Ocotillo Wells to Trifolium (Hwy 86) via Hwy 78
5B–Ocotillo Wells to Fish Creek via Split Mtn Rd
6A–Earthquake Valley to Ocotillo (Imperial Co.) via Hwy S-2
6B–Julian to Earthquake (Shelter) Valley via Hwy 78

Points of Interest and Side Trips:
Sentenac Cienega and Canyon, Grapevine Canyon, Tamarisk Grove, Mescal Bajada, Mine Wash, Narrows Earth Trail, Old Borrego Valley Road, Old Kane

Spring Road, Borrego Springs Road/Texas Dip, Borrego Mountain, Harper Canyon, OWSVRA Ranger Station, Main Street Camp.

Route Summary:
State post mile markers on vertical white "paddle boards," emergency call boxes, and bridges appear approximately every mile. Post mile zero on Hwy 78 is Oceanside, with mileage increasing to the east.

POST MILES FROM:
Oceanside

0.0   Oceanside, junction of I-5 and Hwy 78.

69.7 Earthquake Valley/west Scissors Crossing (elev. 2,300').
      This is the western junction of Hwys 78 and S-2 at the Butterfield Monument, which describes the Vallecito Stage Station 19 miles southeast (see Area 6).

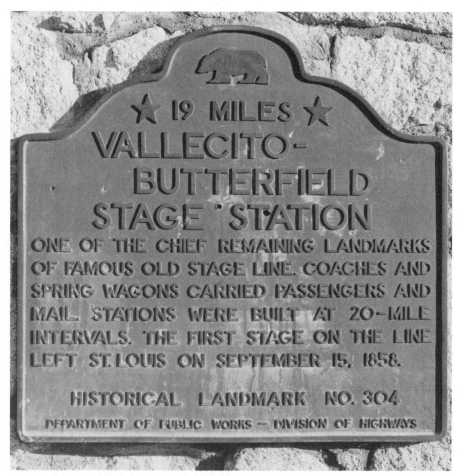

Monument at Scissors Crossing

Vallecito Monument (California Historical Landmark No.304A)
UTM 5-49.0E 36-61.0N

Historic Hwy S-2 follows the long, narrow fault-controlled swath of Earthquake (Shelter) Valley to the southeast and San Felipe Valley to the northwest. Drainages from both valleys meet here at Sentenac Cienega, turning east into Sentenac Canyon, which contains Hwy 78.

70.0 San Felipe Creek and east Scissors Crossing.

The San Felipe Stage Station site and monument is about a half mile northwest up Hwy S-2. The Pacific Crest Trail crosses Hwy 78 just east of Scissors Crossing. It may be seen snaking up Grapevine Mountain, en route to Barrel Spring, 23 miles away on Hwy S-22.

Enter narrow Sentenac Canyon, which forms a partial barrier to water flowing from the San Felipe Valley, forming Sentenac Cienega. The overflow of water continues on through the canyon but goes underground about 2.5 miles farther.

Brothers Paul and Pierre Sentenac lend their name to the canyon and cienega where they raised cattle, goats, and sheep. Paul first came to the area as a prospector and then filed for an 80-acre homestead above the cienega in 1883. Helen Hunt Jackson, writing in *A Century of Dishonor*, published in 1886, reported that he usurped Indians' lands at Scissors Crossing, took their water away from them, and threatened to have them arrested if they stayed on "his" property.

The remains of a stone cabin are found on a promontory overlooking the cienega. Pierre built the rock-walled cabin but Paul lived in it after Pierre's death in 1905. Paul continued to develop his cattle business, establishing a cattle camp at Yaqui Well sometime before 1909. In later years, he acquired property in Wynola, west of Julian, but continued to use his desert property until he sold it in the 1920s and it was incorporated into the San Felipe Ranch.

The state is purchasing a part of this ranch, which will become a part of ABDSP. Before the completion of the Sentenac Canyon Hwy 78 route in 1932, the old dirt road wound from Sentenac Cienega over the hills south of Sentenac Mountain and emerged through Plum Canyon into San Felipe Wash.

72.9 San Felipe Creek bridge #57-96 (elev. 2000').

Some years ago the U.S. Border Patrol maintained a camp here, and the officers constructed a crude swimming pool under the old bridge. The pool has long since washed out. After leaving the bridge area, note the first heavy stands of agave on the hillside to the right. The young flower stalk, roasted in a rock-lined pit, was one of the staple foods of desert Indians. It is said to taste like a cross between baked squash and baked potato.

74.0 Grapevine Canyon/Yaqui Flat (elev. 1760').

To the north (left), at the confluence of San Felipe Creek and Grapevine Canyon, is an Indian area of some distinction. Surface evidence includes pottery fragments and flaking and grinding tools. A flood in 1961 exposed part of a sand bank in which five fire hearths were discovered at different levels, the lowest being 32 feet below the present surface. Archaeologists used carbon samples from the fire in which an arrowhead was found to date the fire as 5,000 years old. The four other fires and surface evidence indicate continuous use since. The turnoff northwest (left) from here is a shortcut to the Grapevine Canyon branch trip described below.

𝕏 Plum Canyon is just east and may be driven south a couple of miles to the start of a short hike to a viewpoint overlooking Earthquake Valley. The name may be derived from the fact that there are a number of desert apricots (*Prunus fremontii*) found in the canyon. The California R&H Trail follows the old route up from the valley, descends north down Plum Canyon and goes up into Grapevine Canyon.

Kenyon Cove is the wide turnout on the south side of the road. Lizard Canyon, at post mile 75.8, is a 4WD road that goes a few miles south.

76.8 Junction of Hwys 78 and S-3/Yaqui Pass Road.

Tamarisk Grove Campground is one-half mile northwest. See branch trips below for details of the Grapevine Canyon route to Ranchita and the Yaqui Pass route into Borrego Valley. Julian is 18 miles west. See Trip 4C for information about Tamarisk Grove Campground. Continue east on Hwy 78, down the drainage controlled by the Aguanga-San Felipe fault.

77.6 Stag Cove on the south (right).

This is a popular RV camping site. The San Felipe fault trace may be seen as a light-colored crush zone on the north side of the valley, on the ridge above wash level.

Stag Cove marks the entry onto Mescal Bajada. This is a pediment, an erosional surface covered with a thick layer of alluvium, lying at the north base of the Pinyon Mountains and extending four miles east to The Narrows. SDSU geologist Eric Frost theorizes that the area may be the denuded footprint of a portion of the Vallecito Mountains, which have moved east as a result of detachment faulting. The name, somewhat of a misnomer, derives from abundant desert agave (mescal) and apparent overlapping alluvial fans (a bajada) from major canyons, including Chuckwalla, Mine, and Pinyon. Chuckwalla Wash, at mile 9.0, is a hiking route into the North Pinyon Mountains.

79.5 Mine Wash turnoff on the south (BM 1,229′).

Side Trip Up Mine Wash.

It is 1.6 miles to the Mine Canyon Indian Village Site, near which are an ironwood tree and an interpretive panel:

Welcome to a Kumeyaay Village (ABDSP Interpretive Panel)
UTM 5-61.2E 36-63.8N   LAT 33°06.75′N LON 116°20.67′W.

Another indication of the extent of Kumeyaay occupation is the hundreds of agave-roasting pits scattered across the flat and on the mountainside. Well-defined trails cross the area in the direction of Yaqui Well, The Narrows, and Harper Flat. Caves in huge boulders a few hundred yards to the east provided shelter for these Indians.

𝕏 Continuing south up the wash, a large canyon capped with gray bluffs joins from the southeast (left) at mile 2.5. An hour's hike up this canyon leads to deposits of water-tumbled cobbles which correlate to the Poway conglomerates of the San Diego coastal plain, according to geologist Charlie Lough. These, and similar deposits in the Hapaha Flat area which have been studied by SDSU geologists under the direction of Dr. Pat Abbott, suggest that this was the route of a major through-flowing river from the east in Eocene times. Such a river has long been theorized from abundant evidence west of the crest of the Laguna Mountains but similar material from the desert side is a recent discovery.

The 4WD road ends in Mine Canyon at mile 4.6, near an abandoned gold-mine tunnel on the northwest bank of the wash. This, at UTM 5-59.2E 36-90.3N (elev. 2310'), is the namesake for the canyon. Hikers may climb another couple of miles to reach the North Pinyon Mountains 4WD road which comes in from Earthquake Valley (see Area 6).

End of Side Trip

79.5 Mine Wash turnoff on the south (repeated from above).

Continuing eastbound, the small ridge on the south side of the road is named "Round Granite Hill." It is an inselberg—a hard, crystalline remnant that resisted the erosion of the pediment surface surrounding it. Were this a true bajada, such a feature would have been buried deep by the alluvial detritus.

80.9 Pinyon Wash on the south (right).

Pinyon Wash dirt road becomes 4WD at the Nolina Wash junction at mile 1.6. Four possibilities from this agave-rich junction are:

1. Nolina Wash (right) goes another two miles before it dead-ends, but it can be hiked from the dead-end. This lower portion of this wash is a favorite of park volunteer naturalists.

2. Bighorn Canyon (hike only), to the west of Nolina, climbs about 4 miles to the sheep guzzler at Blue Spring, high in the Pinyon Mountains. A loop hike may be made by returning by way of Nolina Wash.

3. Sunset Mountain, to the east of Mescal Bajada, is a prominent peak which is a three-mile hike with 2000' elevation gain. Follow the Pinyon Wash jeep trail southeast one mile, then park and hike east (left) up-canyon 1.5 miles to a saddle on the ridge which climbs steeply southeast (right) another 1.5 miles to the summit at elevation 3657 feet.

Optionally hike about 3 miles from this same parking point southeast up a wash and canyon around the southern flank of Sunset Mountain and turn east into Sunset Bowl between peaks 2997 and 3443 on the northwest side of Harper Flat. This sheltered little cove, described in the *San Diego Tribune* by Skip Ruland in the early 1980s, is an excellent dry-camp site and it offers a northwesterly climb onto Sunset Mountain. At least two days and an overnight should be allowed for this alternate hike and ascent of the mountain.

4. The Pinyon Wash 4WD road climbs left from a junction at mile 1.6 for another 3.3 miles into Pinyon Canyon. From the Pinyon Canyon roadhead at mile 4.9, it is a mile hike into Harper Flat, one of the most extensive Indian sites in the entire region. Bedrock morteros and metates, shards, flaking

The Narrows service station (1933)—now gone

and rough hand tools testify to its heavy use. A complex of Indian trails radiates from the area. Harper Flat (average elev. 2600') has abundant high-desert vegetation including Mojave yucca, nolina, ocotillo, agave, desert willow, California juniper, desert lavender, indigo and cassia.

81.5 Narrows Earth Trail south (right).
🏃 This self-guiding geology walk goes about a half mile into Powder Dump Wash, so named for explosive storage here during highway construction in the 1930s. ABDSP brochures are available from the visitor center and may be at the trailhead.

Some of the oldest exposed rocks in this area include those found in Quartz Vein Wash and along The Narrows Earth Trail. These are seen as bands of light and dark material. These pre-Cretaceous metasedimentary rocks were laid down perhaps 500 million years ago as alternating layers of sand and mud in an ancient seabed hundreds of miles to the southeast. They were metamorphosed before and during granitic intrusions; then subsequent northward movement along the highly active San Andreas fault system brought this seabed to its present location. Other outcrops of old rock in this area are found in the San Ysidro and Santa Rosa mountains.

81.6 Quartz Vein Wash is just east of Powder Dump Wash.
This is a sandy 4WD road negotiable for about 0.4 mile. This wash, like the Narrows Earth Trail behind and Nude Wash ahead, displays prominent fault gouging as solid rock has been pulverized into a powdery mass. This is a very complex area where the Aguanga-San Felipe fault zone encounters region-wide detachment faulting of incredible proportions.

As the highway swings to the left into The Narrows, note the large, light-colored pegmatite dikes on the north side.

82.2 Old Borrego Valley Road turnoff north (left).
An electrical substation on the south side marks this turnoff into San Felipe Wash and up into Cactus Valley. This 4WD route, which used to be the only access into Borrego Valley, now passes through a quiet, serene and little visited portion of the desert. The road works east and north to the ABDSP

boundary, where one of several sets of tracks can be followed to the paved Borrego Springs Road near Borrego Air Ranch.

82.4 Nude Wash turnoff south (right).

𝕏 Just east of the substation, Nude Wash offers numerous sheltered campsites in ironwood groves in its half mile of dirt road. Its name may derive from the bare fault-sheared and gouged granitic and metamorphic outcrops visible on a short walk from the roadhead. This is more evidence of detachment faulting. Tinajas—water catchment basins, which are a boon to wildlife—are encountered beyond the stony nudity.

𝕏 One-tenth of a mile east of Nude is Sunset Wash, which is devouring the north face of its namesake mountain. A hike up Sunset Wash reveals towering, exposed sections of mountain fragments, hundreds of feet thick. This dynamic process offers an insight into similar activity eight to ten million years ago which produced the great red fanglomerate ("alluvial fan conglomerate") cliffs at the mouth of Split Mountain.

83.6 Old Kane Spring Road junction. The old 4WD route runs straight ahead to the east.

Side Trip Along Old Kane Spring Road

Mile 0.0 is at the Hwy 78 junction. Mile 2.9 marks the turnoff to Harper Canyon via a 4WD road to the south (see below for description). Continue east, paralleling powerlines on Old Kane Spring Road. Mile 3.0 is at a dirt road which leads north (left) to Hwy 78. Mile 8.5 is the junction with the paved Split Mountain Road in Lower Borrego Valley.
End of Side Trip.

85.6 Borrego Springs Road (BSR) and Texas Dip.

La Casa del Zorro is 6.2 miles northwest (left) at the junction of Yaqui Pass Road (Hwy S-3) and BSR. Christmas Circle in Borrego Springs is another 5.3 miles beyond this junction.

Texas Dip, huge like its namesake state, is just northwest of the junction of Hwy 78 and BSR. The dip is a mile-wide, hundred-foot-deep channel caused by catastrophic flood events. Texas Dip is one of the more dependable locales for desert blooms. Cacti are abundant as well as agave and smoke trees, and annuals are always found here.

86.9 Buttes Pass turnoff north (left) to Borrego Mountain.

A complex of dirt and 4WD roads radiates from here.

Side Trips Into West Butte Section of Borrego Mountain

Mile 0.0 is the turnoff on Highway 78, 1.5 miles east of Borrego Springs Road and 5.2 miles west of Split Mountain Road in Ocotillo Wells. Drive north on the dirt road. Mile 1.0 is Desert Lookout fork. Trips from this fork are described below.

Side Trip to Desert Lookout and Borrego Mountain Wash (mileage continuous from Hwy 78).

0.0 Hwy 78. Drive north.

1.0   Desert Lookout fork. Turn northwest (left) to...

2.1   Desert Lookout.

A hike to the top of West Butte (elev. 1207') begins from this parking area overlooking The Slot. Follow the stub road northeast (right) from the Lookout and then hike north up a faint foot trail to the summit.

Also from the Lookout, a short scramble down leads the hiker into The Slot, a superb example of badlands erosion. In the shadowy defile, red and yellow sandstone walls rise 50 feet or more on either side. At each turn down-wash there are new surprises as the passageway narrows until a large person might have difficulty squeezing through. The hiker may continue west and north about 0.7 mile to rejoin the vehicle trail at the bottom of...

2.9   Borrego Mountain Drop-off. Conventional vehicles must backtrack from the top of the Drop-off to Highway 78. OHVs can negotiate the sandy pitch down into Borrego Mountain Wash. Turn north (left) down-wash. (A right turn dead-ends shortly at The Slot.)

3.1   The Borrego Mountain Wind Caves are visible about 0.3 mile east of the wash. Here the tilted and twisted strata, dark red Diablo formation sandstones which are ancestral Colorado River sediments, have been pierced like Swiss cheese by wind and water erosion. Continue north, down-wash. Sunrise or sunset views from here, across to Fonts Point in the Borrego Badlands and backdropped by the sere Santa Rosas, are superb. A sweeping image of this panorama, by naturalist-photographer Paul Johnson, has long been featured as the lead photo on the state park brochure-map.

4.5   A major tributary from the southeast (right) joins the main wash.

A hike up this tributary leads to a large, dry waterfall in a labyrinth of badland ridges and gorges.

5.6   Junction with San Felipe Wash (see Trip 4D below).

End of Side Trip

Side Trip to Buttes Pass/Goat Trail (mileage continuous from Hwy 78).

0.0   Hwy 78. Drive north.

1.0   Desert Lookout fork. Turn east (right) to...

1.5   Buttes Pass/Goat Trail fork. There are two options from here:

1. East (right) leads 1.9 miles along Goat Trail to Blow Sand Canyon (4WD only) or into OWSVRA near the Ocotillo Wells Ranger Station.

2. North (left) drops over Buttes Pass into Buttes Canyon. Mile 1.9 is the Hawk Canyon turnoff northwest (left).

One-half mile up this turnoff is a beautiful, salmon-tinted bowl which is a fault-formed valley offering many strolls and hikes. The northeast side of the valley is granitic, shot through with bold slashes of pegmatite dikes. The southwest side is a complex sedimentary conglomerate and sandstone suite of rocks, possibly correlated to the Split Mountain Formation. Raptor-nesting areas are visible, high on the southwest cliff side, accounting for the name of the canyon.

Continuing north down Buttes Pass Road, there are three excellent walk-in campsites in coves west (left) of the road. Mile 3.6 joins the San Felipe Wash route (see Trip 4D).
End of Side Trip

86.9 Buttes Pass turnoff (repeated from above).
Continue east on Hwy 78.

87.1 Harper Canyon/Cactus Garden turnoff south (right).
Side Trip to Harper Canyon/Cactus Garden
This turnoff leads 1.6 miles over a dirt road to a junction with the old Kane Spring Road at Cactus Garden. The low point en route, a mesquite-lined shallow wash, may be the old San Felipe Creek drainage before it was beheaded at The Narrows on Hwy 78 by the present-day San Felipe Creek, eroding west from Texas Dip. The terrace northeast of this junction, marked by a faint trail on the west side, was an ancient Indian hunting site.

All of this area is known as Cactus Garden, first named by Horace Parker, guidebook author and state park commissioner. Six of the twelve varieties of cacti indigenous to this part of the Colorado Desert are found here. Also abundant are other desert plants that grow in rocky terrain and dry washes, such as ocotillo, ironwood tree, smoke tree, lavender and indigo bush.

Turn west (right) 0.1 mile to the turnoff to Harper Canyon, a 4WD road to the south (right). It is about two miles from the Kane Spring/Harper Canyon road junction south to the roadhead (elev. 1200'), an area rich with archaeological treasures. An interesting hike goes around the hill to the west (right) of the roadhead. A climb across the wash and up the hillside to the east offers sweeping vistas of Lower Borrego Valley.

A steep three-mile hike from the roadhead climbs narrow, rocky Harper Canyon onto Harper Flat in the heart of the Vallecito Mountains (average elev. 2600'). With suitable shuttle arrangements, one could cross Harper Flat to the west and descend Pinyon Canyon north to the 4WD road described above. Harper Canyon and Harper Flat were named for cattlemen Julius and Amby Harper (see Trips 5D and 6D below).
End of Side Trip

87.1 Harper Canyon/Cactus Garden turnoff (repeated from above).

89.1 Enter OWSVRA, a 40,000-acre OHV playground, funded from "Green Sticker" gas tax fees by the motorists of California (see Trip 5A below).

89.2 Goat Trail/Blow Sand Canyon turnoff.
South (right) leads to Desert Ironwoods Inn RV park and store, well stocked with maps and guides to the local area.

Side Trip Up Goat Trail (4WD road)
North (left) is a 4WD route along Goat Trail toward East Butte. After a mile, the road swings hard left (west) and climbs a steep dugway to Blow Sand Canyon fork at mile 1.7.

Goat Trail leads 1.9 miles west (straight ahead) to Buttes Pass.

The North (right) fork drops into Blow Sand Canyon to Bald Hill at mile 2.5. (The fragile slope is absolutely closed to vehicles.) Mile 3.5 joins the San Felipe Wash route (see Trip 4D).
End of Side Trip

90.1 Turnoff north (left) to OWSVRA Ranger Station.

91.2 Main Street Campground (BM 298').

This well-developed state campground is the most popular base from which to explore the local area. In season, it is a living museum exhibiting the state of the art of off-road automotive engineering and its consumers.

Shell Reef Expressway, a 4WD route which provides access to most of the major natural features of OWSVRA, takes off from the northeast corner of the campground (see Trip 4D below).

92.2 Split Mountain Road junction in Ocotillo Wells.

TRIP 4B:
Tamarisk Grove to Ranchita (S-22) via Grapevine Canyon

From: Tamarisk Grove Campground (Hwy S-3)
To: Ranchita (Hwy S-22) just east of Ranchita store.
Via: Grapevine Canyon Road (dirt road, seasonally 4WD only)

Connecting Trips:
   1B–Montezuma Junction to Borrego Springs via Hwy S-22
   4A–Earthquake Valley to Ocotillo Wells via Hwy 78

Points of Interest and Side Trips:
Yaqui Well, Angelina Spring, Stuart Spring, Jasper Trail junction.

MILES FROM:
Tam.   S-22

0.0   13.2 Tamarisk Grove Campground (elev. 1400').

Drive west on Hwy S-3 0.1 mile to the San Felipe Wash crossing. Turn west (right) up-wash into Grapevine Canyon, named for wild grapes found near springs in the canyon.

The Yaqui Well self-guiding nature trail starts on the north side of the wash from here and climbs over the low ridge to the west. It is a pleasant stroll from Tamarisk Grove to Yaqui Well.

1.0   12.2 Yaqui Well and primitive camp.

Yaqui Well ...a haven for bird life (ABDSP Interpretive Panel)
UTM 5-57.1E 36-66.5N   LAT 33°08.25'N LON 116°23.28'W

Many lost-gold-mine stories and legends of desert ghosts center on this area. One of these stories involves the Indian for whom the area was named. A Yaqui Indian of Sonora who married a Kumeyaay woman from Grapevine Canyon lived in the well area in the 1880s. The Indian later moved to Warner Ranch and worked in the vicinity. Reportedly he made periodic trips into the desert whenever he needed money, always returning with black nuggets. After he was killed in a brawl, $4000 in gold was found in his bunk.

Yaqui Well, a famous old seep in San Felipe Wash a hundred yards north of the parking area, produces water year-round. The well was heavily used by Indians, cattlemen, prospectors and travelers in earlier years. It was first developed as a cattle camp sometime after 1909 by Paul Sentenac. Magnificent desert ironwood and mesquite trees grow here. Bedrock metates and house rings on the rocky rise near the spring indicate that the seeds of ironwoods and mesquite beans were harvested by the Indians.

2.5   10.7 Fork, bear right. The left fork is a poleline access road from Highway 78, 0.4 mile away. The route here passes through a beautiful cactus garden, said to contain one of the largest, densest and most varied displays of succulents anywhere in the park.

4.5   8.7 The California Riding and Hiking Trail (CRHT) joins with a dirt road from the southeast (left). It is 2.0 miles southeast down this road to Highway 78, opposite Plum Canyon. Continue northwest up-wash.

4.6   8.6   Bitter Creek Canyon to the left.

Hikers may go 1.3 miles southwest to Bitter Creek Spring. The spring is located about 150 feet up the side of a hill and is carried to a trough at the bottom by a pipe. The use by animals and birds is heavy.

6.5   6.7   Site of Richter Springs.

Just south of the springs is a large rock with clearly visible morteros.

7.0   6.2   Angelina Spring.

During summer the water may be a foot or so beneath the surface. A small stream generally flows in the wash for some distance before disappearing into the porous sands. This water hole is shaded by cottonwoods, willows, and arrow weed. The plant growth is dense, giving good cover for California quail and many other birds. A flat area adjacent to Angelina Spring had a great amount of Indian use as indicated by the many bedrock morteros and metates, the amount of shards and flaking, and hearth areas.

8.3   4.9   Stuart Spring.

The spring is located on the north hillside in a tangle of underbrush about 20 feet above the wash bed. Water piped down from the spring into a trough is available year-round. The bird life is always good—exceptional during migrations. California quail are in the vicinity at all times, as well as a few mountain quail. The quail, small birds and rodents attract Cooper hawks, red-tailed hawks and owls.

8.7   4.5 Jasper Trail turnoff north (right).

Ӿ   The CRHT also departs Grapevine Canyon at this point. It is about five
miles to S-22 up this very rugged but scenic 4WD road (see Jasper Trail
side trip from Trip 1B.)

The Grapevine route continues west up-wash.

9.3   3.9 Fork, bear northwest (right). The ranch west (left) of the road is the
W-W (Walt and Wanda Phillips) Ranch. Tungsten-mine works are farther
north along the road.

10.3 2.9 Fork, turn north (right). An old cabin is on the northwest corner here.
Climb northeast out of Grapevine Canyon past the Alfred Wilson ranch on the
west (left).

(See Alternate Exit below.)

13.2 0.0 Junction with Hwy S-22 (elev. 4128') just east of Ranchita store and
west of the ABDSP boundary between post mile markers 5 and 6. This
junction is posted Wilson Ranch and W-W Ranch and is readily identified by
the two parallel dirt roads leading south. Oak Grove Lane is opposite.

Alternate Exit From Grapevine Canyon

(Mileage is continuous from mile 10.3 above.)

10.3 Fork marked by old cabin on northwest corner (see mile 10.3
above). Drive straight, hugging the north side of Grapevine
Canyon.

11.7 Turnoff north is another route direct to S-22. Continue straight to
cross, at mile 12.1, a saddle into Hoover Canyon and then drive
through pastures and oak meadows. Take care to shut stock gates.

13.8 Hoover Canyon at Highway S-22 between post mile markers 2 and
3. This point is marked by a metal gate of the Vista Irrigation
District.

TRIP 4C:
Tamarisk Grove To Borrego Springs Via Hwy S-3

From: Junction of Hwys 78 and S-3 near Tamarisk Grove Campground
To: Christmas Circle in Borrego Springs
Via: Yaqui Pass/Hwy S-3 (paved road)

Connecting Trips:

1B–Montezuma Junction to Borrego Springs via Hwy S-22
4A–Earthquake Valley to Ocotillo Wells via Hwy 78

Points of Interest and Side Trips:

Yaqui Well Nature Trail, Cactus Loop Trail, Kenyon Overlook Trail, Yaqui Pass,
Old Borego, Glorietta Canyon.

Route Summary:
County post mile markers start at zero at Hwy 78, reaching mile 12 at Christmas Circle. Odometer mileages are not necessary.

POST MILES FROM:
Hwy 78

0.0   Junction of Hwys 78 and S-3 at Call Box 76.9 (BM 1481').
Drive northeast.

0.1   Drive across the generally dry bed of San Felipe Creek. Turn west (left) here for Yaqui Well Primitive Camp and Grapevine Canyon (see Trip 4B above).

0.3   Tamarisk Grove Campground is a very popular campground with 27 sites each with picnic table, shade ramada, foot locker and barbecue. Drinking water, flush toilets and showers are available. Park staff is in attendance at the entrance station, which offers maps, guides, and interpretive displays. Check at the entrance station for the campfire program schedule. A small garden of typical desert plants with name posts appears in front of the station. Day use picnic tables are also available.

The campground was originally a San Diego County prison camp, established in September 1929 to relieve pressure on the overcrowded county jail. After the camp was transferred to CDPR, Tamarisk Grove served as headquarters for the briefly independent Anza State Park from 1951 to 1957.

Hike Along Yaqui Well Nature Trail
This trail departs northwest across from the entrance to the campground, just west of the ranger residence and palm trees. Follow the trail about 1.5 miles west off the rocky slope and down to the desert wash woodland to the spring, which is encircled by mistletoe-infested mesquite trees and ironwood trees. Note the very different plants found on the rocky slope and in the wash. Key plants in this desert-succulent-scrub community include ocotillo, agave, krameria, brittlebush, teddy-bear cholla, staghorn cholla, fishhook cactus, barrel cactus, chuparosa, cheesebush, jojoba, alkalai goldenbush, trixis, desert lavender, and dudleya. As you drop into the desert wash woodland, typical plants become mesquite, acacia, ironwood, palo verde, smoke tree, indigo bush, desert mistletoe, tamarisk, coyote melon, saltbush, and bladderpod (for a full description of the Yaqui Well area, see Trip 4B).

Hikers can return by walking south from the well to the Yaqui Well Primitive Camp area, where there are pit toilets, an interpretive panel, and the Grapevine Canyon Road. Walk east down the road back to S-3 and the entrance to Tamarisk Grove.
End of Hike

Northeast from the campground entrance, across the highway, is the one-mile, self-guiding Cactus Loop Trail (elev. 1400') which offers a close-up view of the San Felipe fault trace and traverses typical desert

rocky slopes which host superb stands of succulent cacti and related plants. Cacti featured on this walk through the Lower Sonoran Life Zone include: hedgehog, fishhook, staghorn cholla, beavertail, teddybear cholla, and pencil cholla. The walk up to the high point of the trail (elev. 1520') passes through a cholla forest with shrubs almost six feet tall.
End of Hike

Continue driving up the grade to...

1.3   Mescal Bajada Overlook turnout to the south (right).
Just past here, down-slope, can be seen the remnants of the old Yaqui Pass roadbed, constructed during World War II for use by General George Patton's vehicles. Drive across Yaqui Pass (elev. 1750') to...

1.9   Kenyon Overlook Trail (elev. 1720').
The 1.2-mile loop trail begins here and ends at the Yaqui Pass Primitive Camp, with a short walk back along the road to the start. Kenyon Viewpoint is one-quarter mile southwest from the start and a second viewpoint is about one-quarter mile farther to the east. Plants along the trail are typical desert succulent scrub associated with rocky slopes. The trail gently undulates over rocky slopes and down small gullies.

Bill Kenyon Trail (ABDSP Memorial Plaque)
UTM 5-60.5E 36-67.2N   LAT 33°08.6'N LON 116°21.1'W

Orientation & Geography Of Mescal Bajada (ABDSP Interpretive Panel)

2.1   Yaqui Pass Primitive Campground.
As the road drops down from Yaqui Pass, a sweeping panorama of Borrego Valley comes into view. This view focuses on the heart and the most-visited parts of the Anza-Borrego region: the resort town of Borrego Springs and, to the northwest, the park visitor center, park headquarters, the main campground, and Hellhole, Borrego Palm, and Henderson canyons, which drain the San Ysidro Mountains. To the north is the entrance to Coyote Canyon with its year-round running creek, and Coyote Mountain, which separates Coyote Canyon from Clark Dry Lake and Clark Valley. Beyond these are the Santa Rosa Mountains and Toro Peak. Fonts Point, the high point of the badlands, and the buttes of Borrego Mountain can be seen to the northeast.

Toward the bottom of the Yaqui Meadows slope are the fine resorts of Rams Hill and La Casa del Zorro. In 1936 Noel Crickmer purchased the original ranch at the latter location and developed it into the Desert Lodge. This quiet hotel was purchased in 1960 by James S. Copley, whose publishing company still owns the property. It is arguably the premier resort of the entire Colorado Desert south of the Coachella Valley, and is host to many conferences.

6.7   Yaqui Pass Road and Borrego Springs Road (BSR) (elev. 550').
A southeast (right) turn on BSR climbs gently six miles to Texas Dip (elev. 722') and Hwy 78.

The paved road straight ahead becomes Rango Road which leads west past the historic Old Borego Store, the original "Borego Springs" town site. The now-defunct store and post office is on private property and is the site of the annual Borrego old-timers reunion. Rango turns north and becomes Borrego Valley Road, which goes past the Club Circle resort.

Hwy S-3 turns west (left) onto Borrego Springs Road, passing post mile marker 7 at Deep Well Trail.

8.5   Glorietta Canyon turnoff, south (left).

This canyon, popular with park staff and volunteers, is particularly attractive during the spring wildflower season. The unmarked dirt road, between post mile markers 8 and 9, is the southerly extension of DiGiorgio Road in Borrego Valley. It departs from pavement at the east end of the highway curve, climbs south up onto Yaqui Meadows, and swings west (right) into Glorietta Canyon after a couple of miles.

From the roadhead here, hikers may continue west up the fault trace to a saddle overlooking the Tubb Canyon area.

9.5   Solar-powered home.

Observe the home with the steeply sloped, south-facing roof north of post mile marker 9 and just to the east on San Pablo Road. It is 100% solar-powered, the only connection to utilities being the telephone/modem lines. (Woe to the shareholders of power utilities should this technology become widespread.)

12.1   Christmas Circle in Borrego Springs.

TRIP 4D:
Ocotillo Wells to Borrego Valley Via San Felipe Wash

From: Hwy 78 at Ocotillo Wells
To: Hwy S-22 at post mile marker 23 near county dump, junction of Pegleg Road and Palm Canyon Drive (east)
Via: San Felipe and Borrego Sink washes (4WD roads)

Connecting Trips:
4A–Earthquake Valley to Ocotillo Wells via Hwy 78
3A–Borrego Springs to Salton City via Hwy S-22

Points Of Interest and Side Trips:
Southern Borrego Badlands, Cut Across Trail, Borrego Mountain, San Gregorio, Borrego Sink.

MILES FROM:
Oco.   S-22 Wells

0.0   15.0 Ocotillo Wells (elev. 155').

Drive northwest along the west side of Benson Dry Lake and the county airport into OWSVRA. (The east-side route along Benson Dry Lake goes north directly to Devils Slide.)

1.8   13.4 Quarry Road/Shell Reef Expressway intersection.

The Expressway is the main east-west route through OWSVRA. Devils Slide (aka Squaw Peak and Black Butte) is two miles northeast (right), followed by Barrel Springs, Wolfe Well, Shell Reef, Tarantula Wash, Gas Dome Trail, and the poleline Road (BLM Rd SF131) about 11 miles east from Quarry Road. (See Trip 5E San Felipe Hills.)

Quarry Road to the southwest (left) skirts East Butte of Borrego Mountain about a mile to The Cove campsite and, just beyond, to Blow Sand Hill. The unique shape of this east slope of Borrego Mountain acts as a trap for wind-blown sand from the desert floor.

This huge sand dune is very popular for buggy and motorcycle recreation and competition. The bug-eyed headlights from OHVs playing on this dune at night can be seen for many miles out on the desert. Beyond Blow Sand Hill, Quarry Road crosses OWSVRA's major campsite at Main Street and leads to the Ocotillo Wells Ranger Station about two miles from the Quarry Road/Expressway intersection. The somewhat difficult climb to the top of East Butte (elev. 1196') begins from the southernmost ridge of Borrego Mountain, nearest Hwy 78. Climb the crest of the ridge to its highest point for a view of the OWSVRA area, Ocotillo Wells, the Vallecito Mountains, the West Butte of Borrego Mountain, and the Borrego Badlands.

The San Felipe Wash trip continues up the wash north-northwest.

Looking west over the narrows of San Felipe Wash

2.4   12.6 Fault Wash and North San Felipe Wash junction.

The Cut Across Trail is four miles north (right) along Fault Wash. Military Wash, paralleling Fault Wash slightly to the west, was the site of much World War II training activity by General Patton's armored troops, preparing for battle in the deserts of North Africa.

Beware of any unusual looking material and report its presence to park rangers or the county sheriff.

Despite the large military presence here and in Borrego Valley, none of Patton's 11 camps of his Desert Training Center were located in ABDSP. Patton commanded army units on the ground and in the air, while both the Navy and the Marines also conducted military maneuvers in the park.

Continue northwest up North San Felipe Wash and exit OWSVRA into ABDSP.

4.9   10.1 Blow Sand Canyon junction southwest (left).

This leads into East Butte of Borrego Mountain 1.8 miles to Goat Trail.

5.3   9.7   Cut Across Trail/Buttes Canyon intersection (elev. 280').

Side Trip Northeast Up Cut Across Trail.

0.0   San Felipe Wash. Drive north (right) about a mile to the confluence of Big Wash and Third Wash (elev. 336') and swing northeast. Big Wash and Third Wash are hike-only.

2.4   Military Wash (closed, north). Cross Fault Wash to...

3.1   Fault Wash Road. Continue straight ahead northeast. (Short Wash is 4.4 miles north.)

3.8   Palo Verde Wash. Continue straight ahead northeast. (Hwy S-22 is 6.2 miles northwest.)

The route passes Pack Rat Wash, Anopheles Wash, and Bank Wash, each of which leads southeast (right) into OWSVRA to join Shell Reef Expressway about four miles away. Cut Across Trail arcs to the left and enters the mud hills of the Borrego Badlands.

6.1   Basin Wash. Down-wash to the east (right) it passes mud caves and joins Tule Wash after 2.3 miles.

Up-wash to the north (left) it climbs out of Basin Wash, passes Una Palma, and swings east into the headwaters of Tule Wash.

7.9   Five Palms junction to Arroyo Salado.

Tule continues east down-wash to the county line and re-enters OWSVRA at mile 9.2. Pumpkin Patch is just beyond, with a loop-trip possibility southwest to Shell Reef Expressway via Pumpkin Patch Trail. Or continue down-wash about ten miles to Hwy 86 near Salton City.

A north (right) turn climbs out of Tule Wash, passing Five Palms, to drop into ...

9.2   Arroyo Salado. Northwest (left) up-wash passes Seventeen Palms.

13.1   Hwy S-22 at Arroyo Salado Primitive Campground.

End of Side Trip

5.3   9.7   Cut Across Trail/Buttes Canyon intersection (repeated from above).
The Buttes Canyon road, following the split between East and West Butte, climbs south (left) into Borrego Mountain to reach Hwy S-78 after 3.6 miles. The main route continues west up San Felipe Wash another mile to a small wash joining from the southwest (left). An old gold or tourmaline mine is a short walk up this wash at the base of West Butte.

7.2   7.8   Borrego Mountain Wash turnoff to the southwest (left).

7.5   7.5   Hills of the Moon Wash turnoff north (right).
The wash can be explored for several miles north. Like a good badlands wash, Hills of the Moon is virtually devoid of vegetation, creating a real moonscape.

7.8   7.2   Rainbow Wash turnoff north (right).
The vehicle route goes about three miles up this colorful wash, winding between conical, banded, multicolored mud hills until it narrows. A hiker may continue up the wash and then climb the ridge to the northwest (left) about 1.5 miles to Fonts Point.

8.1   6.9   Fork of San Felipe Wash southwest (left) and Borrego Sink Wash west (right). San Felipe Wash crosses the paved Borrego Springs Road at Texas Dip, 4.7 miles southwest. The main route continues due west into Borrego Sink Wash. A large natural amphitheater on the south side of the wash at mile 9.0 offers an excellent, wind-sheltered campsite.

11.1   3.9   The route enters dense vegetation marking the general area of Borrego Spring and what was once the San Gregorio Indian village at the narrowest point of the Borrego Sink drainage. The route forks here. The southwest (left) forks leads about 0.1 mile to the Anza San Gregorio Monument atop a hill on the south side of the wash. The Anza expeditions of 1774 and 1775 made camps near this spot. A series of wells were dug into the sandy wash to provide water for people and animals. The second expedition brought 240 people and 800 head of cattle to California.

> San Gregorio (California Historical Landmark No. 673)
> UTM 5-68.1E 36-75.9N   LAT 33°13.3'N LON 116°16.15'W

The monument is near the old John McCain cabin site, a cattle camp outpost near the turn of the century. The first reported visit to his camp was made in April 1894 by John Kelly, who described McCain in his memoirs, written 24 years later, as "one of the genuine, old-fashioned cowboys of the West—not one of the 'made up' kind that we see among the moving picture outfits of today. He was uneducated and rough, and could get a larger percent of profanity into a sentence than any man I have ever seen, either before or since." McCain was the first to file a homestead at "Borego Spring."
It is from the name of this original spring that the valley, the palm canyon, and the state park take their name. The name on the earliest maps is "Borego." The corrected spelling, with the double "r," first appeared in 1939 when state-park staff decided to reestablish the correct spelling of the Spanish word for

"sheep." In 1950 the U.S. National Board on Geographical Names declared it officially.

11.2 3.8   The site of "Borrego Spring II," 0.2 mile north from the route at the base of some low gray hills, is marked by a dugout depression in the north bank of the wash. Faulting activity probably accounts for the shifting location of Borrego Spring, although no surface water is currently found at the Borrego Spring II site. The road continues west, with Metate Hill about one-half mile south of the road at the outlet from Borrego Sink.

12.7 2.3   Four-way junction just north of Borrego Sink.

Borrego Sink is the low point of the Borrego Valley. The vegetation on the salt flats around Borrego Sink and the old Borrego Spring is a typical example of desert growth in alkaline soil. It is mainly mesquite, which can have a tap root as deep as 150 feet. Besides mesquite, other flora found in the sink include arrow weed, pickleweed, galleta (bunch grass) and various members of the saltbush genus. The main route turns north (right) from the four-way junction, becoming paved at the county dump.

15.0 0.0   Junction with Highway S-22 at the intersection of Pegleg Road and Palm Canyon Drive.

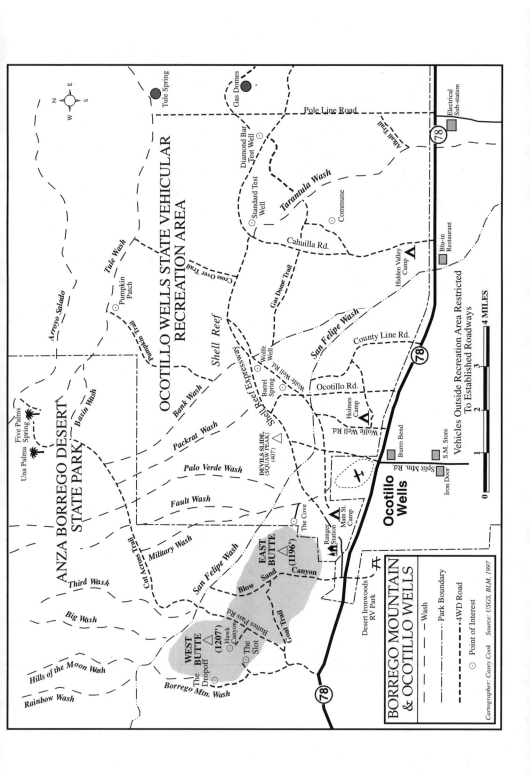

AREA 5-EASTERN:
east Hwy 78, central Hwy 86

T hree public land agencies, each with varying land management missions, offer the visitor a variety of possibilities in the eastern section of
the region. The Ocotillo Wells State Vehicular Recreation Area
(OWSVRA) is administered by the Off-Highway Vehicle Recreation Division of
the California Department of Parks and Recreation (CDPR). Land to the south
is administered by the U. S. Bureau of Land Management (BLM). To the southwest is Fish Creek and Split Mountain, one of the most frequently visited areas
of Anza-Borrego Desert State Park (ABDSP).

Within OWSVRA, OHV travel is generally unrestricted, relying on the driver's sense of responsibility for protecting natural resources. OWSVRA is
bounded by Borrego Mountain and Fault Wash on the west, Cut Across Trail in
San Diego County and S-22 and Surprise Wash in Imperial County on the
north, Highway 86 on the east, and Benson Dry Lake and Hwy 78 on the south.
At approximately 75,000 acres, OWSVRA is the second-largest unit within the
state park system next to Anza-Borrego's 620,000 acres.

OWSVRA is funded by the Off-Highway Vehicle Fund, which derives its
income from "green sticker" registration fees, state-vehicular-area use fees,
miscellaneous sources, and one percent of gas tax, with 50 percent of the fund-
ing coming from the latter.

The philosophy behind OHV use is best summarized by John Quirk, former
chief ranger at OWSVRA and former superintendent of ABDSP:

> *OWSVRA Rangers have a clear sense of their mission, which in no way detracts
> from their role as interpreters and naturalists. The OHV Division Resource
> Ecologists, who assist the Superintendent with resource protection, understand
> that the management of a SVRA is conservation-focused, not preservation-
> focused, and recognize that some consumption of resources is inherent in any
> recreational use of park lands.*

Delivery of public service is no better focused on customer needs anywhere in CDPR than in the "SVRA"s. Accident prevention measures, efficient medical response and diligent law enforcement are provided at levels which often exceed visitor expectations. Interpretive and public information programs foster appreciation of natural and cultural resources.

As a unit of the state parks division, the philosophy guiding ABDSP is that of resource protection. Objectives include providing "stewardship for the vast array of natural and cultural resources found throughout the park" and preserving "the landscape and scenery of the park in a pristine condition." Interpretive programs are designed "to inspire, educate, and instill a sense of wonder in park visitors about the values of the Colorado Desert." This dictates that "the established roadways in the park are Highways," that is, state highways. Therefore all vehicles on dirt or paved roads within ABDSP must be highway-legal vehicles. "Green sticker" vehicles cannot be operated within the boundaries of the park.

BLM and the U.S. Forest Service (USFS) are conservationist rather than preservationist, responsible for multiple use of the land—recreation, mining, timber production, livestock grazing, watershed and wildlife protection. On the other hand, such public land managers as CDPR and the National Park Service are preservationists, opposed to multiple use of the land. "Park" rules are strict in order to protect the land in perpetuity, so that the land will be the same for future generations to study and enjoy. As with state and national parks, the designation of lands as "wilderness" in both BLM and USFS lands shifts from multiple-use conservation to strict resource preservation.

The BLM area here is a portion of the 16-million-acre California Desert Conservation Area (CDCA) which was created by Congress in 1976 "to provide for the administration of public lands in such a way that it would protect its unusual natural and cultural values while providing for the wise use of its resources."

Areas of Critical Environmental Concern (ACECs), such as San Sebastian Marsh, receive special protection. With the passage of the California Desert Protection Act (CDPA) in 1994, federal wilderness areas were created within the CDCA, and as such, do not allow mechanized equipment or facilities for visitors. The Fish Creek Mountains are an example of a BLM wilderness.

TRIP 5A:
Ocotillo Wells to Trifolium (Hwy 86) Via Hwy 78

From: Ocotillo Wells
To: Trifolium (Hwy 86)
Via: Hwy 78 (paved road)

Connecting Trips:
3D–Seventeen Palms—Eastern Borrego Badlands

4A–Earthquake Valley to Ocotillo Wells via Hwy 78
4D–Ocotillo Wells to Borrego Valley via San Felipe Wash
5B–Ocotillo Wells to Fish Creek via Split Mountain Road
5D–San Sebastian Marsh/Kane Spring Area
5E–San Felipe Hills
5F–Trifolium (Hwy 78) to Salton City via Hwy 86

Points of Interest and Side Trips:

OWSVRA (Devils Slide, Barrel Springs, Shell Reef), Los Puertocitos, Old Mine Road, San Sebastian Marsh hike.

Summary:

Highway 78 is paved and level through this area. San Diego County post mile zero is Oceanside. Post miles increase to the east with the county line at post mile 95.3 or, for Imperial County, mile zero. Trifolium (Hwy 86) is Imperial County post mile 13.2. Odometer mileage is used for dirt roads.

POST MILES FROM:
Oceanside

0.0   Oceanside, junction of I-5 and Hwy 78.

92.2 Split Mountain Road, Ocotillo Wells (elev. 165').

This self-styled "Dune Buggy Capital of the World" with a population of less than 200, is strategically located on the southern border of OWSVRA and at the only paved-road entrance to the popular Elephant Tree and Split Mountain areas of ABDSP. It is the focal point for weekend recreational support with its gas station, grocery store, bar and cafes. The Desert Ironwoods Motel is located nearby.

Visit the OWSVRA Ranger Station, two miles west of Ocotillo Wells, for comprehensive information and maps of the area. The $1.7-million complex consists of park headquarters and administration buildings, a water-storage tank, a dump station for RVs, a maintenance shop, restrooms, showers and a pubic telephone. Rangers often lead vehicle tours on weekends. Check the bulletin board on Main Street or check at the ranger station for scheduled events. All three main camping areas—the Quarry, Main Street and Holmes Camp—have vault toilets, shade ramadas, picnic tables, and fire rings. Water is not available. No fees are collected for camping or day use, and open camping is permitted throughout the area for up to 30 days per calendar year. OWSVRA features and points of interest can be reached by a variety of routes that network the area. We offer the shortest side routes from Hwy 78 to these points of interest in the following paragraphs. See Trip 4D for additional descriptions of OWSVRA in the Borrego Mountain area.

92.5 Devils Slide Lane.

A dirt road north (left) on the east side of Benson Dry Lake leads two miles to Devils Slide (the state name), Squaw Peak (the USGS name), or Black Butte (old miners' name). By any name, this is an ancient, decomposing, metamorphic mountaintop with only its tip protruding above the desert sands.

Black Butte is an isolated island of gneiss and schist about one-half mile long, rising some 200 feet above the surrounding flat desert. The dark desert varnish covering its exposed rock makes it appear as a black island in contrast to the light-colored sand of the surrounding desert. There are several old mine shafts and tunnels along the flank and many stories about the area having ghostly apparitions.

Benson Dry Lake was named for an early homesteader who owned a quarter-section of land upon which was a store/restaurant/gas station at what is now Burro Bend Cafe.

92.9 Toner Turkey Ranch.

This ranch in the tamarisk trees was forced to close by noise pollution created by military aircraft using Benson Dry Lake during the late 1930s. The surface rupture of the whopper magnitude 6.5 Borrego Mountain earthquake crossed the highway at this point. This was the 1968 temblor which was so graphically recorded on audio tape by ranger George Leetch in Split Mountain Gorge. This tape and accompanying visuals play continuously in the ABDSP visitor center.

93.4 Wolfe Well Road.

Side Trip Northeast into OWSVRA on Wolfe Well Road (4WD Road) and Shell Reef Expressway East

0.5   Holmes Camp, called El Rancho Ocotillo by ranger Jack Welch in the 1950s, on the east (right). The camp was named for a homesteader who had a large fruit orchard here. The route continues northeast, crossing San Felipe Wash.

1.2   Morton Road joins from the west.

1.9   Barrel Springs Trail north (left).

Side Trip to Barrel Springs

Barrel Springs is 0.7 mile north. Miners used this large mesquite sand dune as a base camp while working their prospects on Black Butte a mile west. Like the ghostly apparitions and flickering lights sighted in the vicinity of the mines, Barrel Springs has had similar reports, known as Borrego fireballs.

End Side Trip

1.9   Barrel Springs Trail (repeated from above). Continue northeast on Wolfe Well Road. Cross Ocotillo Road at mile 2.1 and Pack Rat Wash at mile 2.6.

3.7   Wolfe Well, an abandoned oil-test site marked by pipe and rubble.

At this major intersection in central OWSVRA, Bank Wash runs northwest/southeast, Shell Reef Expressway runs east/west and the Gas Dome Trail runs to the southeast. Wolfe Well Road merges with Shell Reef Expressway which continues east (straight ahead).

4.7   Shell Reef.

This four-million-year-old shell-hash, or coquina, bed has a long trough striking east-west through which the road goes. The five-foot-thick layer of fossil shell fragments, including oyster, pecten (scallop), and clam (*Anomia*), proves that this area was once a shallow sea bottom. Ranger Paul Remeika refers to this type of coquina bedding as a "shoal-deposited death assemblage."

This is a portion of the upper-half (marine-deltaic) Imperial Formation, which was laid down many hundreds of miles to the southeast and transported here by lateral, or strike-slip, fault action. Similar shell-hash beds are found in southwest Imperial County at elevations of a couple hundred feet above sea level in the Fish Creek badlands, Carrizo Badlands, Fossil Canyon in the Coyote Mountains, and the Yuha Buttes. OHV traffic on Shell Reef itself is discouraged in order to preserve these valuable but delicate clues to the past of this dynamic region.

Shell Reef Expressway continues to the east, with several options including Cross Over Trail north to Tule Wash and Pumpkin Patch, or Tarantula Wash southeast to Hwy 78.

6.5   Cross Over Trail forks northeast (left) to Tule Wash. Stay on Shell Reef Expressway (right). Tarantula Wash will cross in 0.2 mile and can be followed south 5 miles to Hwy 78. The Cahuilla Trail crosses Tarantula Wash about 0.3 mile south of Shell Reef Expressway. It can also be taken south 3.5 miles to Hwy 78.

9.5   Gas Dome Trail crosses from southwest to northeast (left). This is the site of the Diamond Bar test well.

10.5   Pole Line Road (BLM Rt SF131) running due north-south. See Trip 5E below for exploration in the San Felipe Hills ahead, including the Gas Domes. Turn south (right) to...

14.3   Hwy 78 at the San Felipe sub-station.

End Of Side Trip

93.4 Wolfe Well Road (repeated from above).

93.8 Los Puertocitos and Ocotillo Badlands.

The Ocotillo Badlands, south of the monument, are a wrinkled, crumpled set of conglomeratic ridges and hidden mudhills elevated in response to left-stepping, right-lateral fault strands which bound the badlands. These badlands can be explored on any of several 4WD routes that transect the area. Anza's second expedition stayed here the night of December 18, 1775. The campsite was named "the little pass" for the low point in the mountains on the northwest horizon which Anza recognized as San Carlos Pass in Coyote Canyon, his exit from the desert.

Los Puertocitos (California Historical Landmark No. 635)
UTM 5-83.6E 36-67.0N LAT 33°08.4N' LON 116°06.25W'

The route passes OWSVRA's Ocotillo Road (three miles north to Barrel Springs) and Alluvial Trail (one mile northwest to Holmes Camp) and crosses...

95.3/0.0 San Diego/Imperial County line (elev. 82').

A BLM sign advises "Entering the California Desert Conservation Area."

POST MILES FROM:
County Line

1.2   Old Mine Road turnoff south (elev.42').

This is an elevation of note in the "bathtub" of the Salton Trough. It marks the approximate high stand of prehistoric fresh-water Lake Cahuilla, fed by the Colorado River in flood. This elevation is encountered on several trips while exploring the Anza-Borrego region, including Trip 3F (Travertine Rock), Trip 5B (Gypsum Railroad), and Trip 7B (Superstition Mountain).

Side Trip South on Old Mine Road

At mile 1.5 down this dirt road, and then about one-half mile east from it, is a most curious collection—the "Airplane Graveyard." Several acres, behind barbed wire and "Look but don't enter" signs, are covered with parts of WW2-era warplanes and transport aircraft in a very lonely and vacant corner of the desert. A wind sock flaps beside a large dirt air strip that seems frozen in time over a half century ago—is this North Africa, circa 1944?

The sparse wooden ruins of Baileys Well (elev. 0') are a few hundred yards southwest of the graveyard. The ground is covered with the shells of fresh-water mollusks, reminders of the presence of the great inland sea of Lake Cahuilla and its death as recently as four hundred years ago.

Old Mine Road continues south, intersecting Old Kane Spring Road at mile 2.1, and reaching the Gypsum Railroad at mile 6.5. The "old mine" is the Imperial Gypsum Company quarry up against the Fish Creek Mountains across the railroad. From this point it is two miles west to Split Mountain Road (paved).

End Side Trip

2.1   San Felipe Wash and Blu-In store, Bridge #58-124.

4WD vehicles can drive northwest up the wash into OWSVRA or southeast down the wash to Old Kane Spring Road. Cahuilla Road turnoff north (left) is about a mile east. It goes north past Hidden Valley Camp and northeast to the old Commune area to connect with Gas Domes Trail. The old (hippie) Commune was home to about 15 young adults and children from about 1972 to 1974. Today, the Commune's old windmill can be seen at the Blu-In store.

Verdant, tree-shaded Allegretti Farms is next, on the south side of the highway. Tarantula Wash/Alkali crossing is at mile 8.1.

5.6   Pole Line Road, BLM Rt SF131 (BM 19').

This, formerly known as the Texaco Oil Well Road, is well marked by an electrical substation on the south (right) side of the road. See below for Trip 5D south to Kane Spring Road, San Sebastian Marsh and Harpers Well. See also below for Trip 5E north into the San Felipe Hills and the Gas Domes. The double culvert crossings at post miles 8.2 and 8.3 are named Condit/Bondit ditches. Just east of here is a closed 4WD road which strikes south and provides a good two-mile hiking route to the north edge of San Sebastian Marsh. The BLM brochure notes that...

> *This unique water-based habitat along San Felipe Creek has supplied a permanent, dependable source of water since ancient times. The site of an early Indian village, the marsh was a stopping place for the Spanish explorer Anza, who named it after his Indian guide Sebastian Tarabel. The marsh is the only designated critical habitat in California for an endangered species, the desert pupfish. Because of its importance in sustaining this unique marshland environment, San Felipe Creek is a registered National Natural Landmark and Area of Critical Environmental Concern. The marsh is closed to vehicle use. Removal of objects of antiquity such as arrowheads and pottery fragments is prohibited.*

Hwy 78 continues east, past a wash and 4WD trail at mile 11.8, which leads into the southeast sector of the San Felipe Hills. This is named "Oil Well Wash" on old maps and "Jim Jacklitch Creek" on the AAA county map. It leads several miles northwest to the Artesian Well and Pole Line Road. Deep sand drifts can block this wash from time to time.

13.2 Trifolium (Hwy 86) (BM -179).

This junction is named for the Trifolium Extension Canal, which terminates here where San Felipe Creek enters the Salton Sea. The Trifolium Canal services southwest Imperial Valley off of the West Side Main Canal near Brawley, which in turn taps the Colorado River's All-American Canal from Calexico.

Before the completion of paved Hwy 78 in the late 1930s, this locale was known as Kane Spring for the mesquite-formed sand dune 1.6 miles southeast on Hwy 86. This name is reflected in Old Kane Spring Road, aka Julian-Kane Spring Road, and the USGS topographic-map title.

Hwy 86 crosses San Felipe Creek just southeast of the junction at a U.S. Border Patrol checkpoint. The author has seen this creek, usually a three-season trickle, become a raging bank-to-bank torrent during late summer *chubascos* (Spanish for "hurricanes"). Not even these river banks can contain the waters of major flood years. The flat desert becomes an angry, mobile sea, churning and swirling down into the basin, dissolving the highway surface as if it were cube sugar.

Salton City and Hwy S-22 are 12.6 miles northwest, offering a loop trip back to Borrego Springs.

TRIP 5B:
Ocotillo Wells to Fish Creek via Split Mountain Road

From: Ocotillo Wells
To: Fish Creek
Via: Split Mountain Road (paved)

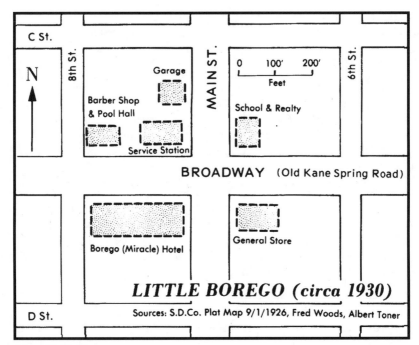

Map of Little Borego

Connecting Trips:

5A–Ocotillo Wells to Trifolium (Hwy 86) via Hwy 78

5C–Split Mountain to Hapaha and Harper Flat via Fish Creek

Points of Interest and Side Trips:

Little Borego, Old Kane Spring Road, Halfhill Dry Lake, Elephant Trees Discovery Trail, U.S. Gypsum Mine, Fish Creek to Carrizo Wash (and extension to Plaster City) via Gypsum Railroad.

MILES FROM:
Ocotillo Wells

0.0   Ocotillo Wells, Hwy 78 (elev. 170').

Drive south from Burro Bend cafe and gas station on Split Mountain Road (once known as Gypsum Mine Road), past Split Mountain Store and the Iron Door Saloon. These are the last outposts to stock up and tank up for trips into the Fish Creek and Vallecito mountains.

2.6   Little Borego (site).

Old Kane Spring Road leads west (right) from here along a pole line, 5.5 miles to Cactus Garden in ABDSP and another 3.0 miles to Hwy 79 near Nude Wash.

This intersection, formerly known as Main and Broadway, is the heart of Little Borego. The only signs left of this town, an early victim of the 1930s Depression, are several concrete slabs which now host private residences. The largest of these slabs was the base of the 14-room Miracle Hotel.

Miracle Hotel in Little Borego—now gone

The paved road swings east (left), onto the alignment of the Old Kane Spring Road. A half mile down, a dirt road angles due east (left) off the paved road, through a surprisingly upscale desert community consisting of about 10 homes, and over the southern shoulder of the Ocotillo Badlands. This dirt road intersects Old Mine Road after four miles and, just beyond, the "Airplane Graveyard" and Baileys Well (site).

Split Mountain Road swings right at an electrical substation to...

4.0   Old Kane Spring Road (east) and Halfhill Dry Lake (left).

The old dirt road strikes east, paralleling Fish Creek Wash and San Felipe Creek past San Sebastian/Harpers Well to reach Hwy 86 some nineteen miles east. Farmers began entering the area after 1910, soon after the completion of the Old Kane Spring Road. In 1918, San Felipe City, between the Fish Creek Mountains and Harpers Well near San Felipe Wash, consisted of a derrick, a house, an old shed and a couple of enterprising men. Although other hopeful settlers, especially veterans after World War I, homesteaded land in the San Felipe City area, the heat, flash floods, high winds and drifting sand soon caused them to give up the struggle.

Halfhill Dry Lake is a popular staging area for ultralight aircraft.

Continue southeast on the paved road, entering ABDSP at mile 5.6. The state park occupies two square miles of Imperial County here, thanks to a surprising westward jog in the county line. (Surveyors fiddle with lines to correct historical errors.)

5.9   Elephant Trees Discovery Trail (right), Ranger Station (left).

The Lost Herd of Elephant Trees (ABDSP Panel)
UTM 5-83.8E 36-59.4N LAT 33°04.28N LON 116°06.15W.

The dirt road goes west about a mile to a parking area where the 1.5-mile loop nature trail begins. Descriptive brochures found at the trailhead are keyed to numbered posts along the self-guiding trail on this low-desert alluvial fan spread at the mouth of Alma Wash. It is one of the first areas in the park to

Borego schoolhouse

Dr. Woillard at Broadway and Main

Upstairs at the Miracle Hotel

Grocery store at Borego

flower early in spring. A wide variety of plants, in addition to the rare elephant tree (*Bursera microphylla*), are found on this fairly level walk through a desert wash woodland. Perennials to note include barrel cactus, smoke tree, ironwood, indigo bush, desert lavender, creosote, acacia, desert mistletoe, staghorn and teddybear cholla, ocotillo, chuparosa, brittlebush, jojoba, cheesebush, beavertail cactus.

The tree can be recognized by its large, swollen trunk and tapered branches, appearing like octopus tentacles reaching for the sky. The small, reddish-brown, widely spreading upper branches and twigs appear stunted, thereby giving the tree a shrub-like appearance. Generally the tree doesn't exceed a height of 6-8 feet, but some have attained heights of up to 20 feet. The tree is highly aromatic and its odor has been described as reminiscent of turpentine, cedar, or a combination of orange peel and pine needles. The yellow-green papery bark peels in thin flakes exposing an inner green bark, below which are reddish layers that can exude a blood-colored sap if the tree is cut or damaged. The tree is a very able drought resister, capable of maintaining life in

Elephant tree near Split Mountain

a very arid and rocky environment. Its thick, pulpy trunk readily absorbs and stores water, giving it a swollen appearance suggesting the trunk of an elephant.

The tree is in the Torchwood family (Burseraceae) and is related to frankincense and myrrh. Like its biblical relatives, it had special significance to the indigenous people of the area. The Cahuilla, who collected elephant-tree sap from the "herd" located in the Santa Rosas, called the plant *kelawat eneneka* "bitter wood." Because of the sap's power, only shamans handled the blood-red substance, which was considered too dangerous to be kept in the open and was always hidden. The Seri of Mexico considered the tree holy and a tea made from the tree was drunk during a vision quest by those seeking to become a shaman, or medicine healer.

The tree also had practical value for those whose culture allowed the handling of it. The sap was rubbed on the skin to cure skin diseases and heal insect bites and scorpion stings. The sap has been used to caulk boats, glue furniture, mend broken dishes, and preserve wood from attacks by worms. Mexicans still use the bark for tanning and dyeing, and a tea is made to cure stomach ailments. The smoke from a burning tree was inhaled as a remedy for headache. Today, medical researchers are investigating its curative possibilities. Remember, these and all the plants within the state park are protected.

8.2   Fish Creek Wash (BM 224').

Turnoff west (right) leads to Fish Creek Primitive Campground and the Split Mountain area (see Trip 5C below). Straight ahead is the U.S. Gypsum mine, the nation's largest gypsum quarry. Hundreds of tons of ore are freighted twice daily 25 miles southeast to Plaster City for processing into finished wallboard, as an ingredient in cement, and as an agricultural soil conditioner. For railroad buffs, this is a nostalgic reminder of many long-gone narrow-gauge operations serving mining towns throughout the Old West.

Side Trip to Carrizo Wash and Extension to Plaster City (dirt road)

This trip follows the dirt road paralleling the USGC railroad.

0.0　Fish Creek/Split Mountain Road. Cross the wash and turn southeast (left). Exit ABDSP into BLM public lands at mile 1.0. Note the huge chunks of almost pure gypsum, calcium sulfate, which provide ballast along the railroad. This, and related salts, precipitated out of warm, shallow seawater which was here in the late Miocene/early Pliocene epoch, four to five million years ago.

2.1　Intersect Old Mine Road (BM 115'). Workings of the Imperial Gypsum Company quarry are visible about a mile south (see Old Mine Road side trip above in Trip 5A). Pass "First Trestle" at mile 3.1, now replaced by eight massive culverts, which afford drainage to much of the northeast Fish Creek Mountains. These mountains contain the Fish Creek Wilderness Area, closed to all vehicular travel and probably the most road-free, least-visited area in western Imperial County. The BLM DAG notes that *these rugged mountains offer challenging canyon hikes and back country camping. Evidence of early Indian trails, campsites and rock-ring fish traps are found along ancient Lake Cahuilla shoreline at the base of the mountains.*

4.0　At a slight jog in the road to the left, cross the high-water beach line of old freshwater Lake Cahuilla (elev. 42'). This is an opportunity to walk for about a mile south to the water line on the cliffs, across fields of shells that tell of invertebrate life in these waters as recently as 500 years ago. BM 38' is at mile 4.6 and sea level at mile 5.8. Continue southeast, briefly below sea level but not underwater, thanks to the 42-foot-high Colorado River delta dam south of Mexicali which keeps the Gulf of California at bay, for now. Bottom out at minus five feet and climb imperceptibly, rounding the prominent northeast tip of Fish Creek Mountains to...

9.5　Carrizo Wash/Second Trestle (elev. 38').

The picturesque old wooden trestle of the 1970s has been replaced by concrete. Carrizo seasonally has water and occasionally rages in full torrent after late-summer/early-fall hurricanes from the Gulf of California. This point is the focus of hundreds of square miles of watershed from southern San Diego County and southwestern Imperial County. (If thunderheads you're seeing, you'd better be fleeing.)

Choices here are three:

1. 4WD trail south (right): Drive up Carrizo Wash six miles to the hummock where Carrizo Wash swings west into the forbidden Carrizo Impact Area. Just west of the hummock, pick up BLM route SF361 at UTM 5-97.0E 36-41.0N and work south about three miles to the old Butterfield Stage Route, thence southeast about 11 miles to Plaster City.

2. Dirt road southeast (straight): Cross Carrizo and parallel the rail-road fifteen miles to Plaster City. *Do not* get off this road because it cross-es U.S. Navy Target #103, a live bombing area.

3. 4WD trail north (left) down Carrizo and under the pole line: Tamarisk groves, mesquite thickets and shifting sand dunes make this route interesting but difficult to travel. Select the most traveled route in the wash or along the bank. Intersect Old Kane Spring Road after seven miles at UTM 5-94.8E 36-59.3N. This can be difficult to identify on the ground. If you encounter thickets with substantial water, you've gone too far and have entered the San Sebastian Marsh ACEC, which is closed to vehicles and is illegal and impassable. Backtrack to Old Kane Spring Road. From this point it is nine miles east (right) to Hwy 86 and six miles west (left) and north via Pole Line Road to Hwy 78.

End of Side Trip

TRIP 5C:
Split Mtn to Hapaha and Harper Flats via Fish Creek

From: Split Mountain Road/Fish Creek Wash junction
To: Hapaha and Harper Flats
Via: Fish Creek Wash (dirt road through Split Mountain becoming 4WD road)

Points of Interest and Side Trips:
Fish Creek Primitive Campground, Anticline, Wind Caves, Elephant Knees, Loop Wash, Sandstone Canyon, Olla Wash.

MILES FROM:
Split Mountain Road

0.0   Split Mountain Road/Fish Creek Wash junction.
Drive west (right) and cross the unsigned county line. The abandoned mine operation on the hill to the right is the Robertson-Peeler deposit of stron-tium sulfate, a salty variation of the calcium sulfate from the U.S. Gypsum Mine across the valley.

1.4   Fish Creek Primitive Campground (left).
As supervising ranger Fred Jee says, "Welcome to George Leetch coun-try," recognizing the late ranger who presided over this popular area for so many years in the 1950s through 70s. Tens of thousands of campers, including the authors, received their introduction to Anza-Borrego from the legendary Leetch, whose trailer/ranger station occupied this site for decades.

Fault Lines and Flash Floods (ABDSP Panel)
UTM 5-83.2E 36-54.1N   LAT 33°01.42'N LON 116°06.55W

1.7 Split Mountain Gorge, southern entrance.

For the next several miles, cliff walls tower several hundred feet on both sides. This "split" separates the Vallecito Mountains on the west from the Fish Creek Mountains on the east.

The gorge of Split Mountain is, geologically speaking, an antecedent stream canyon. Less than a million years ago, a stream flowed through this area and, as the mountain rose, the stream continued on its same course and cut into the slowly rising land.

2.5 The Amphitheater.

𝆙   A wash on the left, penetrating high sandstone and conglomerate walls, climbs steeply into a large bowl. SDSU geologist Pat Abbott describes this bowl as a Miocene battleground between alluvial fans advancing east from the rising Vallecitos and north-flowing streams from the Fish Creeks. The story is told by the reddish conglomerates from the west interfingering with light-colored, coarse sandstones from the south.

3.5 Split Mountain Landslide and Waterfall Canyon.

𝆙   The massive, chaotic jumble of boulders on the left, topped by whitish gypsum beds on the skyline, is one of at least three huge, long-runout landslides that are major features of Split Mountain. Area geologists have recently begun using the term *sturzstrom* (German for "fall stream") for these features, as detailed in the SCGS 1996 guidebook. Recent observations from the emerging science of planetary geology have detected similar features on the Moon and Mars. A "beheaded" boulder, a rock cut cleanly in half horizontally by the slide, can be seen in the east canyon wall, just to the left of the slide area near a barrel cactus.

The Split Mountain sturzstrom is terrestrial, originating miles to the west in the Vallecitos. A natural trench east through the core of this landslide, seasonally containing water-filled tinajas, is Waterfall Canyon. A dry-waterfall series starts after a few hundred yards and gets progressively more challenging. Rock climbers can hike about 1.5 miles into Waterfall Canyon before crumbly rock fabric precludes further travel.

3.8 The Anticline, Submarine Landslide, and Split Mountain Fault.

The ABDSP Panel found here mentions that the anticline in Split Mountain has long "confounded" geologists. Dr. Pat Abbott, in the SCGS 1996 guidebook, says otherwise and offers this for the panel's update:

> *If you were standing at this site five million years ago, you would be floating in a shallow sea, the ancestral Gulf of California. To the west, you would see the ancestral Vallecito Mountains standing high and shedding a large cone of eroded sediment that extended into the sea toward you as an alluvial fan/fan delta— today, the sandstone layers around you in both walls of the Gorge are part of that fan. Looking east you would see the ancestral Fish Creek Mountains.*
>
> *About five million years ago, a great earthquake shook loose 300,000,000 cubic yards of rock from the steep face of the Fish Creek Mountains, the mass fell, shattered on impact, and flowed at high speeds for seven miles to the northwest*

Split Mountain

toward the Vallecito Mountains. Lobes of rocky debris detached from the fast-moving mass and injected downward into the sediments on the sea floor, pushing and buckling the sand layers into the anticline in front of you—today, some of the once fast-moving rocky debris that caused the anticline is exposed above and alongside it.

UTM 5-82.7E 36-51.2N LAT 32°59.85N LON 116°06.88W.

4.1   Crazycline Canyon, exit of Split Mountain.

A short walk east offers close scrutiny of the contact between the submarine landslide and the sandy marine bottom along which it traveled. A ledge about 300 yards up precludes travel for non-climbers. The upper reaches of Crazycline must be accessed from the Wind Caves trail (below).

4.4   Split Mountain Wind Caves.

The Wind Caves trail climbs steeply to the east (left). The faint path which drops into upper Crazycline Canyon departs from the main Wind Caves trail about one-half mile up from Fish Creek Wash. The crazyclines (geologist Charlie Winker's takeoff on "anticlines" and "synclines") are a rugged mile up this canyon. Here the submarine Fish Creek sturzstrom, falling and streaming from the eastern highlands, dug deeply into the seabed to produce the crazy, carpet-like folds which are now frozen in sandstone.

It is another steep mile to Wind Caves, marine beds of the Imperial Formation, which include "The Phantom" and other fantasies in sandstone. The view from the Wind Caves is a spectacular panorama of the folded and wrinkled Carrizo Badlands. The view to the southwest presents the image of a choppy sea, with undulating, crashing waves frozen in motion. Imperial Formation wind caves, like these but larger, are south across the Carrizo Badlands in BLM's northwest Coyote Mountains (see Trip 7B).

4.5   North Fork Fish Creek.

The 4WD turnoff west (right) is the North Fork of Fish Creek Wash. 4WD vehicles can drive up-wash about four miles, exploring such self-descriptive tributaries as Oyster Shell, Lycium/Jig Saw/Stone, and Mollusk washes. The clay hills surrounding these washes are highly fossiliferous, containing masses of sea shells from the ancient sea bottom. Here also is the foot of the submarine sturzstrom which originated at peak 2121' in the Fish Creek Mountains and raced seven miles west to run up onto butte 1134' between Stone and Coral washes.

As you drive up-canyon, be on the lookout for the purple-hued Orcutt's aster. Although it is commonly seen in Fish Creek, it is rare in other areas of the park. Other plants to note are the white tissue-paper-like prickly poppy, the slender, inflated desert trumpet, and the low, yellow trixis.

4.6   Wind Caves Wash and "Dinosaur Tracks".

Just east of a sandstone buttress, at the junction of Wind Caves and Fish Creek washes, a small arroyo climbs northeast up to Wind Caves. In this arroyo, often with a muddy tenaja at its base, are eroded sandstone depressions. To an early surveyor, these five-million-year-old features appeared like 65-million-year-old dinosaur tracks and thus they were labeled on a USGS map. To this day, where murky myth becomes silly science, some people and some maps maintain that these marine erosional features are indeed dino tracks. The coming attraction may be, as has been seriously claimed by some in Dinosaur Valley State Park in Texas, the discovery of human prints contemporary with those of dinos. (Welcome to Anza-Borrassic Park. Farewell Darwin.)

4.7   Mudhills Wash, Elephant Knees.

This old route to Carrizo Marsh, described by Parker as a miners' route between San Felipe City and the Carrizo area, has long been closed to vehicles. It is about a half-mile hike to the "Elephant Knees" formation.

A Fossil Reef High and Dry (ABDSP Panel)
UTM 5-82.4E 36-50.3N LAT 32°59.38'N LON 116°07.10'W

7.2   Loop Wash (east entrance) north (right).

Note the prominent coquina-shell beds atop the yellowish mudstones of the Imperial Formation. Ledges in the wash bed are other layers of coquina.

Boulders in the wash bed are likewise composed of solid masses of shell hash. The Loop Wash road rejoins the main wash about two miles west.

7.5   Camels Head Wash, south (left).

This is a transitional area from fine, yellowish marine sediments to the red sandstones and green claystones of the ancestral Colorado River delta deposits. Fragments of *Dinohippus*, an early horse, were found here in 1965, helping to reconstruct the evolution of large mammals in this area.

9.0   Loop Wash (west entrance).

Blackwood Basin, named by paleontologists for the abundance of petrified wood, is the open setting to the north. REMINDER—all natural features are protected as a heritage of the land and a valuable resource for scientific study in their original location; arrest and fines are the consequences of collection or disturbance.

9.9   Diablo Dropoff Wash, south (left).

The dropoff down from Arroyo Seco del Diablo is a very narrow and rough mile south. It should be considered one-way-only coming out, as vehicles cannot pass in the wash. It is a good hike to investigate fascinating concretions embedded in the walls of the wash.

10.7 Layer Cake.

This multi-colored ringed pedestal is a striking example of three-million-year-old Colorado River sandstone interfingered with green and gray lagoon muds and clays shed from the rising Vallecito Mountains ahead. The bank on the right at mile 12.1 is an interesting exhibit of unconforming and cross-bedded sediments where alluvial gravels overlie mudstone and claystone which in turn overlie massive sandstone at an angle—all evidence of a turbulent flooding and tectonically active environment.

12.5 Sandstone Canyon, west (left).

This fine example of a badlands canyon with towering, near-vertical sandstone walls and narrow width has been a popular destination for off-road explorers since the 1940s. Ranger Leetch called it "the queen of all desert washes." The canyon could be driven for several miles. Campers were often seen enveloped in the shadows and recesses of the twisting, turning cliffs. Then, in a few moments in 1992, thousands of tons of debris, perhaps triggered by a quake in this highly active area, crashed onto the floor of Sandstone near its mouth.

For years this canyon has been hike only. However, just recently small jeeps have breached the slide. Camping or resting under unstable cliffs? Not a good idea. The desert a land of peace and calm? Generally—until we reflect on the evidence of massive landslides, fierce flash flooding, and devastating earthquakes that we've seen in the last ten miles.

Speaking of flash floods, it was probably the Hatfield flood of January 1916 that wiped out the pupfish of Fish Creek. The torrential downpour within the county has been attributed to rainmaker Charles M. Hatfield, who was urged by the San Diego City Council to create rain to fill the city's reservoirs.

Sandstone Canyon

For $10,000, Hatfield promised to fill Morena reservoir. After he set up his rain-inducing equipment, it began to rain on January 14. By January 27, Lower Otay Dam broke, sending down 13 billion gallons of water to the sea. When Hatfield demanded his payment, the city offered to settle if Hatfield assumed responsibility for the $3.5 million in lawsuits filed against the city for damages. Hatfield was never paid. The results of the rain were felt as far away as the desert, where flood waters rearranged desert features. The only pupfish in the park today are those found at the visitor center pond and at the Borrego Palm Canyon pond next to the trailhead. The June Wash saddle at the head of Sandstone Canyon is a good destination about three miles from Fish Creek. Follow the remnants of the old vehicle trail to its end. Take the west (left) fork, and climb to the saddle, just north of high point "Diablo" at UTM 5-69.6E 36-50.7N (elev. 2100'). Survey point "Diablo" is the high hill which you keep on your left as you ascend to the saddle. This high point is significantly at or near the headwaters of several major drainages in the Fish Creek and Vallecito badlands: Sandstone, June, Arroyo Seco del Diablo, and Arroyo Tapiado. From the saddle it is about five miles south down June Wash to Hwy S-2, making this loop a great shuttle hike.

13.2 Olla Wash (elev. 1360'), northwest (left).

The entrance is marked by a large pinnacle between Olla and Fish Creek. This wash can be driven about two miles to a dead end at the huge monoliths of clay and rock known as the Mud Palisades. Vegetation is sparse, mostly desert willow, mesquite, cat claw, and desert agave.

Fish Creek winds to the right where, at about mile 14, a very nice late-afternoon view of the upper Fish Creek badlands unfolds after a short walk over a low saddle. The road soon passes a large syncline feature in towering conglomeratic cliffs and continues climbing to the northwest to break out into...

Split Rock in Hapaha Flat

17.1 Hapaha Flat (elev. 2200′).

Tom Lucas, the last full-blooded Kwaaymii Indian, a band of the Kumeyaay whose permanent village sites were mostly located on the edge of the Laguna Mountains, reported that all of his people came together here each spring (see Trip 6B).

Interesting exploration beckons from the hillside to the northeast at UTM 5-72.16E 36-54.39N. Mesquite is found up the left tributary, a sure sign of near-surface water. Carbonate or caliche rock formations are also here, a sign of possible spring water.

17.7 Dave McCain Spring Turnoff north (left).

. McCain, a cattleman who lived in Julian and was the grandson of pioneer cattleman George McCain, piped water down from this spring to a tank for his cattle which grazed in Hapaha Flat, at the head of Fish Creek. The spring had previously been used by Kumeyaay and was known to them as Hapaha or Hapawa. The spring has been dry for several years. Pat Abbott reports a valley to the northwest of the dry spring that displays the aspect and cobble evidence that suggests a remnant channel of the Eocene through-flowing rivers discussed above in Mine Canyon. Perhaps, bit by bit, the rugged Vallecito Mountains will yield the necessary evidence to reconstruct these old river channels in the desert area and infer their connection to well-known channels on the San Diego coastal slope of the Lagunas.

20.0 Split Rock (elev. 3000′).

This prominent boulder bears pictographs of colored lines as well as petroglyphs. This old Indian campsite is a good one for today's campers. Junipers start appearing at this elevation.

20.7 Saddle of Fish Creek and San Felipe watersheds (elev. 3170′).

The road suddenly deteriorates to a difficult 4WD route, descending steeply over boulders. A hike is recommended into...

21.8 Harper Flat (elev. 2600′).

This southwest corner of the flat is a good point for orientation. The 4WD trail cuts straight west for about a mile to the base of the Pinyon

Mountain Dropoff, one-way-down only (see Pinyon Mountain side trip in Area 6). Pinyon Wash flows due north along the western edge of Harper Flat and then northwest down Pinyon Canyon to a 4WD road that climbs across Mescal Bajada from Hwy 78 (see side trip in Area 4). Harper Flat itself spreads out to the north and east and invites exploration afoot.

This huge, gently sloping, bowl-shaped valley in the heart of the Vallecito Mountains was a favored cattle-grazing area. It is now absolutely closed to vehicular traffic. This was the site of one of the largest Indian camps in the Anza-Borrego region.

A complex of Indian trails radiates from the area. There are also cupule petroglyphs, pock-marked rocks, with the pocks resembling little mortero holes with diameters up to three inches. They are considered one of the oldest styles of petroglyphs. What makes these in Harper Flat unusual is that there is a definite pattern to them. The holes are in a straight line, with several holes in a ball at one end of the line.

Pinyon Canyon west offers a hike a short distance from here to the ruins of an outpost constructed by Julius and Amby Harper. Over a couple of years, they constructed two concrete-and-rock dams for water storage. They also constructed a road from Earthquake Valley. One of the dams is dated June 17, 1922. Today, the two old concrete dams are now filled with sand to form two smooth, giant steps on the canyon floor.

The ruins of the Harper cabin can still be seen about 200 yards below the lower dam. It was a one-room structure measuring about 12 x 25 feet, with the back and ends quarried out of rock. Agave stalks formed the studs and the rafters for the roof, and the front and the roof were made from corrugated sheet iron.

TRIP 5D:
San Sebastian Marsh/Kane Spring Area

From: Hwy 78, San Felipe Substation
To: Kane Spring
Via: Pole Line Road south (4WD road)

Connecting Trips:
5A–Ocotillo Wells to Trifolium (Hwy 86) via Hwy 78
5E–San Felipe Hills

Points Of Interest:
Tarantula Wash, Harpers Well.

Note: According to latest BLM information, the Old Kane Spring route is increasingly difficult to follow and may be closed to vehicles sometime in the near future, especially between Harpers Well and Kane Spring/Hwy 86. Follow signs, as always, and be prepared to hike into San Sebastian Marsh. See Tarantula Wash (mile 1.6 below), or Trip 5A for the best trailheads.

San Felipe, Fish and Carrizo creeks are generally dry washes except when occasional flash floods bring torrents of water rushing down their winding courses. But beneath the sandy surfaces of these washes, underground streams flow east and surface about 80 feet below sea level to form small streams and ponds. The muddy but verdant San Sebastian Marsh, with a unique desert riparian-aquatic habitat, is formed at the general confluence of these three creeks, five miles west of Hwy 86 and two miles south of Hwy 78 near an area called Harpers Well. It is a permanent and dependable source of water used by the wildlife that abounds in the area, by migratory birds that must have a dependable watering stop in their annual flights, and by people since ancient times.

No Vehicle Traffic Is Permitted within the Marsh Area.

All roads are adequately signed, so visitors should have no difficulty determining when they have reached the boundaries. The marsh covers about six square miles around the confluence of the Fish, Carrizo, and San Felipe washes. Such a fragile and unique ecosystem deserves the best of care from its visitors. This marsh area has been designated a National Natural Landmark by the National Park Service and an Area of Critical Environmental Concern (ACEC) by BLM, which patrols it regularly. Call BLM El Centro for latest information and road conditions.

MILES FROM:

Hwy 78   Hwy 86

0.0   13.8   Hwy 78 San Felipe electrical substation (BM 19').

This is seven miles west of Hwy 86 and nine miles east of Ocotillo Wells. Drive south along Pole Line Road. Beware of sand traps, especially when crossing washes. Consider everything east of the Pole Line Road and north of Old Kane Spring Road as the ACEC and prohibited to vehicles.

1.6   12.2   Tarantula Wash is a good camping area for heavy trailers and campers. This is the best place from which to hike into upper San Sebastian Marsh. The marsh starts about three miles east, down-wash.

Continue south along the pole line. San Felipe Wash crosses at mile 2.3 and Fish Creek at mile 3.3. Watch for mile 3.7, where the pole line jogs east (left) 50 yards. 0.2 mile farther is...

3.9   9.9   Junction with Old Kane Spring Road. Turn east (left). The route was originally marked with posts stamped with the letter K. Some of these posts as well as old culverts can still be found, although much of the route has been obliterated by blowing sand and numerous flash floods since it was abandoned about 50 years ago. The general rule is to head east and look for the latest wheel tracks. *Note:* This route may be closed to vehicles by BLM. Observe posted signs. Drive east.

The Pole Line Road goes south about five miles to the Gypsum Railroad.

5.3   8.5   Cross Carrizo Wash. Hikers can hike about three miles northeast
🏃 (left) down-wash to view the marsh. Giant reeds and cattails are found on the western end of this marsh, where San Felipe Creek merges with

Carrizo Creek. This is the most impressive viewpoint for the marsh. The vehicle route continues straight ahead to the east.

6.0   7.8   "Salk" survey point. Remains of a windmill are found on the site of San Felipe City (see Trip 5B for history).

8.2   5.6   Mesquite Drill Hole (yellow pipe south of the road) was an oil-test site of the early 1900s.

9.2   4.6   Harpers Well (elev. -120') was an oil-test well in the early 1900s and
𝕜   earlier that that, a campsite used by Spaniards who blazed a road to
𝕜   California. The road drops steeply into Mark Wash and climbs out the other side. Lower San Sebastian Marsh is about a mile northwest of here. Water flows faster at this end, providing a better habitat for desert pupfish and leopard frogs. The marsh is home to a large variety of birds, reptiles and mammals. Common plants found in the marsh include cat-tail, three-square bulrush, giant reed, and tamarisk. Common plants found on the marsh edges include saltgrass, pickleweed, inkweed, quailbrush, mesquite, and fourwing saltbush. Walk along the embankment to truly appreciate the uniqueness of the area and look for the tracks of animals who daily drink at the water's edge.

San Sebastian Marsh was named by Juan Bautista de Anza, during the first trail-blazing expedition in 1774, in honor of his Cochimi guide, Sebastian Tarabal. Tarabal was born at Mission Santa Gertrudis, north of San Ignacio, and came north as a young man with Captain Gaspar de Portola and Father Junipero Serra in 1769 in the epic expedition which founded San Diego and commenced mission-building in Alta California. Tarabal, having traveled from Mission San Gabriel to Altar, Sonora, via Coyote Canyon, San Sebastian Marsh, and Yuma, knew the route which Anza had vaguely envisioned.

Here at San Sebastian, Anza found an Indian village with more than 400 people. The Indians all recognized Tarabal, and they greeted him. Anza reported there was plenty of water and pasturage although both were quite salty except for one spring. It was also here that Anza discovered that he was not the first Spaniard to pass this way. Two years earlier, Captain Pedro Fages had passed through San Sebastian while in pursuit of deserters from the San Diego presidio. He had entered the desert from the Cuyamaca Mountains by way of Oriflamme Canyon, Mason Valley, and the Carrizo Corridor. From here, he had crossed Borrego Valley and entered Coyote Canyon en route to San Gabriel Mission. Father Francisco Garces, who accompanied Anza on the 1774-75 expedition, correctly surmised that the road to California had already been discovered. Garces had, himself, explored the area south of the border, just below Yuha Well, some years earlier. Anza's original route contribution, then, was only the area from the border to San Sebastian. Later, in Coyote Canyon, Anza would come across hoof-print evidence confirming that Fages had passed this way two years before.

San Sebastian Marsh is rich in history and legend and the twilight zone between the two. See Choral Pepper's *Desert Lore of Southern California* for such local treasures as: Buck's Black Gold, the Pegleg Placers, the Abominable Sandman, and the Lost Spanish Galleon. Here's a teaser for one of the tales, perhaps for that magic time when the shadows of a dying day stretch long across the desert and the campfire flickers into life.

One or more Lost Ships of the Desert sailed up the Gulf of California and the Colorado River and into the flooded Salton Basin only to become stranded in an inland sea after the water receded. The ship has been variously described as a Viking ship, a Spanish pearl ship and an English pirate ship loaded with Spanish treasure. Sightings have been reported at San Sebastian, Yuha Desert, Carrizo Badlands, Split Mountain, and Agua Caliente. Shreds of historical data support the lost ship story. The periodic flooding of the Salton basin is certainly historic fact. It isn't impossible for a ship to have entered over the Colorado River Delta during a particular combination of high tides, southerly gales, and basin flooding from major Spring run-off from the Rockies. (As you will see, at the end of Trip 7C, the legend of the lost ships is a siren call for those officials who would like to see the Laguna Salada breached at its northern end to admit sea-going ships into the Salton Basin from the Sea of Cortez.)

13.8   0.0   Junction with Hwy 86 atop the Kane Spring mesquite dune hill (elevation minus 150'). If you are going west along Kane Spring road from the Hwy 86 toward Harpers Well, take care to select the route that goes around the north side of the low hills west of the Kane Spring dune hill. It is 1.7 miles northwest to the Hwy 86/78 junction. *Note again:* This route may be closed to vehicles by BLM. Observe posted signs.

———————————

TRIP 5E:
San Felipe Hills

From: Hwy 78, San Felipe Substation
To: Hwy 86 at Tule Wash
Via: Pole Line Road north (4WD road)

Connecting Trips:
5D–San Sebastian Marsh/Kane Spring Area
5F–Trifolium (Hwy 78) to Salton City via Hwy 86

Points of Interest:
Artesian Well, Gas Domes.

MILES FROM:
Hwy 78

0.0   Hwy 78 San Felipe electrical substation (BM 19').
Drive north along Pole Line Road (BLM Rt SF131). Alkali Trail, a 4WD route southwest to Tarantula Wash, crosses at mile 1.3.

3.2   Intersection of Pole Line Road and Shell Reef Expressway.
Ocotillo Wells is about 11 miles west on the 4WD Expressway.
Turn east (right) for entry into San Felipe Hills. Many spring-formed dunes in this area have developed where rising seep water allows growth of

vegetation, which in turn traps blowing sand so that it accumulates. Sand piles up so high that water cannot rise through to the surface and the spring or seep is then completely sealed. The core of such a dune is a black, mucky mass of soil and decayed vegetation.

The remote and lonely valley that is the heart of San Felipe Hills unrolls from atop a ridge line. The road descends to...

5.3   Artesian Well.

This well began in the 1920s as an oil-test hole. At the 4000' level drillers struck hot water, which ended the operation. It was abandoned, and ran wild and hot until about 1935, when it was capped off and designated a U.S. Dept. of the Interior water reserve.

There are two route options from Artesian Well. The route down-wash goes south and east to reach Hwy 78 after about four very sandy miles. This was called "Oil Well Wash" on early maps, and now "Jim Jacklitch Creek" on the AAA Imperial County map. The route to the gas domes proceeds north up the valley and northwest over a low ridge of red mud formations.

6.3   Gas Domes.

The site is atop a fairly flat hill covered with bermuda-like salt grass. The ground is whitened with alkali and is damp in many places. At the top of the hill is a small dome, perhaps four feet tall, conical and composed of hard gray clay from periodic water eruptions. From a vent, gas bubbling through water can be heard. These are presumably similar to the far more extensive and active carbon-dioxide mud pots on the southeast edge of the Salton Sea, near the Salton Sea National Wildlife Refuge on the corner of Davis and Schrimpf roads.

Continue northwest and west, past sand dunes south (left) of the road to..

8.2   Rejoin Pole Line Road.

The steep, mesquite-covered bluff several hundred yards southeast of this junction marks McCain Spring, undoubtedly a favored Native American camp in earlier days. The OWSVRA Gas Domes Trail proceeds west about 11 miles to Ocotillo Wells. Approximately one mile southwest of this junction, at the head of the South Fork of Tule Wash, are the remains of the Diamond Bar test well, or A.C. Routhe well.

Turn north along the pole line to...

9.8   Enter Tule Wash and drive northeast (right) to...

13.6   Hwy 86/Tule Wash junction at Bridge #58-14, post mile 53 on Hwy 86.

TRIP 5F:
Trifolium (Hwy 78) to Salton City via Hwy 86

From: Trifolium (Hwy 78)
To: Salton City (Hwy S-22)
Via: Hwy 86 (paved)

Points Of Interest and Side Trips:
Salton Sand Dunes, Tule Wash, Arroyo Salado.

Connecting Trips:
  5A–Ocotillo Wells to Trifolium (Hwy 86) via Hwy 78
  3A–Borrego Springs to Salton City via Hwy S-22
  3F–Salton City to Travertine Rock via Hwy 86
  3D–Seventeen Palms—Tule and Arroyo Salado washes
  5E–San Felipe Hills

POST MILES FROM:
Heber

0.0   Heber (elev. -15'). Junction of Hwys 86 and 111 southeast of El Centro.
Post miles increase to the northwest until the Riverside County Line.

43.6 Trifolium (elev. -179').
Drive northwest on Hwy 86 from this junction with Hwy 78, just north of San Felipe Creek and a U.S. Border Patrol station.

47.6 U.S. Navy road (elev. 10').
The Salton Sand Dunes, largest in the Anza-Borrego region, are about two miles east on the north side of this road. These are "barchan" type dunes, crescent-shaped dunes, which form and move in response to the prevailing westerly winds. The gentle slope of a barchan dune is concave upwind, the steep slope is convex downwind. The direction of movement is downwind to the east, led by the two "horns" on the "outboard" leading edges. Barchan dunes in this area are destined to die at the shore of the Salton Sea.

Hwy 86 crosses the eastern shoulder of the reddish San Felipe Hills at elev. 17' and descends. When fresh-water Lake Cahuilla was full at elev. 42' earlier in the millennium, these eastern hills would have been a significant peninsula, jutting into the lake with a steep bottom dropoff.

51.9 Campbell Wash Bridge #58-15 (BM -113).
This wash is the drainage for the northern San Felipe Hills. It curves south, reaching the Gas Domes after about four miles.

9.7   2.9 Tule Wash Bridge #58-14 (BM -135'). Post mile marker 53.1.

Side Trip West Up Tule Wash (4WD Route)
  0.0 Hwy 86. Mile 2.4 is South Fork Tule Wash. Bear right up the main wash. Pass alkaline Tule Spring at mile 2.5.
  3.5 Pole Line Road (BLM Rt SF131). Enter OWSVRA. Road junction to southwest (left) at mile 6.0 is Cross Over Trail to Shell Reef Expressway. (Don't confuse Cross Over Trail with Cut Across Trail, which is several miles west.)
  9.5 Pumpkin Patch. Collecting of concretions is illegal. The Pumpkin Patch Trail leads southwest (left) to East Bank Wash near Wolfe Well. Continue west up Tule Wash.

10.4 County line, enter ABDSP. (See Area 3 for details of route northwest from here.)

16.3 Hwy S-22 at Arroyo Salado Primitive Camp

End of Side Trip

53.9 Air Park Drive.

This small airport had a brief burst of attention in the early 1990s when it was proposed as a regional super-port to serve San Diego via high-speed commuter rail.

The foundation of the old Squeaky Springs Service Station, called Winona on early maps, is on the west (left) side of the road at mile 10.9. It was mentioned in early logs as a tow out and repair facility for travelers stuck in "Blake's Ravines," arroyos to the west.

54.7 Arroyo Salado Bridge #58-13 (BM -131).

Side Trip West Up Arroyo Salado (4WD Route)

1.6 Tule shrubs at "spring" (was moist soil on 6-7-70).

2.5 Pole Line Road (BLM Rt SF131). A 1941 log notes "large smoke trees and one palm" here. Fork to the northwest leads about a half mile to Salt and Soda Springs on the northeast bank. Enter OWSVRA and continue west, bearing left up Arroyo Salado.

3.9 Confluence of main Arroyo Salado and North Fork Arroyo Salado at One Palm (aka Lone Palm). The Oh-My-God Hot Springs site (the old Soda Springs) is just north of this confluence. Just northwest is a well-built abandoned mud house of recent origin. The old Truckhaven Trail in ABDSP is about eight miles northwest (right) up-wash from this wash junction.

The main route bears left up Arroyo Salado. At mile 4.4 is another tributary of North Fork. Bear left again.

10.0 County line, enter ABDSP. (See Area 3 for details of route northwest from here.)

15.9 Hwy S-22 at Arroyo Salado Primitive Camp

End of Side Trip

56.1 Salton City (elev. -87') at So. Marina Dr.

Borrego Springs is 28 miles west on Hwy S-22.

AREA 6-SOUTHWESTERN:
west Hwy 78, Hwy S-2

The theme of this area is the development of transportation corridors—trail, road, and rail. The most visible feature is Highway S-2, which generally follows the route of the historic corridor, which brought thousands of California-bound emigrants to the Golden State. To the south are the tracks of the San Diego and Arizona Eastern Railroad—"the impossible railroad"—designed to connect San Diego to the agricultural wealth of Imperial Valley and link it directly to major rail connections east. It is a route that has been challenged continuously by the wilderness it dared to penetrate.

The history along Highway S-2 reads like some pages from a Who's Who of Southern California Explorers—a list of those who passed this way en route to somewhere else—Pedro Fages, Santiago Arguello, Jedediah Smith, Jonathan Trumbell Warner, Kit Carson, Kearny's Army of the West, the Mormon Battalion, gold-crazed Argonauts, riders on the Jackass Mail, and drivers and passengers on the Butterfield Overland Mail stage and perhaps you, the reader.

We cannot see the trail of bones and rotting carcasses on the *Jornada del Muerto*, or the missing Indian villages, or the changes in native vegetation caused by the introduction of non-native grasses, which would choke out many of the less aggressive native species.

We do see curious road scars from wagon wheels, and old trails that have blended in with still-older Indian trails and today's animal trails. We still see the grinding holes, rock art, and kitchen middens of the Kumeyaay who called this home. More importantly, we can still share a feeling of awe with those who came before when we find hidden oases or glimpse a view that has remained for eons. We can romanticize the past in the comfort of today and so easily forget the sacrifices, the struggles for survival, and the unforgiving nature of the desert for those who are not prepared for it.

TRIP 6A:
Earthquake (Shelter) Valley to Ocotillo Via Hwy S-2

From: Earthquake Valley/Scissors Crossing
To: Ocotillo (I-8, Imperial County)
Via: Hwy S-2 (paved)

Connecting Trips:
1A–Warner Junction to Earthquake Valley via Hwy S-22
4A–Earthquake Valley to Ocotillo Wells via Hwy 78
6B–Julian to Earthquake Valley via Hwy 78
6C–Blair Valley and Smugglers Canyon
6D–Mason Valley to Banner via Oriflamme and Chariot Canyons
6E–Vallecito Creek and Carrizo Badlands
6F–Mortero Wash and Dos Cabezas
7A–Jacumba to Seeley via I-8
7B–Ocotillo to Superstition Mountain via Hwy S-80
7C–Ocotillo to Yuha Basin via Hwy 98

Points Of Interest and Side Trips:
Pinyon Mountains, Box Canyon, Vallecito, Agua Caliente, June Wash, Indian Gorge, Mountain Palm Springs, Bow Willow, Carrizo Gorge, Sweeney Pass, Canyon Sin Nombre, Jojoba Wash, Dolomite Mine, Volcanic Hills, northwest Coyote Mountains (wind caves), Fossil Canyon.

Summary:
Trip 1A started at the beginning of Hwy S-2 at the Warner Junction on Hwy 78 and proceeded 17 miles southeast through San Felipe Valley to Scissors Crossing (east). This trip, 6A, picks up the S-2 route at this point and continues another 48 miles southeast to the end of Hwy S-2 at Ocotillo (I-8) in Imperial County. Trips 1A and 6A are thus a continuous route along Hwy S-2.

County post mile markers appear almost every mile along Hwy S-2 until the San Diego/Imperial County Line from where continuous odometer mileage is used along Imperial Highway into Ocotillo.

The southern segments of Hwy S-2 are particularly subject to flash flooding during late summer and fall thunderstorms. Be especially wary of Bow Willow, Carrizo Wash, and low desert washes near Ocotillo. High water running across the road generally subsides rapidly.

POST MILES FROM:
Warner Junction

0.0   Junction of Hwys S-2 and 79 (Warner Junction).

17.0 Scissors Crossing (east) and Sentenac Cienega (elev. 2254').
County Hwy S-2 intersects State Hwy 78 on the northwest edge of Sentenac Cienega. See connecting trips 4A and 6B above for east-west options on Hwy 78. Trip 4A has information about the cienega. This is post mile 70 for Hwy 78 (i.e. it's 70 miles east of Oceanside). Turn west (right) and cross San

Felipe Creek. The big cottonwood on the north side of the bridge is a popular rendezvous and picnic site.

17.3 Scissors Crossing (west) and Vallecito Monument (elev. 2300′).

This monument commemorates the Vallecito stage station 19 miles south-east (see Trip 4A for text). The route turns southeast (left) on Hwy S-2.

19.0 Earthquake Valley.

Stewart Hathaway, an early cattle rancher from Julian and a landowner here, recalled that there was once a large natural lake in the valley that was drained by an earthquake early in the century. (A Richter magnitude 6.0 quake rocked Imperial Valley on April 19, 1906.)

Granite Mountain to the west stands alone. It rises abruptly from the floor of Earthquake Valley at elevation 2200′ to the summit at 5633′ and is pierced by many old mine shafts and tunnels.

21.1 Stagecoach Trail RV Resort with a well-stocked store including area maps and publications. (See Appendix 2.)

21.9 ABDSP Boundary/Pinyon Mountain Turnoff (BM 2360′).

Side Trip into Pinyon Mtn (dirt road to The Squeeze, 4WD beyond)
0.0 Hwy S-2/Pinyon Mountain Turnoff east (left).
0.1 Fork.

Side Trip into North Pinyon Mountains (dirt road)
Dirt road northeast (left) crosses the playa and then it climbs up the alluvial fan about three miles into the North Pinyon Mountains, a little visited but attractive section of the park. A saddle at a road fork (elev. 3100′) is a good area for a quiet, isolated camp.

From the camp area, hikers can descend northeast about two miles into Mine Canyon to a roadhead. This road leads about five miles north to Hwy 78 (see Mine Canyon side trip in Trip 4A). The namesake mine is on the northwest side of the road at about elev. 2175′.
End of Side Trip

Dirt road east (right) crosses the playa and then climbs through increasingly luxuriant stands of Mojave yucca, nolina and agave into the pinyon-juniper belt.
4.0 Pinyon Mountain Valley. A low saddle marks the entrance into this secluded mountain vale, which has an average elevation of about 3500′. The road crosses several more washes and then offers numerous excellent campsites nestled among the pines.
5.7 High Point (elev. 3950′). Just beyond High Point, on the north side of the road, are huge single-needle pinyon pines (*Pinus monophylla*). Kumeyaay Indians gathered pinyon nuts from such trees in late summer. They were picked not fully ripened, before animals and insects were attracted to them. A walk up the gentle slope on the north side of the road

will yield superb vistas of Borrego Valley and Borrego Badlands, with the Santa Rosas etched against the sky on the far horizon.

6.4 Whale Peak Trail Head. To the south is the departure point (elev. 4000') for the hike up Whale Peak to the southeast (right). Whale stands like an island surrounded by a sea of desert. The hike goes about three miles through a narrow, rocky wash, across open meadows and up brushy slopes and ridges to the flat summit at elev. 5349'. There is no well-defined trail. Head generally for the highest area. A small cairn, found in a crack on the topmost boulder of the peak, near the Geodetic Survey marker, has a visitor's register which marks Whale Peak as one of the Sierra Club's 100 notable desert peaks in southern California. Allot about five hours to complete the round trip of six miles at a moderate pace. Lack of a major fire in the area has allowed plant life to grow into large, well-developed specimens. The nolina and Mojave yucca have trunks 10-12 feet tall. Pinyon pines and California junipers are large and abundant. From the top, look across to Harper Flat and Blair Valley and beyond to Borrego Valley, the Salton Sea, and Mexico.

7.4 The Squeeze (small 4WD only beyond here).

The route passes between two rocks just a few feet apart, marking the end of travel for fat vehicles, many 4WD sport-utes included. Don't go through The Squeeze unless you are prepared to negotiate the dropoff ahead, because it is very difficult to return back through it.

8.0 The main route makes a sharp right turn up out of the main wash into a rocky path. (One can continue down the main wash about one-half mile to a dead-end at a 35-foot dry water chute.) The main route tops a small ridge, just beyond which is...

8.3 The Pinyon Mountain Dropoff, also known as "Heart Attack Hill."

One of several drop-offs in the Anza-Borrego region, this is the most hazardous. Put passengers out to walk down. Put the vehicle in lowest gear. Keep headed downhill and don't apply brakes until the bottom where there is a right-angle turn left. A fishtail action or a sideways slide can result in a rollover.

From here the route leads a couple of miles into Pinyon Wash over a series of smaller ridges and gullies to the southwest edge of Harper Flat. Road turns south (right) and climbs steeply out of Harper Flat and over a saddle into Hapaha Flat. From the saddle down into Fish Creek and east through Split Mountain, the route is again a regular 4WD road (see Trip 5C).

End Of Side Trip

21.9 ABDSP Boundary/Pinyon Mountain Turnoff (repeated from above).

22.0 Cool Canyon turnoff, west (right).

This route is good both for canyon exploration and for those wanting to climb to the top of Granite Mountain. Drive one mile over a rough road to the trailhead. Many of the boulders show signs of Indians' having used this canyon in years past to grind seeds and prepare food. Local resident T. Curtin, known by many for his Big T Desert Tours, recommends staying in the right main, fork which leads to "a huge juniper, perhaps the biggest you've ever seen." This Granite Mountain canyon has many exposed pegmatite dikes. It is within dikes such as these that prospectors have found gold and tourmaline to the west. Cool Canyon also has a wide variety of plants, including desert apricot, jojoba, Mormon tea, agave, yucca, creosote, white sage, various cacti, mosses, and lichens. This canyon is within the park. Do not collect rock specimens.

About one mile from the trailhead, the canyon splits into three forks. A climb up the west ridge would lead to the top of peak 4624'. It is another 1000' climb to the west to the egg-shaped granitic boulder that is the cap of Granite Mountain. A bench mark is on top of the boulder. The climb up Granite Mountain can also be approached from Rodriguez Canyon (see Trip 6D).

22.7 Little Blair Valley Turnoff.

The dirt road left goes about two miles over a low rise into Little Blair Valley (see Trip 6C). Hwy S-22 continues south over Little Pass to...

23.0 Blair Valley turnoff.

(See Trip 6C for detailed descriptions of Blair Valley, Ghost Mountain, Little Blair Valley, and the Smuggler Canyon hike.) The turnoff southeast (left) leads a half mile to the Foot and Walker Pass monument on the stage route.

> Butterfield Overland Mail Route (California Historical Landmark No. 647)
> UTM 5-55.8E 36-55.2N   LAT 33°02.19'N LON 116°24'08.13'W

The establishment of the Butterfield Overland Mail in 1858 between St. Louis and San Francisco was one of the major factors in the development of transportation in the West. John Butterfield of New York was awarded the overland mail contract to convey mail and passenger twice each week, each way, between San Francisco and the Mississippi River. A year was spent in making preparations, laying out the route, planning stations, digging wells in the desert, equipping stations, and procuring coaches and stock. During 1858, Warren F. Hall was employed by Butterfield to establish the route and locate stations between Tucson and Los Angeles. Carrizo Creek and Vallecito were originally selected by James E. Birch as stations for the interim mail and passenger service before the regular contract was awarded to Butterfield, and they were retained as stage stops. A new station between the two was established at Palm Spring. Box Canyon was widened to permit easy passage of the coaches. A station was also added in San Felipe Valley, midway between Vallecito and Warner Ranch.

By the time the first stage rolled, the company had 1,500 employees, over 80 stations already constructed, 200 mail wagons, and over 1,200 head of stock. The first mail left Tipton, Missouri, and San Francisco, California, simultaneously, on September 16, 1858, and took 24 days between the two points. As service improved, the overland mail became faster than that provided by ocean-going vessels. Travel on the southern Butterfield route was not interrupted until the beginning of the Civil War in 1861, when a more northern route through Salt Lake City and Sacramento was begun and the southern route was discontinued.

Hwy S-2 traverses the southern edge of the Blair Valley basin for the next couple of miles over a low divide and rapidly descends to...

25.7 Box Canyon Overlook pullout south (left).

Box Canyon (California Historical Landmark No. 472)

Southern Emigrant Trail History (ABDSP Interpretive Panel)
UTM 5-52.1E 36-52.9N   LAT 33°00.9'N LON 116°26.5'W

The Mormon Battalion hacked out the road with a few hand axes and a small crowbar. They are credited not only with opening a wagon road to California, but also with completing the longest infantry march ever made in United States military history.

Even after the trail through the canyon was widened for the larger coaches on the Butterfield line in 1858, the hubs of the wheels would often scrape the solid rock wall on the uphill side. Both roads had to be routed up and around to avoid the 30-foot dry waterfall. This waterfall and the intricately patterned metamorphic rock walls can be viewed via a short walk down into the canyon. Walk the canyon and the old wagon roads to get a feel for the history of this area. See if you agree with one of the canyon's old names—Devils Canyon.

25.7 Box Canyon (repeated from above).

Continue the descent past post mile marker 26 and exit Box Canyon into the Mason Valley cactus gardens. The tallest cholla specimens in the Anza-Borrego region grow along the northwest edge of this valley. This towering bronze-colored cholla is known as Mason Valley cholla and is a hybrid between

Box Canyon

teddybear cholla and silver cholla. The hybrid is sterile, but it spreads itself by dropping joints, which generally take root.

26.9 Oriflamme Canyon dirt road (elev. 2272).

The Oriflamme Canyon route was the short cut from San Diego to the desert, first used by presidio commander Pedro Fages in 1772 (see Trip 6G for the Fages monument on Sunrise Hwy, 10 miles west). This was also the route of the first U.S. mail service between San Diego and Yuma, a biweekly service established in 1854 by Joseph Swycaffer and Sam Warnock.

See Trip 6D for the trip from here to Banner via Chariot or Rodriguez Canyon.

27.1 The large road clearing east (left) has an interpretive panel on the southeast side near the road.

> The San Antonio-San Diego Mail Line...the Jackass Mail
> (ABDSP Interpretive Panel)
> UTM 5-51.1E 36-51.7N   LAT 33°00.23'N LON 116°27.20'W

Congress had passed legislation in 1856 creating a mail and passenger service between San Francisco and the Mississippi River. Authority for the selection of both the route and the contractor was given to the Postmaster General, Aaron V. Brown, but Congress specified that an interim service should begin at once. John Butterfield of New York and James E. Birch of California submitted bids. Birch was awarded the interim service while the regular mail contract was awarded to John Butterfield. The San Diego Jackass Mail portion of the line continued in operation until terminated in 1861 due to Civil War.

A rugged old wagon road from Mason Valley up Salt Creek into the Laguna Mountains brought hay and wild oats for animals and wood for cooking and heat to the Vallecito, Palm Spring, and Carrizo stage stations when they were in operation. The old wagon route is on the same alignment as the Mason Valley Truck Trail.

27.5 Rainbow Canyon.

Hike Up Rainbow Canyon

The entrance is northeast (left) opposite a sharp turn in Hwy S-2 which is marked with directional arrows. Stands of Mason Valley cholla appear to be guarding the entrance to the canyon. Follow the sandy wash to the first of several dry waterfalls. The spectacular swirled and foliated marine metasediments, sliced with pegmatite and other granitic dikes and veins, give the canyon its name. Experienced hikers can negotiate some steep ledges about a half mile into the canyon. An old gold or tourmaline mine in a pegmatite dike is about a mile in on the left. More steep ledges make a transition from banded metamorphics to a granitic regime as the canyon opens into a bowl. The saddle at the east end of the bowl, south of peak 3279', is about 2.5 miles from Hwy S-2.

Hikers can descend northeast from the saddle into southern Blair Valley. It is about two miles from the saddle to the camping sites in Blair Valley at the north end. Arrange a shuttle and allow about 5 hours if you are planning to hike from the mouth of Rainbow Canyon to Blair Valley. Besides the spectacular geology, Rainbow Canyon is outstanding for its variety of vegetation. Raptors' nests and wood-rat nests are other delights to be found. There are 13 dry waterfalls in Rainbow Canyon.

29.1 Butterfield Ranch (Elev. 2,040').

This attractive destination offers a store, gasoline, restaurant, swimming and jacuzzi pools. RV, camping, and mobile home sites are available.

See Appendix 2 in the Appendix for reservation information.

30.2 Campbell Grade Viewpoint.

Everett Campbell constructed this road in the 1930s with an easier grade than the Butterfield route, which parallels it 100 yards north (left). The sinuous tracks in the valley below are said to be some original ruts of the stage line.

34.7 Vallecito Regional Park (elev. 1550').

This mesquite-shaded 71-acre public campground offers piped water, flush toilets, a covered picnic area, group sites, and 44 primitive campsites with tables, fire rings, and barbecue stoves. The park is administered by the San Diego County Department of Parks and Recreation. See Appendix 2 for reservation information. Vallecito has been a campsite for literally hundreds of years, beginning first with the native Kumeyaay.

The Kumeyaay had continuously occupied this area from about 1000 A.D. to 1906, when the village site was abandoned. Lt. Pedro Fages, in 1772, was the first white man to pass through the area, pursuing deserters from the San Diego presidio. It was not until 1782, however, that he specifically mentioned the area and recommended the site for a future presidio. He had found

Vallecito Stage Station

"plenty of pasture and two pools of water." He also mentioned the Indian village, which he said was occupied by 500 Indians. Fortunately for the Kumeyaay, Indian hostilities on the Colorado River precluded extended contact at this time, giving the Kumeyaay a few years of respite before the full impact of the white man's arrival was truly felt. But by the time John Audubon, Jr., encountered these Indians in 1849, only a small village existed. He made a sketch of the Kumeyaay village, called *Hawi*, which was located near a spring. In 1916, a flash flood covered the site of the old village with sand.

Fifty years after Fages discovered Vallecito, Lt. Santiago Arguello rediscovered it when he chased Indian horse thieves into the desert following the old Fages route down Oriflamme Canyon. Arguello also discovered the route up San Felipe Valley to San Gabriel and Los Angeles, and in 1825 it became the Sonora Road and the official Mexican mail road to Alta California, the predecessor of the Southern Emigrant Trail and the Butterfield Overland Mail.

The outbreak of war with Mexico in May 1846 brought increased use of the road by Americans, beginning with the arrival of Brigadier General Stephen Watts Kearny and his Army of the West in November. Two months later, the Mormon Battalion followed Kearny and opened the wagon road to California. A year later, on February 2, 1848, the Treaty of Guadalupe Hidalgo officially ended the war, a week after gold was discovered at Sutter's Mill.

The Butterfield Stage Station was erected in 1858 with a barn, crammed with hay for horses, not far from the station.

Vallecito Stage Depot (California Historical Landmark No. 304B)
UTM 5-60.8E 36-48.5N   LAT 32°58.55'N LON 116°20.95W

Through the years, the Vallecito station was occupied by one tenant after another but it was not until James E. Mason (the younger) that the valley had a legal owner. In 1884 Mason received patent to 160 acres that included the old station. Later owner Christian F. Holland deeded six acres in 1934 to San Diego County to begin the restoration process of the crumbling stage station. Today, one room and its roof are parts of the original structure.

37.2 Bisnaga Wash.

The highway commences a sharp turn to the south (right) at a turnout on the northeast (left) marking the entrance to Bisnaga Wash. (This is not the same as Bisnaga Alta Wash, shown on topographic maps west of here and north of post mile marker 36.) "Bisnaga" is Baja-Spanish for any barrel cactus, which here is *Ferocactus cylindraceus*, "fierce cylindrical cactus."

A hiking route leads north from the parking area about two and a half miles to the base of the Vallecito Mountains, passing through excellent displays of barrel cactus, with cholla, ocotillo, chuparosa and some elephant trees at trail's end.

38.2 Agua Caliente Regional Park (BM 1233').

This 910-acre park on the eastern flank of the Tierra Blanca Mountains is operated by the San Diego County Department of Parks and Recreation, as is Vallecito Regional Park. The natural 96°F. mineral waters have long attracted people suffering from arthritis and rheumatism who are seeking the curative powers associated with hot springs. The mesquite-shaded campground features both indoor and outdoor natural hot-water bathing pools, an indoor jacuzzi, showers, a picnic area, a playground, a recreation hall, a campfire circle, nature trails, and 140 campsites, most of which have full or partial hookups, tables, fireplaces, and ramadas. A caravan area can also handle large groups. County rangers offer excellent, seasonal programs. See Appendix 2 for camp reservation information.

Agua Caliente Springs Store is a half mile from the campground entrance and has a great selection of camping supplies, guidebooks and maps for the local area.

Hiking Route to Moonlight Canyon and Inner Pasture

The Moonlight Canyon Trail is a 2.5-mile loop, with an option to climb through the Tierra Blanca Mountains to Inner Pasture. The trail departs from the south end of the campground, at campsite 140, near the shuffleboard courts (elev. 1350'), ascends south over a saddle into Moonlight Canyon, turns north (left) down-canyon and passes some water seeps. At the mouth of the canyon the trail narrows and turns west (left), following a rocky path to return to the east end of the camp at campsite 63. The highpoint of this loop is peak 1882', which can be climbed from the highpoint of the trail by continuing up about 300'.

A southwest (right) turn at the saddle will work up Moonlight Canyon about 1.5 miles to a low pass (elev. 2190') overlooking Inner Pasture. This isolated and picturesque desert valley, a fault-controlled feature along the main strand of the Elsinore fault between the Tierra Blanca "white earth" and the Sawtooth Mountains, was a favored cattle-grazing area.

A longer but most interesting loop return route is to drop into the valley and hike about a mile east to the arroyo that drains upper Inner Pasture. This arroyo is guarded by a knoll on each side of the entrance (elev. 1820'). Turn north and drop northeast two miles through this narrow, winding canyon to intersect Hwy S-2 near post mile 41.0 (elev. 1100'). Hike northwest (left) about three miles back to Agua Caliente. Total loop-trip distance is about nine miles. (Take care not to leave Inner Pasture to the southeast via the private dirt road into Canebrake Canyon).
End of Hike

Ocotillo Ridge Nature Trail, Desert Overlook Trail, and Squaw Pond Trail

Northwest of the Agua Caliente entrance station is the start/end of the 0.5 mile Ocotillo Ridge Nature Trail, which skirts the campfire circle. The Desert Overlook Trail and the Squaw Pond Trail follow the Ridge Trail up to a fork just above the campfire circle. The south (left) fork climbs a steep trail one-quarter mile to Desert Overlook (1450'). The north fork (right) branches again to head either east along the ridge trail or west one-half mile up a sandy wash and past a growth of honey mesquite to Squaw Pond, a small, boggy oasis shaded by willow and a palm tree.
End Of Hike

38.2 Agua Caliente Regional Park (repeated from above).

Hwy S-2 swings southeast, paralleling the paved airstrip.

41.5 June Wash turnoff is north (left).

Side Trip Up June Wash

This 4WD route goes about two miles north up the main June Wash into the middle of Section 15 and then veers to the northeast (right) up a tributary for another 1.4 miles. According to ranger Bob Thierault, the old route due north up June Wash has been wiped out by flash flooding and the entrance blocked by smoke trees.

Hikers, carefully navigating with the *Agua Caliente* topo map, can go northwest and then north from the center of Section 15 up main June Wash to mile 4.5 which is due west of survey point "Diablo." This survey point is on the north boundary of Section 3. Pick out the saddle to the north (left) of "Diablo". From the saddle (elev. 2100') at UTM 5-69.6E 36-50.7N the hiker looks down into Sandstone Canyon. It was from this point that rangers first observed the high vertical walls of Sandstone Canyon in the 1950s. Sandstone Canyon debouches into Fish Creek about three miles east.

This saddle and ridge line, at the headwaters of the Sandstone Canyon/Fish Creek drainage system and the June Wash/Vallecito drainage system, is a significant divide between the San Felipe watershed of the northern Anza-Borrego region and the Carrizo watershed of the southern region. It confounds logic to have such a divide on the south side of the mile-high barrier of the Vallecito Mountains. The explanation is that Fish Creek cuts through the Vallecito Mountains at Split Mountain to join the San Felipe Wash system to the north. Fish Creek, as an antecedent, or pre-existing, stream, has been able to maintain its course by cutting downward faster than the Vallecitos are being uplifted.

End Of Side Trip

43.1 Palm Spring/Vallecito Creek turnoff.

See Trip 6E, which describes the route to View of the Badlands, Palm Spring, Arroyo Tapiado, Arroyo Seco del Diablo and on down Vallecito Wash Creek to Carrizo Cienega.

44.0 South Canebrake Turnoff.

The Canebrake ranger station is just up this turnoff to the northwest in the private community of Canebrake.

45.5 Well of the Eight Echoes, north (left).

The reverberating echoes of a yell down this 15-inch-diameter, 20-foot-deep iron pipe support its name. The well was reportedly drilled for water to irrigate proposed cotton crops.

46.1 Indian Gorge/Indian Valley Turnoff, southwest (right).

Side Trip Up Indian Gorge (dirt road becoming 4WD road)

0.8 Entrance to Indian Gorge, a narrow defile with smoke trees.

𝕏   **1.7**   Torote Canyon northwest (right).

El Torote....the elephant tree (ABDSP Interpretive Panel)
UTM 5-71.7E 36-37.0N   LAT 32°52.23N LON 116°14.05'W

Hike a mile to a large bowl where dozens of elephant, or "torote," trees are found. Arc west and south up-canyon another three miles and cross the ridge into the North Fork of Indian Valley.

2.0   Indian Valley. An old Indian trail begins here and leads southeast (left) over a low saddle, descending steeply into the wash of Palm Bowl. Palm Bowl Grove is up-wash (to the right). Mountain Palm Springs campground is another mile east down-canyon, past Surprise Canyon Grove to Southwest Grove, and then down the main trail to the roadhead.

2.7   Indian Valley fork.

𝕏   North Indian Valley road goes right about three miles, ending at the mouth of a narrow canyon guarded by native palms. Near the palms is a silted-in rock tank inscribed with the name "McCain"—an early-day cattle and pioneering family.

𝕏   South Indian Valley road also goes about three miles. There are more palms in this fork than in North Indian Valley. 0.2 mile from the valley forks is a huge granite boulder a few hundred feet to the left, on the back side of which is a smoke-blackened cave that was used as an Indian shelter. Bedrock morteros are also found behind the shelter.

End of Side Trip

46.1 Indian Gorge/Indian Valley Turnoff (repeated from above).

46.2 Old County Road turnoff (BM 713').

The old county road continues straight ahead southeast. The Southern Emigrant Trail went this way, east through the Carrizo Gap between the Coyote Mountains and Fish Creek Mountains. This was the historic *entrada* to southern California until ABDSP and BLM permanently closed the route to through-travel after 1960, a result of the use of the Carrizo Impact Area as a U.S. Navy bombing range.

Side Trip to Vallecito/Carrizo Creek Junction

From Hwy S-2, continue straight, southeast, on decaying asphalt about a mile to Bow Willow Creek. Bear left into the creekbed, passing the tree-shaded site of the 1950s Bow Willow ranger station to the north (left), and continuing east, with the South Carrizo Creek 4WD road joining at mile 3.8. The major junction with Vallecito Creek, Carrizo Creek and Canyon Sin Nombre is at mile 3.9.

End Of Side Trip

Hwy S-2 turns south (right), and now has a new name, Sweeney Pass Road, as the previous road, "The Great Overland Stage Route of 1849" continues to the east.

46.2 Old County Road turnoff (repeated from above).

47.1 Mountain Palm Springs (elev. 667').

The turnoff west leads about a half mile to Mountain Palm Springs campground. There are five main palm groves with about four hundred native California fan palms in this area. The lyrical description of "the desert palm whose feet are in the water and head is in the sun" alludes to the hydrologic fact that palms are compelling evidence of near-surface water. As is the case throughout the badlands of the Colorado Desert, the presence of such water is related to the relationship of water table and impermeable rock barriers through faulting.

> Native Palm Groves....remnants of ancient savannas
> (ABDSP Interpretive Panel)
> UTM 5-7.3E 36-36.1N   LAT 32°51.73'N LON 116°13.10W

The Surprise Canyon/north fork of Mountain Palm Springs Canyon leads about one-half mile from the campground up a rocky arroyo to North Grove, which is visible from the campground. Mary's Grove is offset from the north fork to the northwest. Continuing west up the canyon you reach Surprise Canyon Grove. Southwest of this, the canyon suddenly opens into a magnificent amphitheater called Palm Bowl, where more than 100 palms fringe the edge of the bowl and a tiny spring is at the north side of the oasis. An old Indian trail leads north between Surprise and Palm Bowl over a saddle about one-half mile into Indian Gorge. An alternate loop trip is to climb the saddle south of Palm Bowl into the south fork of Mountain Palm Springs Canyon and descend east to Southwest Grove.

The southern fork of Mountain Palm Springs Canyon, which is the trail beginning at the trailhead, offers two palm groves, the lower of which is Pygmy Grove, with about 50 trees. These trees are stunted to about half the size of normal *Washingtonia* palms. The upper and larger oasis is Southwest Grove. A sign at Southwest Grove points the way to Torote Bowl, about a mile south and west up the rocky slopes. The trail that leads to Torote Bowl also leads over to Bow Willow Canyon. The distance from Mountain Palm Springs roadhead via Southwest Grove to Bow Willow campground is about 1.5 miles, making this a popular one-way shuttle hike or a comfortable round trip via a paralleling return trail just to the east.

47.1 Mountain Palm Springs (repeated from above).

48.4 Bow Willow Campground turnoff.

Dirt road west (right) passes south of Egg Mountain and goes 1.6 miles to the campground. The canyon's namesake desert willows, probably used by the Kumeyaay for bows, are among the largest in the park. ABDSP Interpretive Panels, found beneath the shaded ramada near the old ranger station, describe

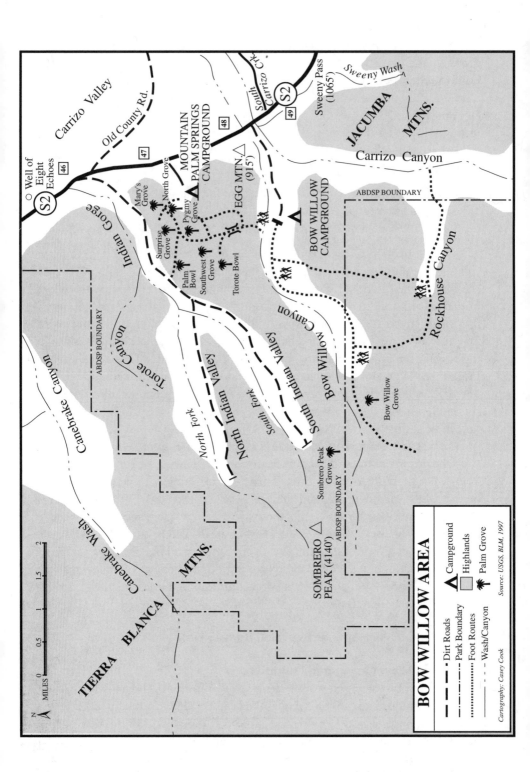

BOW WILLOW AREA

Campground ▲
Highlands ☐
Palm Grove ✹

Source: USGS, BLM, 1997

Dirt Roads
Park Boundary
Foot Routes
Wash/Canyon

Cartography: Casey Cook

the area with the following titles: You Are Surrounded, Chuckwalla, Mountain Palm Spring, Elephant Tree, Kumeyaay.

UTM 5-72.4E 36-33.9N

Hike Up Bow Willow Canyon

0.0 The campground (elev. 950') is on the site of an ancient Indian village. Morteros can be seen up in the granite boulders at the west end of the site. Mountain Palm Springs is about a 1.5-mile hike north over a low saddle and then east (see above).

0.5 Just west of the first ridge up the wash from the campsites, a trail leads south up an arroyo, exits ABDSP onto BLM land, and leads over a broad saddle via Single Palm about 2.5 miles to a junction with Rockhouse Canyon. Rockhouse Canyon goes west about a mile from this junction to the rockhouse, an old cattleman's line shack.

The main route swings south and west up-wash and exits ABDSP at about mile 2.0.

2.5 Enter a huge and beautiful bowl, elev. 1350'.

An arroyo leading southeast goes over a saddle at elev. 1730' and drops into upper Rockhouse Canyon after about a mile. The line shack mentioned above is opposite on the southwest edge of the bowl. West of the Bow Willow bowl, the canyon steepens into bushwhack city, although a delightful seasonal stream is an encouraging sound here.

3.5 Fork at elev. 1700'.

The northwest (right) fork climbs steeply another half mile to Sombrero Peak Palm Grove (elev. 2751'). There are about 90 tall, slender California fan palms in this grove in the eastern shadow of 4229' Sombrero Peak.

The main canyon straight ahead climbs into the Bow Willow Palm Grove.

End of Side Trip

48.4 Bow Willow turnoff (repeated from above).

48.6 Carrizo Creek (elev. 700').

4WD turnoff southwest (right) leads up Carrizo Canyon. Carrizo is a generalized Spanish word for reeds, cattails, or tall grasses growing in cienagas or along watercourses in the arid Southwest and Mexico. Carrizo Canyon drops in elevation from 2,800 feet at Jacumba and descends between the Jacumba and the In-Ko-Pah mountains to the desert floor at 700' at Bow Willow.

The old San Diego and Arizona Eastern (SD&AE) Railway, a Southern Pacific subsidiary, is now the San Diego and Imperial Valley Railroad (SD&IV) operating on San Diego Metropolitan Transit District (MTB) right-of-way. San Diego councilman Juan Vargas is a leading proponent of re-opening the line to connect San Diego with inland markets, including the lucrative international trade which now flows through Mexicali/Calexico to San Diego's historic rival port of Los Angeles.

Revenue freights operate daily eastbound from Plaster City to the SP main in El Centro and westbound from Tecate to tidewater and the Santa Fe main. The Pacific Southwest Railway Museum, based in Campo, regularly operates excursion trains from Tecate to the head of Carrizo Gorge. Plans are afoot to run a railcar from there across Goat Trestle and from Plaster City to Indian Hill. But for the need to restore a tunnel or two, Mr. Spreckels' "Impossible Railroad" seems poised to roll into the millennium.

Side Trip Up Carrizo Canyon (4WD trail)

0.0   Junction with S-2. The entrance to Carrizo Canyon is a wide, sandy arroyo, covered with a forest of smoke trees and desert willows.

2.5   Rockhouse Canyon Wash to the west (right). Hike about three miles west (right) to the line-shack-rock house (see above in Bow Willow).

4.0   Tributary canyons (elev. 950') climb to the east and west. A hike up the east fork leads about two miles to Carrizo Palms (elev. 1600-1800'), below the big north bend of the railroad. The 170 palms found here, between tunnels 20 and 21, can also be reached from Indian Hill in the Dos Cabezas area of the park. When construction crews were blasting tunnels between 1912 and 1919, the water in these palm oases was crucial to the work crews, who installed a pump to boost water to their camp 400 feet up from the groves.

The roadhead here will vary according to storm activity.

End Of Side Trip

48.7 South Carrizo Creek Road.

The 4WD turnoff (left) is another route to Carrizo Cienega and stage site. The Vallecito/Carrizo/Canyon Sin Nombre confluence and road junction is about 4.5 miles east.

49.0 Sweeney Canyon and Pass.

Hwy S-2 enters Sweeney Canyon and starts up the steep grade of Sweeney Pass to top out at elev. 1200'. This climb was long a barrier to most vehicles trying to follow the rough Imperial Hwy route in the 1930s and 1940s. In 1952, county engineers constructed a sinuous route snaking along the hillside which finally enabled conventional vehicles to negotiate Sweeney Pass. By the early 1960s the entire Imperial Hwy had been paved.

The canyon and pass were named for Lt. Thomas W. Sweeny who was in charge of Camp Independence on the Gila River. (His name has long been misspelled.)

51.3 Canyon Sin Nombre.

This turnoff is the beginning of "The Journey Through Time" field trip featured in introductory geology classes and natural-history tours. Thanks to the southwestward tilt of the sediments in the Vallecito-Fish Creek and Carrizo basins, this 20-mile journey across the basin to the northeast and into Split Mountain is an orderly progression down the stratigraphic column, back through time, from recent sediments to about ten million years ago. A few time blips in the otherwise orderly story at the beginning of the trip, at the entrance to Canyon Sin Nombre, provide flashbacks to a half-billion years ago, the earliest rocks in the region.

Old Sweeney Grade about 1940   *Canyon Sin Nombre*

The following ABDSP Interpretive Panel, located at Bow Willow Campground, paints the picture:

CANYON SIN NOMBRE

The Carrizo Badlands hold many mysteries within their sedimentary layers. Today they appear arched and lifeless, but three million years ago the scene was dramatically different. The Colorado River spilled over its banks many times through the centuries and deposited thousands of feet of silt in the Borrego Desert. This delta region of the Colorado teemed with life. Fossils found in these layers tell us that lakes formed and streams meandered through the valleys while trees and grasslands covered much of the surrounding landscape. Mastodons, camels, horses, and rhinos roamed the savanna, while overhead vultures soared on wings 17 feet across!

Side Trip Down Canyon Sin Nombre

4WD road northeast (left) drops off the mesa into Canyon Sin Nombre ("Canyon Without Name"), which winds about four sinuous miles to the Vallecito/Carrizo Creek confluence.

The light-colored wash at about mile one, just before the narrow entrance to the canyon, marks the concealed trace of the Elsinore fault, one of southern California's three great fault zones. The canyon descends through ancient metasedimentary rock portals and marble outcrops, past 100-million-year-old granitic intrusions and 75-million-year-old pegmatite dikes to a sudden unconformity in time—the awesome fold at about mile two in three-million-year-old sandstone. The geologic wonders con-

tinue to unfold down-canyon until the walls fall away and the road passes through a dense smoke-tree forest.

The major confluence of Carrizo and Vallecito creeks is reached at
about mile four. Approximate mileages from here are:

1. Four miles west or southwest (left) to Hwy S-2 via Bow Willow
or Carrizo Creek road, respectively.

2. Eight miles northwest (straight ahead) to Hwy S-2, mile 43, via
Vallecito Creek and Arroyo Seco Del Diablo junction, Arroyo Tapiado
junction, and Palm Spring.

3. Four miles east (right) to Carrizo Cienaga and stage station site,
dead-end at boundary of Carrizo Impact Area (CIA). See Trip 6E.
End Of Side Trip

A slot canyon tributary to Canyon Sin Nombre

51.3 Canyon Sin Nombre (repeated from above).

51.5 Carrizo Badlands Overlook.

The dirt turnout northeast (left) goes along the old county road 0.3 mile to a posted ABDSP interpretive panel:

THE CARRIZO BADLANDS...a journey through time

Marine reefs, lake deposits, and silt from the Colorado River delta have been cast into layers over millions of years. These deposits, once horizontal, have been tilted up and exposed like the pages of a book. The elements of erosion have sculpted the desolate badlands in front of you. Paleontologists studying the fossils of the Carrizo Badlands have discovered this is one of the richest deposits of its kind on Earth. The time period of one-half million to five million years ago is represented by the hardened bones of mastodons, llamas, horses and tapirs. Grasslands and scattered forests supported large animal herds.

Hwy S-2 tops out at BM 1325' at post mile marker 53 and descends.

53.5 Jojoba Wash (elev. 1200').

4WD road southwest (right) is Jojoba Wash, named for its abundant goatnut shrubs. The Jojoba Wash road loops through the Volcanic Hills for about six miles back to Hwy S-22. A rugged connecting 4WD route at mile 4.0 climbs up a steep dugway to join the Dos Cabezas road after a couple more miles (see Trip 6F). Travel direction recommended is from Dos Cabezas to Jojoba because of this dropoff, which should be attempted only by high-clearance/short-wheelbase 4WD.

53.6 West Dolomite Mine Road/Coyote Mountains.

The road northeast (left) leads 1.6 miles to the Dolomite Mine, clearly visible on the slope of the Coyote Mountains. The abandoned mine once yielded dolomite marble, a magnesium calcium carbonate, which was trucked eight rugged miles south to the rail siding at Dos Cabezas.

55.5 Volcanic Hills.

The highway passes through a water gap eroded into the lava flow. This area, with tell-tale names like Red Hill and Lava Flow Wash, offers the most accessible examples of volcanic activity in the Anza-Borrego region. Variously called Jacumba basalt and Alverson andesite, approximate dating on these flows ranges from 15 to 22 million years ago. The separation of compositionally similar Table Mountain near Jacumba, some ten miles away, as the crow flies, and three thousand feet higher, is an indication of major regional dip-slip and strike-slip faulting along the Elsinore fault zone.

55.8 Mortero Canyon/North Mortero Wash.

A dirt road crosses the highway. The southwest (right) 4WD trail leads through Mortero Canyon about four miles to the Dos Cabezas station (see Trip 6F). This is a sandy route, definitely 4WD. The northeast road (left) is another Dolomite Mine road, which crosses North Mortero Wash and then proceeds northwest to the quarry.

Hwy S-2 crosses Lava Flow Wash to...

56.5 San Diego/Imperial County Line (elev. 914′).

A dirt road bearing true north-south at the Imperial Hwy monument marks the county line and the boundary between ABDSP and BLM's Yuha Desert Recreation Area. The plaque that was here until the 1980s was placed by the Boyce Aten post of the El Centro American Legion in 1933, when the reality of their dream of a "First class roadway from El Segundo on the coast to El Centro" was a set of meandering, sand-bound tracks, passable to little more than animal-drawn vehicles.

There are no post mile markers along this portion of Hwy S-2 so odometer mileage below is continuous southeast from Warner Junction as well as northwest from Ocotillo (Imperial County).

POST MILES FROM:
Warner
Junc.   Ocotillo

56.5 8.4   San Diego/Imperial County Line (repeated from above).

58.0 6.9   Northwest Coyote Mtns—Wind Caves turnoff (elev. 894′).

The dirt road northeast (left) leads about two miles to the base of the northwest Coyote Mountains, designated by BLM as an Area of Critical Environmental Concern (ACEC) for the rich fossil molluscan fauna in the marine Imperial Formation. This is a Gulf of California fauna, much of which is related to Caribbean taxa, evidencing a submerged Panama isthmus during early Pliocene times. (Collecting is illegal under federal law. The area is patrolled and heavy fines will be issued to violators).

From the roadhead an old mining trail can be climbed northwest and then northeast into the wind-cave area UTM 5-87.9E 36-31.1N in southeast section 32 near peak 1662′. One-way hike is about three miles.

58.7 6.2   South Mortero Wash (BM elev. 798′)

The BLM-signed jeep trail southwest (right) leads into an interesting complex of routes, all of which offer intriguing, isolated campsites. These routes eventually dead-end at the heads of box canyons after several miles. The box canyons are evidence of continuing uplift along the Elsinore fault zone, as the steepening gradient causes headward erosion into the desert uplands above.

60.1 4.8   "Big Bend Crest" (elev. 814′).

This rise at a bend in the highway marks the crest between the large drainage systems of Mortero Wash to the north and Palm Canyon Wash to the south. A dirt road leads along the crest southwest a couple of miles to the Dos Cabezas Road at "The Big Bend" of the SD&AE Railroad (see below).

61.0 3.9   Dos Cabezas Road (elev. 673′ BM)

A BLM-signed dirt road leads southwest (right) three miles to "The Big Bend" of the SD&IV (SD&AE) Railroad, where Palm Canyon Wash crosses under the railroad. In 1976 summer Hurricane Kathleen slammed into much of the Colorado Desert. At this point, two hundred feet of roadbed and trestle were completely washed away to leave rails and crossties suspended high in the air with no visible means of support. The dirt road continues four more miles west to the Dos Cabezas station site (see Trip 6E).

61.8 3.1 "KV Line" and Palm Canyon Wash.

High-tension powerlines, measured in kilovolts (KV), cross the highway southeast of Palm Canyon Wash.

63.6 1.3 Shell Canyon Rd/Hwy S-2 Intersection (Elev. 420').

Side Trip North to Fossil Canyon

0.0 Shell Canyon Rd/Hwy S-2 intersection. Cross the multiple channels of the combined watercourses of Mortero and Palm Canyon washes which from here to the Salton Sea is called Coyote Wash.

1.5 County dump—three roads diverge from this point.

The northeast (right) jeep trail goes several miles to join the Painted Gorge road (see Trip 7C). After the first mile it passes tilted coquina beds of oyster, pectin (scallop), barnacle, clam and other shell hash, evidence of an early Pliocene, warm-water, shallow marine environment, much like the Gulf of California today.

The west (left) paved road goes a couple of miles to a rock-and-gravel quarry, one of several which exploit alluvial products shed from the Coyote Mountains.

The northwest (left-bearing) road leads into Fossil Canyon, aka Alverson Canyon and Shell Canyon. Just past the transmission lines, yellowish marine Imperial Formation sediments with invertebrate fossils can be explored on the ridge east (right).

2.4 Fork to a second quarry and Fossil Canyon.

The second quarry is straight ahead. Bear right onto a dirt road, past a flat area suitable for large-group camping, and then hard right into a canyon where the route becomes jeep-only. A large cove on the right at mile 3.0, just past a large dark-green outcropping of metamorphic amphibolite, offers excellent wind-sheltered campsites.

Jeep road continues northwest.

3.3 Entrance to Fossil Canyon (elev.800').

The route into the canyon turns northeast (right) and becomes hike-only when it enters BLM's Coyote Mountains Wilderness (posted). At mile 3.6 a coquina (shell hash) ledge crosses the wash on a north-south strike. Fossil animal remains which can be observed (but not collected) include coral, cone shell, pectin (scallop), oyster, turret shell, clam, and barnacle. These taxa represent a rich marine environment with at least three invertebrate phyla: mollusks, echinoderms, and arthropods.

The dark lava flow on the left at mile 4.0 is a volcanic breccia, associated with the 18 million-year-old Alverson Andesite observed in the Volcanic Hills along Hwy S-2.

4.3 "Tunnel" trail climbs steeply right up a highly mineralized and colorful slope to a mine prospect. Just past this point on the left are conglomerates correlated with the Split Mountain Formation, interbedded with lava flows. At mile 4.6 an old mining trail proceeds up a small, dark volcanic wash to the left, eventually gaining the west ridge for a superb view deep into Baja along the Sierra Juarez crest.

4.7   As the main canyon suddenly narrows, two large dikes of marble at elev. 1200' guard the entrance to a narrow chasm, which rapidly ascends past scour holes, mud walls, gypsum beds, and dry waterfalls.

The saddle at mile 5.4 (elev. 1459') (UTM 5-91.0E, 36-30.0N) offers a sweeping view northwest across the Carrizo Badlands.

End Of Side Trip

63.6   1.3   Shell Canyon Rd/Hwy S-2 Intersection (repeated from above).
Swing south (elev. 368'), past the Lazy Lizard Saloon (Ocotillo's answer to Ocotillo Wells' Iron Door Saloon), into...

64.9   0.0   Ocotillo (I-8 junction).
It is about 70 miles west to El Cajon. Ocotillo offers stores, auto services, restaurants, sheriff, motel, and fire station. This is a great little desert town but don't expect much open after sundown (except for the Lazy Lizard).

TRIP 6B:
Julian to Earthquake (Shelter) Valley via Hwy 78

From: Julian
To: Earthquake (Shelter) Valley
Via: Hwy 78 (paved)

Connecting Trips:
1A–Warner Junction to Earthquake Valley via Hwy S-2
4A–Earthquake Valley to Ocotillo Wells via Hwy 78
6A–Earthquake Valley to Ocotillo (Imperial County) via Hwy S-2
6D–Mason Valley to Banner via Oriflamme/Chariot Canyons

Points Of Interest and Side Trips:
Side Trip to Fages Monument and Kwaaymii Point via Hwys 79 & S-1; Banner Store and Recreation Ranch.

Summary:
This is the middle, or central, gateway into the Anza-Borrego region from the San Diego area. Trips 1A and 1B described the northern gateways along Hwys S-2 and S-22. Trip 7A will describe the southern gateway along I-8.

A major side trip is described from Julian southeast on Hwys 79 and S-1 "Sunrise Highway" past the Fages Monument, to Kwaaymii Point. This trip is included in this book because, little known to most, ABDSP actually extends up into the Laguna Mountains and crosses the Sunrise Highway.

POST MILES FROM:
Oceanside

0.0   Oceanside, junction of I-5 and Hwy 78.

51.1 Santa Ysabel (elev. 2984'), junction of Hwys 78 and 79.

57.9 Julian (elev. 4220').
Having survived ghost-town candidacy, Julian is now a compelling tourist town featuring fine shops, restaurants, lodging, the Pioneer Museum and the original Eagle Mine. Drive southeast through town.

58.1 Cuyamaca Junction and U.S.Post Office.
The main road log continues straight ahead (east).

Side Trip to Kwaaymii Point via Sunrise Highway.
0.0   Cuyamaca Junction, Hwys 78 & 79, Hwy 79 post mile marker 20.2. Drive south toward Cuyamaca Rancho State Park on Hwy 79.
2.6   Inspiration Point (elev. 4600'), post mile marker 17.6.
This lofty perch, also known as Desert View Park and Vista Point, has a bird's eye view of the central Anza-Borrego region, just as Crawford Overlook on Hwy S-22 has of the northern gateway and Desert Tower on I-8 has of the southern gateway.
5.8   Hwy S-1 "Sunrise Highway" junction, Hwy 78 post mile 14.4, Hwy S-1 post mile 37.7. Turn southeast (left).
7.5   Fages Monument (elev. 4700'), CRHT, Hwy S-1 post mile 36.

Pedro Fages Trail (California Historical Landmark No. 858)
UTM 5-42.8E 36-50.6N LAT 32°59.65'N LON 116°32.5'W

Hike To Mason Valley Truck Trail
From Lake Cuyamaca to the west, the CRHT crosses Hwy S-1 just north of the monument (BM 4666') and trends east across a pleasant meadow. It then wraps northeast around a hill to the intersection of the PCT, the ABDSP boundary, and the roadhead of the Mason Valley Truck Trail (MVTT), elev. 4690'(see Trip 6D). This is 1.4 miles from Hwy S-1. If you stroll through this pastoral verdant meadow, with its tilting headstones of ancient Julian schist, be sure to close all gates. Hikers and riders can thus enter ABDSP via yet another mountain gateway from the west. This important junction, featuring old cattle water works and a pleasant grove of planted pines, is referred to below as the MVTT roadhead.
The hiking trail from the MVTT roadhead drops northeast into Chariot Canyon via a "little used, rocky track on a bone-jarring descent" per *The Pacific Crest Trail*, which provides details of the PCT through this area.
The dirt road east from the MVTT roadhead is the MVTT itself. It goes two miles to a dirt-road T-junction and is recommended for riders. This basically was the route to the desert for Fages, the Jackass Mail, and many other pioneers. From this T-junction, the

northwest (left) route goes via Chariot Canyon to Hwy 78 at Banner. East (right) drops precipitously via MVTT into Oriflamme Canyon to Hwy S-2 at the mouth of Box Canyon. See Trip 6D for details of these dirt roads.

Each of the routes noted above provide options to drop hikers or riders at Fages Monument on the Sunrise Highway and pick them up in Chariot or Oriflamme canyons.

End Of Hike

7.5   Fages Monument on Hwy S-1 (repeated from above). Post mile 36.0.

Hwy S-1 ascends gently about two miles to a summit (elev. 5018') and enters the central montane portion of the Anza-Borrego region. It then drops to the Lucky 5 (Rattlesnake Valley) turnoff southwest (right) and proceeds on southeast (left) to...

10.1   Oriflamme Mountain turnoff, east (left). Hwy S-1 post mile 33.5.

The Oriflamme turnoff is a 4WD trail which crosses the PCT and quickly enters BLM land. The gate is locked except during hunting season. After crossing the headwaters of Oriflamme Canyon it climbs onto a little-known mesa which is Oriflamme Mountain. Oriflamme offers a complex of 4WD routes and trails for exploration. Call BLM for dates of hunting season.

13.1   Kwaaymii Point turnoff. Hwy S-1 post mile 30.3.

Drive 0.3 mile east to the overlook (elev. 5468') from where Cottonwood Canyon drops precipitously down to the desert floor far below. The PCT runs both ways from this point. The Kwaaymii were a local band of Kumeyaay of which the late Tom Lucas was the last full-blooded member. His story is recorded in Lora Cline's *Just Before Sunset*. The Kwaaymii had permanent villages along the edge of the Laguna Mountains, at Vallecito, Agua Caliente, Palm Spring, and Mason Valley.

End Of Side Trip

58.1 Cuyamaca Junction and U.S. Post Office (repeated from above).

Continue east on Hwy 78 and commence the descent down Banner Canyon. Good desert visibility, sans vegetation, starts just below the pine-tree line at post mile 62. Commence naked geology. The main trace of the Elsinore Fault is visible on the canyon wall opposite to the north (left). This right-lateral fault line is marked by several features: the brighter green strip of vegetation where the water table is forced nearer the surface, flat benches cut into the descending ridges beneath "faceted" ridge faces, and the linearity of the canyon. "Right-lateral," typical of most of southern California's great faults, refers to the apparent direction of movement of any object on the opposite side of the fault from the observer.

Just beyond the old Madden mill site, Hwy 78 makes a left hairpin turn to cross Chariot Canyon creek.

A few yards before Banner Store is...

65.0 Chariot Canyon dirt road, (elev. 2770'), southeast (right).

The dirt roads, utilizing Chariot, Rodriguez, and Oriflamme canyons and the MVTT, are described in Trip 6D.

65.1 Banner Store and Recreation Ranch (elev. 2760').

This friendly outpost offers fuel, phone, maps and books, supplies, and a campground open to the public. See the Appendix 2 for camp reservation information. The town of Banner was established during the Julian gold rush days when Louis Redman discovered gold in 1869 while looking for wild grapes in Chariot Canyon. He marked the site with a small American flag, giving the name of the town that developed there. Banner City, as it was called, had a population of 600-1,000 with several stores and hotels, and many saloons. The *Julian Sentinel* of 1894 reported that the school had 30 students and that "the graduating class equaled that of National City and exceeded Escondido." Banner Creek, which runs through the canyon of the same name, flooded in 1874, 1916, and 1926, each time washing away most of the town. The town wasn't rebuilt after the last flood.

68.0 Cigarette Hills. The name is attributed to truckers for the first light-up point after the hairy descent down Banner Grade.

69.7 Earthquake Valley (Shelter) Valley, (elev. 2330').

This is Scissors Crossing (west) at the Vallecito Monument.

TRIP 6C:
Blair Valley and Smuggler Canyon

From: Hwy S-2/Blair Valley turnoff
To: Hwy S-2/Little Blair Valley turnoff (dirt road)

Points Of Interest and Side Trips:
Ghost Mountain/Yaquitepec, Morteros Trail, Smuggler Canyon/Pictographs

MILES FROM:

Blair Val. T/O	Little Blair Turnoff

0.0 7.9 Hwy S-2/Blair Valley Turnoff (elev. 2550').

Post mile marker 23 on Hwy S-2 is six miles southeast of Hwy 78 at Scissors Crossing. Drive east around the north end of the playa, which is always closed to vehicle travel. Headward erosion from Box Canyon will someday breach the low southwest divide and drain the shallow, enclosed Blair basin into the Vallecito Creek system.

Although this is a popular area for large groups, parties of 25 or more must obtain a permit from ABDSP park headquarters. A designated group site is the long, narrow cove which parallels the playa's south end about a mile from the paved road. "Pack it in, pack it out" is the custom and the rule here.

0.5 7.4 Foot and Walker Pass.

Ӿ   A monument here describes how passengers on the Butterfield Overland Mail walked over the low pass separating Blair Valley from Earthquake

Blair Valley with lenticular cloud

Valley and occasionally even pushed the stage over the pass, hence the name. Climb to the top of the ridge that overlooks Blair Valley, and look south-west toward Box Canyon to see the tracks of the overland stage. It has been over 100 years since the last stage rolled along this once-major thoroughfare, but still the drama and excitement of this period of history remain alive in this desert where little of the surrounding landscape has changed. Ghost Mountain's itinerant poet, Marshal South, captured the romance of this bygone period:

> There's a valley I know in the wastelands,
>> Where, down through the greasewood and sage,
> Like a dim, ghostly thread from the years that have fled
>> Stretch the tracks of the Overland Stage.
> Lone, ghostly and dim in the starlight;
>> Grey, desolate and pale in the dawn,
> Blurred by heat-waves at noon—still o'er mesa and dune
>> Wind the tracks of the wheels that have gone.
> Old coaches whose wheels long have mouldered,
>> Old stage-teams whose hoofs long are dust;
> Still, faint and age-greyed, wind the old wheel-ruts made
>> By tires long since crumbled to rust.
> And down where the silence lies deepest—
>> Like a lone, crumbling bead on a thread—
> In the mesquite-grown sands the old stage-station stands,
>> Hushed with memories—and ghosts of the dead.
> The desert rays wake not its brooding.
>> But oft 'neath the star-powered sky,

Round the walls on dark nights there move dim, ghostly lights,
　　As once more the old stages sweep by.
And again, across dune, wash and mesa,
　　As the dead years turn back on their page,
Pass the dim, racing teams from a ghost-world of dreams,
　　Down the tracks of the Overland Stage.

2.7　5.2　Ghost Mountain Fork.

The southwest fork (right) is a dirt road which leads one-quarter mile to the parking area and trailhead for Ghost Mountain. No other homesteaders of the region have garnered as much interest as the Marshal South family. Beginning in 1940, *Desert Magazine* readers followed monthly installments about the family's day-to-day life on Ghost Mountain. In 1947, publisher Randall Henderson announced the following:

> *For eight years Desert Magazine has been printing a highly controversial feature entitled "Desert Refuge." It was the month by month story of the experiences of Marshal and Tanya South and their three children—living alone on Ghost Mountain....They turned their backs on civilization and together undertook an experiment in primitive living....Marshal, being a colorful writer, has dramatized it in a way that fascinated many of Desert's readers—and was quite disgusting to a few of the less tolerant....Then one morning recently the following headline in a San Diego newspaper glared at me: "Divorce Plea Breaks up Hermit family." Tanya had filed a complaint against Marshal. After 14 years, the Ghost Mountain experiment in primitive living had failed.*

Marshal South Homesite (ABDSP Interpretive Panel)
Yaquitepec ... one family's attempt to live off the land
UTM 5-57.1E 36-51.6N　　　　　　LAT 33°00.2'N LON 116°23.3'W

Tanya and the children moved to San Diego and reentered civilization. The children enrolled in school for the first time. Marshal moved to Julian and continued to write articles for *Desert Magazine* until he died in October 1948.

The South family's home at Yaquitepec on Ghost Mountain

Henderson wrote in the December 1948 issue: "We'll miss Marshal South. He was a dreamer—an impractical visionary according to the standards of our time, but what a drab world this would be without the dreamers."

The east fork goes over a low saddle into Little Blair Valley.

3.5   4.4   Morteros Trail

A short quarter-mile walk leads to a boulder-strewn village area which was heavily used by Kumeyaay women. A rock pestle was used to pound seeds in the bedrock mortar (mortero). A smaller hand-size smooth rock (mano) was used to grind seeds or dried plants into flour by using roller-pin action, which creates slicks (metates) in the bedrock. Look for both morteros and metates in the village ahead. Note areas of dark earth while walking toward the village. These were agave roasting pits. Agave, which is commonly seen about the hillsides, was the only plant gathered and prepared by the men because of the difficulty of digging them up and preparing the roasting pit. The agave was ready to collect from April through summer, after it reached a height of four to five feet but before it blossomed. The stalk was removed from the plant base by digging it out, then was baked in a rock-lined pit at the bottom of which were coals that had a covering layer of rock or leaves to protect the stalks from burning. The stalks were covered with more leaves and material, and then were allowed to bake naturally for up to three days before they were opened and the sweet, molasses-flavored agave was consumed or dried and stored for future use.

Morteros & Village Scene ... lasting memories of the Kumeyaay
(ABDSP Interpretive Panel)
UTM 5-58.2E 36-52.2N   LAT 33°00.5'N LON 116°22.6W

The road continues 0.1 mile east to...

3.6   4.3   "Pictograph" or Smuggler Canyon Fork in Little Blair Valley.

Side Trip Up "Pictograph" or Smuggler Canyon (dirt road)

Continue east, straight ahead, climbing the alluvial fan 1.5 miles to the roadhead, which offers excellent campsites hidden in boulders. Whale Peak has been climbed from this area, but that route is longer and has a greater elevation gain. See Pinyon Mountain Road in Trip 6A for the shortest route.

Pictograph Trail (ABDSP Interpretive Panel)
A Message on the Rocks
UTM 5-59.9E 36-53.4N   LAT 33°01.2'N LON 116°21.5'W

The hiking route goes over a low divide into Smuggler Canyon, then bears right down the valley about a mile to a very prominent boulder on the west side of the streambed, on which the pictographs are well displayed. This Indian rock-art has been painted on (pictograph) rather than etched into the rock (petroglyph) by early-day Kumeyaay. The colors used were derived from minerals, ground into a powder, and then a binder and carrier, such as tree pitch, animal fat, or sap was probably used. (Similar rock art in central Baja California, however, did not use a binder or carrier according to Harry Crosby in *The Cave Paintings of Baja California*.)

The pictographs here are unusual for their well-executed yellow and red symbolic designs consisting of interlaced elements in a diamond-chain motif. The diamond chains and chevrons are typical of Luiseno rock-art and show the influence this Indian group had on the neighboring Kumeyaay.

Ken Hedges, curator of archaeology at the San Diego County Museum of Man, was the first to do a detailed rock-art study of southern California. Hedges defined five rock-art styles in southern California, three of which are found in the Anza-Borrego and Yuha Desert region.

The three found in this region are:

1. Southern California Rectilinear Abstract—a pictograph style consisting of diamond chains, zigzag lines and tally marks, chevrons, and geometric designs. No stick figures ever occur at the same site as these. This style is also commonly known as San Luis Rey because it was first identified in that area. The Smuggler Canyon rock-art site is in this style. This was also the style commonly used by the Cahuilla who lived to the north of the Kumeyaay.

2. Peninsular Range Representational—a pictograph style consisting of anthropomorphic figures, predominately men and animals as stick figures. This style occurs with other designs but not with diamond design. The most famous representation of this style in the park is found in the Dos Cabezas area. An exact replica of it is found on the wall of the visitor center. This style is commonly known as La Rumorosa, named for that border area of Baja where it was first clearly identified.

3. Great Basin Abstract and Colorado Desert Representational are both petroglyph styles, but only the Great Basin Abstract, which has intangible designs, is found in San Diego County. The Colorado Desert Representational has anthropomorphic and zoomorphic figures.

In some places, the rock-art existing today might be the only record of early people that has survived, other artifacts having long disappeared. If something is to be learned of these early people, then their rock-art must be preserved for future study. It is believed that the pictographs existing in the park today are about 200-300 years old, although the styles themselves can be much older.

Look at the rock-art, ponder what it might mean, photograph it, but do not touch it—natural oils in your hand and fingers will destroy the pigment as would chalk. Do not chalk over the drawings to get better pictures. All Native American artifacts are protected by law. For those who would like to learn more about the rock-art of Anza-Borrego, see Manfred Knaak's *The Forgotten Artist*.

A half-mile farther down the canyon is a seasonal Kumeyaay camp on the right in the flat boulder ledges where many bedrock morteros have been worn. The low point, where the canyon narrows, probably had pooled water, which would account for the sizable presence of Kumeyaay here in years past.

Pass through a narrow, bouldery defile to a superb overlook into the Carrizo Valley, backdropped by the rugged peaks of the Tierra Blanca, Jacumba and Coyote mountains. Vallecito is clearly visible as the green patch in the tans and browns far below. (In reverse, this overlook can be picked out from Vallecito Stage Station as a light-colored patch in the vee of a brown gorge.)

Experienced climbers can ascend and traverse the challenging cliffs to the left and work carefully down 3rd-class pitches over huge boulders into lower Smuggler Canyon and to Highway S-2 just east of Vallecito Stage Station. Total one-way distance of this through-hike is about six miles. (This hike gives the lie to the possibility of this route being a true smuggler's canyon—it's way too much work for anything other than fitness fun.)
End Of Side Trip

3.6   4.3   "Pictograph" or Smuggler Canyon Fork in Little Blair Valley
(repeated from above).

Route continues northwest (left) farther into Little Blair Valley and around the west and north sides of another dry lake. There are several excellent, secluded campsites up against the rocky ridge to the left. Cross a low divide and bear west (left) along the hillside to...

6.9   1.0   The north side of Foot and Walker Pass. Turn north along the tracks of the old stage route to...

7.9   0.0   Hwy S-2/Little Blair Valley turnoff at mile 22.3.

TRIP 6D:
Mason Valley to Banner via Oriflamme and Chariot Canyons

From: Highway S-2 in Mason Valley
To: Highway 78 at Banner Store
Via: Oriflamme and Chariot Canyons (dirt road)

Connecting Trips:
  6A–Earthquake Valley to Ocotillo (Imp. Co.) via Hwy S-2
  6B–Julian to Earthquake Valley via Hwy 78

Points Of Interest and Side Trips:
Rodriguez Canyon, Ranchito Mine, PCT/CRHT to Fages Monument, Chariot Canyon mining district.

MILES FROM:
S-2
Mason Hwy 78
Valley Banner

0.0   11.4   Oriflamme Canyon turnoff from Hwy S-2 (elev. 2272').

This is just north of post mile marker 27 at the mouth of Box Canyon. It also marks the beginning of the Mason Valley Truck Trail (MVTT) which will end at a locked gate very near the Fages monument on the Sunrise Highway. Hikers and riders can be dropped at this locked gate to be retrieved later on the Sunrise Highway.

0.3   11.1   Enter ABDSP and Vallecito Wash.

Be wary of sand traps next mile. Not every state-park boundary crossing will be noted in this trip description. Boundaries are clearly posted.

2.1   9.3   Junction of Rodriguez and Oriflamme canyons.

The MVTT goes southwest (left) up Oriflamme Canyon. The Rodriguez Canyon side trip below offers an alternative parallel route to Banner Store or a loop route through the Chariot Canyon mining district.

Side Trip Up Rodriguez Canyon (dirt road)

0.0   Junction (elev. 2520'). Bear northwest (right), following the pole line.

0.3   The rutted hiking trail to the north (right) leads 1.5 miles to an old mining prospect and cabin ruins (elev. 3500') on the southeast flank of Granite Mountain. This is a good point from which to climb this barren, rocky massif. Work up the barren ridge to the north about two miles to the summit (5633').

A set of rockhouses, history unknown, is about a half mile northwest of this rutted trail junction on a high point at elev. 2900'.

The road enters a narrow canyon with a seasonal stream and climbs onto a broad flat to...

2.2   The Guy Urquhart turkey ranch. Ruins of the ranch buildings east of the road can be explored. Desert willow, sugar bush, tamarisk and screwbean mesquite predominate here.

The road crosses from private land into BLM land at the section line at mile 2.8. Faint roads lead left to campsites on the flat while the PCT winds along the ridge line above.

3.7   Saddle of Rodriguez Canyon (elev. 3650').

The PCT crosses the road and saddle, en route east to Scissors Crossing. It can be followed east about a half mile to look down on the ruins of the Desert Queen Mine.

4.8   Ranchito Mine and mill. The ruins of a large five-stamp mill and the mine workings, in a quartz diorite and schist matrix, are across a meadow to the northeast. Ownership in 1957 was with the family of Lt. Cave J. Couts, an Army officer who figured prominently in San Diego history during the Gold Rush. Couts' son, Cave J. Couts Jr., created his own Gold Rush when he purchased the Ranchito Mine in 1895 for $5,500 cash. The Ranchito produced about 2,500 ounces of gold and about 100 ounces of silver between 1895 and 1948. At today's price, that would approach a million dollars.

5.5   Junction with Chariot Canyon. Hwy 78 and Banner are 1.5 miles north (right). A loop trip south (left) up through Chariot Canyon goes about 10 miles back to Hwy S-2 via the MVTT Trail.
End Of Side Trip

2.1   9.3   Junction of Rodriguez and Oriflamme canyons (repeated from above).
Bear left up Oriflamme Canyon via the MVTT.

3.0   8.4   The site of state-operated Camp Carlton is among the alders and sycamores along Oriflamme creek. CCC crews based here in the 1930s hacked out the MVTT with hand tools.

The route enters ABDSP at mile 3.5 and climbs steeply to...

5.8   5.6   Chariot Canyon/MVTT junction (elev. 4100').
This is the divide between the major San Felipe Creek and Carrizo Creek drainage systems. The main route continues northwest (straight) down into Chariot Canyon.

> **Side Trip to The MVTT Roadhead Near Fages Monument (dirt road)**
> **0.0**   Chariot Canyon/MVTT junction. Drive southwest (left)
> **0.7**   A faint track cuts steeply up through thick chaparral to the southwest leading toward the Fages Monument. This approximates the old Lassitor hay road, which functioned from 1857 to 1861. James R. Lassitor used this and the Salt Creek route to the south to freight hay, wild oats and firewood from his ranch in the Cuyamaca Mountains down to the stage station at Vallecito. (Over 100 years later the process is still the same, only the product has changed. Today, trucks roar down Banner grade just a few miles north carrying fuel to service stations along the old Butterfield Trail.) To the east, the Lassitor hay route roughly parallels the MVTT down Oriflamme Canyon to Hwy S-2.
> **2.0**   MVTT roadhead (elev. 4701).
> This is a major trail junction, marked by a water tank and a grove of trees south of the road, and is the end of travel for motor vehicles due to a locked gate (see Trip 6B.) The PCT crosses nearby—look for its trail markers. Hikers and riders have two choices here:
> 1. Drop steeply north (right) 1.3 miles into Chariot Canyon and on into San Felipe Valley 5 miles farther.
> 2. Hike west (straight ahead) through a closed gate, then south (left) and west through another closed gate to...
> **3.4**   The Fages Monument on Sunrise Highway S-1.
> **End Of Side Trip**

5.8   5.6   Chariot Canyon/MVTT junction (repeated from above.) The PCT, headed for Chariot Mountain and the Rodriguez Canyon saddle (see above), departs northeast from the road at mile 6.0. It will reach the Rodriguez Canyon saddle, near the Desert Queen mine (see above), after 4.6 miles.

6.3   5.1   A trail joins from the southwest in the bottom of the canyon at
elev. 3860'). The PCT and CHRT ascend this grade 1.3 miles southwest to
the MVTT roadhead noted above. Sycamore and cottonwood trees along
a small stream with lavish spring wildflowers make this one of the most
inviting canyons in the entire area. Continue down-canyon to the north.

7.0   4.4   Exit ABDSP into the Chariot Canyon mining district.
Gold was discovered in the San Diego mountains on Coleman Creek,
west of Julian, in late 1869. With the discovery of the Washington Mine, staked
out on George Washington's birthday in 1870, a full-scale rush to the Julian area
was on.

As soon as the town of Julian was laid out, prospectors began searching
the canyons surrounding the town. In February 1871, George V. King was
searching for gold along the Banner grade and up Chariot Canyon. He passed
the Ready Relief and Redman diggings, and climbed upward out of the dense-
ly wooded canyon to the mountainside covered with scrub oak and manzanita, where he noticed a large white quartz boulder. There he discovered one of
the richest veins in the Banner area, and named it the Golden Chariot Mine.
About $2 million worth of bullion was eventually taken from the mine. It was
the richest single strike in southern California.

The next few miles are San Diego's answer to the Mother Lode highway
in the Sierra. The names stir some long-ago frontier memories: the Golden
Oaks mine, Freedom II mill site, Ben Hur mine, Cold Beef, the fabled Golden
Chariot, the Golden Sugar, the Lucky Strike, and Golden Ella. The richest of
these have been reopened and are being worked. All are on private property
and visitors are not welcome off the road.

9.9   1.5   Junction with Rodriguez Canyon road to the northeast.

11.4   0.0   Hwy 78 and Banner Store and Recreation Ranch (elev. 2755').

TRIP 6E:
Vallecito Creek and Carrizo Badlands

From: Vallecito-Palm Spring turnoff/Hwy S-2
To: Carrizo Stage Station (site)
Via: Vallecito and Carrizo Creeks (4WD roads)

Points Of Interest and Side Trips:
Palm Spring, Arroyo Tapiado, Arroyo Seco del Diablo, Diablo Dropoff, Carrizo
Cienega.

MILES FROM:
Hwy S-2

0.0   Vallecito-Palm Spring Turnoff/Hwy S-2.
Post mile 43 marker is at the entrance at "Carrizo Corridor Overlook," so
named by naturalist Paul Johnson. The sand traps here are deceiving—there's
lots of it, sand. Stay in vehicle tracks.

0.4   View-of-the-Badlands turnoff, northwest (left).
Main route continues down-wash southeast, down Vallecito Creek.

Side Trip To View-Of-The-Badlands (4WD road).
0.0   Turnoff to the northwest. If you took the right set of the tracks in the
wash you'll pass...
0.2   "Pelvis" survey point and a Mormon Battalion marker. Road right is
a short alternate up and over "Pelvis Pass" to Mesquite Oasis and
Palm Spring. Continue straight northwest up View-of-the-Badlands
Wash.
1.6   A small arroyo joins from the northeast (right). The hogback ridge
forming the left bank of the arroyo marks the two-million-year-old
Plio-Pleistocene depositional boundary in the Vallecito Badlands. Several
hundred yards up on a ridge to the right of the arroyo is is a small stone
cairn which is mis-labeled "View-of-the-Badlands" on topographic maps
at UTM 5-72.2E 36-44.7N. This is an OK view but it is not "The View."
For the latter, continue jeeping north.
3.5   End of road and the real View-of-the-Badlands. Arroyo Hueso, the
large wash system to the east (right), is beheading View-of-the-
Badlands Wash at this point, in the geologic process known as headward
erosion or stream piracy. A June Wash tributary is committing a similar
act several hundred yards northwest of this point at UTM 5-70.9E 36-
46.2N.
End Of Side Trip

Carrizo Badlands

1.0   Turnoff to Palm Spring and Mesquite Oasis, 0.6 mile north (left).

Many excellent mesquite-shaded campsites are a few hundred yards
northeast of here at the mouth of the Palm Spring arroyo and a little farther east
at the mouth of Arroyo Hueso. Both arroyos are blocked to vehicle travel up
from the campsites but can be explored on foot for several miles into the
Vallecito Badlands. Please respect and don't disturb the mesquite residents of
this area. After thousands of years of tranquility, they are taking a beating from
campers.

Water has existed at this mesquite-surrounded watering spot since Indian
times, as is shown by the scattering of shards and the remains of cooking fires
and camp middens. This was also a very important watering stop on the
Southern Emigrant Trail, midway between the water at Carrizo Cienega and
that at Vallecito. When Butterfield Stage stations were erected at Carrizo and
Vallecito, a relay station was established at Palm Spring. The small adobe
building and corrals have long since disappeared, leaving the oasis again quiet
for the desert wildlife. The monument marks the site of the way station, which
was in operation from 1858 to 1861.

PALM SPRING (California Historical Landmark No. 639)
UTM 5-73.1E 36-42.4N   LAT 32°55.17'N LON 116°12.07W

Southern Emigrant Trail and Butterfield Stage (ABDSP Interpretive Panel)
Palm Spring....rest stop on the Butterfield Stageline

*"It was bright moonlight while we remained here, and the beauty and the singu-
larity of the scene will not soon fade from my memory."*

—*J.M. Farwell, Newspaper Correspondent for "Alta California" 1858*

UTM 5-72.4E 36-33.9N   LAT 32°50.56 LON 116°13'33.55W

Lt. Pedro Fages passed here eastbound in 1772, having come down
Oriflamme Canyon, and continued on to San Sebastian Marsh. He passed
westbound in 1782, returning from the Yuma uprising, and headed for San
Diego. It was on the second trip that he recorded the presence of this oasis,
apparently having been in too much of a hurry to note it on the first trip. He
wrote that he found "a small spring of good water, near which there were three
or four very tall palm trees."

While the original palms are long gone, three short California fan palms
were planted here several years ago and seem to be thriving.

The side road continues west past Palm Spring 0.2 mile to the Mesquite
Oasis turnoff (right), another excellent camping tuckaway. Beyond this turnoff
the road crosses a low rise for another mile to join View-of-the-Badlands Wash
at survey point "Pelvis." The prominent line of mesquite from here to Palm
Spring is clear evidence of near subsurface water along the Vallecito Creek
Fault.

Continue southeast down-wash.

2.4   Arroyo Hueso ("bone wash") joins from the north (left). It was named in the 1950s by vertebrate paleontologists from the Los Angeles County Museum (LACM) under the supervision of Dr. Theodore Downs.

2.6   "Hollywood and Vine," the prominent mud hummock northeast (left), offers sheltered camping behind the mesquite-formed sand dune. James A. Jasper, a San Diego county supervisor, was responsible for signing this and many other places about a mile apart along several of the dim and dusty trails threading the San Diego backcountry in 1895. The old emigrant trail from Teofulio (San Felipe) Pass southeast to Carrizo gap was marked in such a manner by Jasper's iron signs. Directions painted on the signs gave distances to settlements and water holes. Long ago a wag painted the words "Hollywood and Vine" on the metal plate of Jasper's sign here, and the name (but not the original sign) stuck.

4.6   Turnoff north (left) is Arroyo Tapiado.
Parker (see Appendix 1) translates this as Concretion or Mudwall Wash.

Side Trip up Arroyo Tapiado (4WD road)
0.0   Arroyo Tapiado/Vallecito Wash junction.
0.8   The ridge on the left marks the entrance to Rainbow Basin. Ranger Paul Remeika describes this colorful area of tans and greens, rich in scientific value, as a two-million-year-old lake bed surrounded by sloping plains, much like Lake Henshaw of today. Evidence points to such vegetation as California laurel, walnut, black willow, cottonwood, sabal palm, and native avocado.

The road now swings right and then left at mile 1.8, where the ancient lake-bed deposits are replaced by even older pinkish deposits derived from the ancestral Colorado River. High walls now enclose the canyon, which offers numerous mud caves and natural bridges in the next couple of miles. ABDSP may contain the largest and longest mud caves in the world. Researcher Dwight Carey notes that subterranean streams are buried at depths of up to 180 feet. The erosion rate is low, indicating that the caves are mature, perhaps thousands of years old. At least 22 caves are known. The largest caves are over 1,000 feet long, with rooms up to 80 feet high and 30 feet wide. Some of the caves have dry waterfalls.

"Karst" refers to the kind of topography that is formed in limestone, dolomite or gypsum by dissolution and is characterized by sinkholes, caves, and underground drainage. This is a pseudokarst area, meaning that it is karst-like but not formed in limestone. It is composed of gypsiferous claystone known as mudstone. Flash floods have played a major role in carving out these caves. The biggest threats facing these caves today are "weekend warriors and flashlight cavers," who do not understand either the fragile beauty of the caves or the inherent dangers of exploring mud caves with crumbling walls. If you are interested in seriously exploring this area, contact a local chapter of the National Speleological Society. Otherwise, limit your exploration to those caves mentioned below, and use caution to protect both yourself and the fragile features of the area.

The following ABDSP Interpretive Panel is slated for placement in this canyon.

ARROYO TAPIADO MUD CAVES

The canyon you are about to enter is laced with caves and tunnels hollowed out by water in the wrinkled sediments. The badland sediments here are considered unstable and subject to collapse. Some of the caves wind into the hillsides for more than 1,000 feet in an environment much like the karst geography of the limestone country of Kentucky and Tennessee with its many caverns and tunnels. The soft crust of the mudhills is very fragile and will hold the tracks of humans and vehicles for years. For this reason please exercise special care when walking and picnicking in Arroyo Tapiado. Please consider those who will come after you to explore this fascinating canyon. All vehicles must remain on the dirt roadway and all foot traffic should be restricted to the canyon bottoms. Please leave the mudhills unscarred and consider camping outside of the canyon to help reduce our impact on this fragile setting.

3.1 Big Mud Cave, also known as Cave Canyon, is on the right, inviting exploration for about a quarter of a mile. Not really a cave, it is a canyon with mudstone arches and bridges. A 30-foot-high entrance makes it very visible from the road. Because of the number of caved-in "skylights," Cave Canyon can be explored without any lights.

Just to the right of Cave Canyon is the 20-foot-high, three-foot-wide slot opening of Plunge Pool Cave, also visible from the arroyo. Note the white ash layer at the entrance to this cave. This volcanic ash was laid down hot in shallow fresh water about 2.3 million years ago. This is a true cave and lights are necessary if you wish to explore. About 100 feet from the entrance is the Plunge Pool Room, which has a 50-foot-high dry waterfall that plunges down from a skylight entrance. A small side canyon, to the right of the entrance, can be followed for about 40 feet.

6.3 Cut Across Trail climbs right onto West Mesa and goes 2.3 miles southeast to Arroyo Seco del Diablo, offering a loop trip back down to Vallecito Creek.

End Side Trip

4.6 **Arroyo Tapiado (repeated from above).**

5.3 **Little Devil Wash (hike only).**

6.1 **Arroyo Seco del Diablo turnoff (Spanish for "Devil's Dry Wash").**

Side Trip up Arroyo Seco Del Diablo (4WD road)
0.0 Turnoff
1.0 Diablo Seep, marked by mesquite and bees. Water here is certain evidence of an earthquake fault. It also makes the name of the wash a misnomer.

2.5   High walls close in. These are red channel sandstones from the ancestral Colorado River and are sediments possibly transported from the Colorado Plateau/Grand Canyon area. Abundant arrow weed, mesquite, and smoke trees indicate a year-round near-surface water supply. The high walls decrease to low walls by mile 5 of this side trip.

5.7   Diablo Dropoff turnoff to Fish Creek. The following side trip can hook up with Trip 5C through Split Mountain for a through route to Ocotillo Wells.

Side Trip To Diablo Dropoff

0.0   An east (right) turn here climbs out of the arroyo onto Middle Mesa. At mile 1.0 a short trail leads right for an overview of Deguynos Canyon.

1.5   Diablo Drop-off at elev. 1078'. This route is absolutely for experienced off-roaders only. The first stage is in heavy sand. The second stage is the crux move and demands study and perhaps road work prior to the descent. Shift into compound low, stay headed straight down the slope, and do not brake until the bottom. Expect less than four wheels on the ground for a few incredibly long moments. A narrow, rough trail leads out to...

2.5   Fish Creek. Note large sandstone concretions weathering out from the reddish Diablo formation walls. A northeast (right) turn goes through Split Mountain out to pavement.

End of Side Trip

5.7   Diablo Dropoff turnoff to Fish Creek (repeated from above). Main route continues northwest up the wash.

5.8   Cut Across Trail climbs left onto West Mesa and goes 2.3 miles northwest to Arroyo Tapiado. This offers a loop trip back down to Vallecito Creek.

Tilted three-million-year-old sandstone layers, several miles northwest, mark an ancient delta where the ancestral Colorado River met a Pliocene sea. Concretions in myriad fantasy shapes are abundant here.

(Remember: collecting or disturbing natural features is illegal.)

End Of Side Trip

7.4   **Vallecito/Carrizo Creek junction.** There are three alternatives back to Hwy S-2 from here, each of which is about four miles long.

1.   Straight ahead (south) is Canyon Sin Nombre, leading through a superb smoke-tree forest and into high sandstone cliffs before climbing steeply to Hwy S-2 at post mile marker 52 near Carrizo Badlands Overlook.

2.   0.3 mile west is the Bow Willow/South Carrizo Creek junction. From there, northwest (right) leads up Bow Willow through thick vegetation, past the old ranger-station site and up the old county road to Hwy S-2 at post mile marker 46.

3.   West (left) leads up Carrizo Creek, through lush green mesquite thickets and past old homesteads marked by lines of tamarisk trees to Hwy S-2 at post mile marker 49 at the mouth of Sweeney Canyon.

The main route bears east (left) downstream toward Carrizo Cienega and enters heavy tamarisk thickets. Water, abundant underground, will soon appear on the surface. The wetter the season, the farther upstream water surfaces. In a wet spring, it is not unusual for Carrizo Creek to be running all the way from Carrizo Gorge, across Hwy S-2, and through here to the cienaga.

The thick growth of tamarisk (*Tamarix chinensis*-possibly *amosissima*) was not always here. This is an exotic, originally from the Mediterranean area, that was one of eight species of *Tamarix* brought to the western United States in the latter part of the 19th century as an ornamental, as a windbreak, or for erosion control. This particular species has become wild, and is now a weed found along rivers and riparian areas throughout the West. It is also called salt cedar because it has small, scaly, cedar-like leaves that exude salt carried up from the soil through the roots. Salt cedar can out-compete most native species for available water, creating tamarisk forests wherever surface water is found. It has an extensive root system that can tap a water table as well as surface roots that can soak up rainwater. It can also tolerate drought, fire, flooding, heat, and salinity. In a little over 100 years, it has invaded over one million acres of sensitive habitat in the West. Herbivores, such as bighorn sheep and deer, do not eat the plant and so will avoid water holes where visibility is limited. Its eradication from water sources and drainages within ABDSP has been a priority for resource ecologists, who hope to restore native plants to the area. The large tamarisk trees (*Tamarix aphylla*) found at Tamarisk Grove Campground and along the fields in Borrego Springs are another species and are not a problem. They provide shade and act as a windbreak.

10.1 Graves Cabin turnoff to right. A half mile down this road is an overlook of the very dense and large Carrizo Cienaga. The view here is very different from that seen by emigrants who came to California over 100 years ago. They would not have seen the salt-cedar thickets before you. Instead, they would have seen a marsh choked with tall reeds or tule with cattails and ringed with creosote, mesquite, and burro-weed.

Main route bears left over a rise to...

10.6 End of eastbound route at the beginning of the Carrizo Impact Area, a 27,000-acre no-man's land which has been closed to the public since 1942 except for a brief period. The military leased the land from the state for use as a bombing range beginning in 1942 and lasting through 1959. In 1959 the Navy sent in special teams to remove any dangerous explosives and then returned custody of the land to the state. The area was once again open to the public. Soon afterward, however, park visitors began finding live bombs and other ordnance, and in 1962 a man was injured in an explosion while trying to remove some scrap materials from the area. The range was then closed and has been so since then. Live bombs continue to be found in the area, and periodic clearing of live ordnance continues.

Turn south (right) 0.3 mile and park to commence exploration of the marsh area around the old Carrizo Stage Station site. The large square, four-room adobe station probably nestled up to the low ridge to the right (west). The

melting adobe walls below a Jasper water-hole marker on the ridge are pic-
tured in a 1935 photo in Parker's classic *Anza-Borrego Desert Guide Book*.

11.0 This station was an important stop for all travelers on the Southern
Emigrant Trail because it was the first station reached after crossing the
hardest and driest part of the Colorado Desert. It was also the first desert stop
where something green was visible, and abundantly so.

TRIP 6F:
Mortero Wash and Dos Cabezas

From: Highway S-2
To: Dos Cabezas Spring and Devils Canyon
Via: Mortero Wash (4WD roads)

Points Of Interest and Side Trips:
Dos Cabezas RR station, Indian Hill, Piedras Grandes, Mortero Palms, Syd
Hayden Spring, Devils Canyon.

MILES FROM:
Hwy S-2/
Mortero Wash

0.0   Hwy S-2/Mortero Wash turnoff.
The checkpoint is between post mile markers 55 and 56, about eight miles
northwest of Ocotillo and I-8. A dirt road north leads to North Mortero Wash
and then northwest one mile to the Dolomite Mine.
Drive southwest on 4WD road, immediately crossing Lava Flow Wash.
The road climbs gently over a spur of the Volcanic Hills and bears right into
main Mortero Wash at Mortero Canyon. The volcanic genesis of this land is
most apparent here where massive lava flows—andesite and red and black
basalt—and airborne ash solidified 18 million years ago. As you exit the
canyon, an old quarry is visible on the right side of the bowl to the right. A post
at mile 3.1 marks the departure from main Mortero Wash over the South
Mortero Canyon Crossover to arrive at...

3.9   Dos Cabezas Railroad Siding.
This is a fascinating stop for minutes or hours of exploring the historic
remnants of a site on the SD&AE Railroad. The ruins of the Dos Cabezas station, water tower, and loading ramp harbor the ghosts of the SD&AE which
hover over this lonely and forlorn scene. One can conjure the image of double-
headed steamers on the point of hundred-car freight trains, pounding up the
valley into the maw of Carrizo Gorge. After 12 years of heartbreaking setbacks
and near superhuman labor, the "golden spike" was driven marking the completion of the line on November 15, 1919. The first through-train rumbled
through Carrizo on November 30, 1919, but it was the returning train, on

December 1, which was the "official" grand opener. San Diego magnate John D. Spreckels' line traversed 147 miles of sparkling seacoast, snowbound mountains, treacherous canyons and blazing desert, even dipping into Mexico, to freight the great agricultural wealth of the Imperial Valley west to tidewater.

Although passenger service ended on January 11, 1951, the railroad continued as a vital freight artery until September 10, 1976. On that day tropical storm Kathleen slammed into the desert mountains to deal a near-final blow to dozens of trestles and bridges and nearly end the half-century contest between railroad men and mother nature. Although the line was reopened briefly in 1982, tunnel and trestle fires closed it in 1983. While new operators San Diego & Imperial Valley (SD&IV) Railroad dream yet of rebuilding, it would seem that nature's intent is clear. The line and the land have reverted to wilderness, where man afoot is only a visitor. Neither he nor his machines are to remain.

Ghostly whistles of long-gone locomotives echo in the Carrizo Gorge between crags and peaks which continue to carry the fanciful survey names of Grunt, Moan, Groan, Puff, and Windy. They still sing the saga of "the impossible line."

Dos Cabezos Station on the old SD&AE Railroad (looking north)

SD&AE Railroad tracks washed out by Hurricane Kathleen in 1976

Side Trip To Indian Hill (dirt road)

0.0   Dos Cabezas siding near the loading ramp.

Drive northwest (right) up the dirt road paralleling the railroad, past abandoned Dos Cabezas Mine on the right. Limestone used for roofing materials was quarried here.

Side Trip To Jojoba Wash (4WD road)

A 4WD turnoff at mile 0.5 leads northeast (right), takes a nasty drop into West Mortero Wash and climbs over into Jojoba Wash to reach pavement six miles from the railroad. This route would have been part of what Horace Parker called the Old Freight Road running from Dos Cabezas Spring to Sweeney Canyon at "the popout," post mile marker 50 on Hwy S-2. His associated references to nearby lost mines bear some resemblance to the Reedy Lost Gold report by Choral Pepper. (See Appendix 1.)

End Of Side Trip

Continue northwest along the railroad to ...

1.3   Indian Hill trailhead.

Indian Hill is about one mile west (left) across the railroad tracks. Hike up the obvious wash. The hill, one of several large rock outcrops in this upland valley, is in the northeast corner of section 29, UTM 5-77.6E 36-24.1N. It is misidentified on the topographic map.

The huge granite boulders of Indian Hill have tumbled together to form usable caves, which made the area attractive to Kumeyaay and earlier people. Numerous pictographs, smoke-blackened caves, pottery fragments, and unique ceremonial yonis attest to concentrated Native American use of this area. It has the distinction of being one of the oldest occupied areas in Anza-Borrego Desert State Park.

Indians sheltered here about five thousand years ago. They used darts but lacked the bows and arrows of later Indians. They also lacked pottery. This is a sensitive area because of the cultural resource.

Do not move or remove any Indian artifacts as its original location is important for future study. Do not touch any rock-art sites because contact will destroy the pigment.

Over the low rise on the northwest edge of the upland valley are the circa 1910 remains of the main construction camp for crews working the lower portion of the Carrizo Gorge route. An old jeep trail, just north of the Indian Hill marked on the topographic map, ran directly east to west and connected the RR camp with the road from Dos Cabezas.

Farther northwest, below the railroad bed and about 1.5 miles from Indian Hill, is an east fork of Carrizo Canyon with several palm tree groves. Jerry Schad describes a hike through this tributary and Choral Pepper places the Reedy Lost Gold nearby (see Appendix 1.)

Road ends at a wash at mile 2.2. A hike southwest from this point is an alternate approach to Indian Hill.

End of Side Trip

3.9 Dos Cabezas railroad siding and railroad crossover #1.

Dirt roads on both sides of the tracks lead southeast 1.6 miles to crossover #2. From here the Dos Cabezas Road strikes east (left), crossing the county line into BLM public lands and passing "The Big Bend" of the SD&IV (SD&AE), to reach Hwy S-2 about seven miles from the Dos Cabezas siding. This point on Hwy S-2 is about four miles west of Ocotillo.

The main route continues south from Dos Cabezas, away from the railroad.

4.9 Piedras Grandes turnoff.

Side Trip into Piedras Grandes

The dirt road climbs about two miles into the massive granitic boulders which are the namesake of the area. An excellent, wind-sheltered campsite is about one-quarter mile up, where deep bedrock morteros suggest that people have appreciated this site for many centuries.

A pleasant three-mile loop hike is possible up the road north and west from the campsite, over the ridge line and left down the valley to the main road and left again back up to the campsite.

The famous Dos Cabezas pictograph, a life-size replica of which hangs in the lobby of the visitor center, is from this area. A series of figures are depicted, but the figure on the left is of great interest. It depicts a man standing on horseback—the only known representation of a horse and rider in Kumeyaay rock art. Some archaeologists surmise that the drawing may record the first encounter with Spaniards, possibly Anza's first expedition in 1774.

End of Side Trip

Main route continues south (straight ahead). Road from the left at mile 5.2 is from Dos Cabezas Road at crossover #2 (see above). Continue south, crossing Palm Canyon Wash. Rocky outcrops to the east (right) harbored a line shack which was a sheep-tending outpost, built in 1920 by Robert D. McCain. These boulders today offer pleasant campsites.

6.0   Mortero Palms Turnoff.

This isolated and inspiring grove is about one-half mile up the valley. A steep trail leads to the palms, which are tucked away in a canyon rimmed with brown and white granite. Over one hundred palms stand closely grouped together. There is an intermittent small waterfall at the end of the grove. The bedrock mortar holes, which are the namesake of the canyon, are found about 300 feet down slope from the fronds.

Schad describes a hike from here to Goat Trestle, said to be the largest wooden trestle in the world.

6.1   Dos Cabezas Spring/Syd Hayden Spring Junction.

Dos Cabezas is 0.3 mile straight ahead. Dos Cabezas Spring is located in a cove surrounded by fractured and decomposed old granites of the Jacumba Mountains which are covered with desert varnish. From a distance two rock masses can be distinguished against the skyline above the spring—hence Dos Cabezas ("two heads"). This area has been known as Dos Cabezas since at least 1891, when the *San Diego Union* reported a silver rush to the area, which never panned out. Desert Willow is the predominant tree in this cove, while mesquite and sugar bush are also common. Cholla and ocotillo cover the desert floor.

The main route continues southeast (left) toward Syd Hayden Spring. At mile 7.0 the remains of a cabin are 0.3 mile south (right) in a cove in the hills.

7.7   Syd Hayden Spring is 0.7 mile south (right) up an arroyo in a mesquite thicket.

The route swings northeast from here to exit ABDSP at the county line.

8.7   Devils Canyon turnoff.

Side Trip Up Devils Canyon (4WD road)

The turnoff leads southeast (right) about a mile over a low ridge and into Devils Canyon (elev. 1350'). The canyon was the original route of the Mountain Springs cutoff, built by John G. Capron, from the Southern Emigrant Trail in the Yuha desert over the mountains west to Jacumba and San Diego. It was in use from 1865 until completion of the new (now abandoned) concrete Hwy 80 in 1913. See Pepper (Appendix 1) for a photo of surreys and buckboards, circa 1900, preparing for the hard climb from here to Mountain Springs. The old trail climbs 1,000 feet in 3.8 miles to Mountain Springs (BM 2292'), where California Historical Landmark No. 194 notes that "This spring is said to be the location used by the Army as a campsite in 1846. The area was later used as a stage station."

Hikers can follow the old route south up-canyon and under the high bridge carrying Interstate 8 traffic westbound. Remnants of cut and fill and rock-built roadbed can still be found. The last recorded vehicle transit was a mountain biker in 1995 who walked and carried his bicycle almost all of the way from the desert up the mountain over massive boulders and through entangling vegetation. It is not likely that Devils Canyon will ever see wheels again.

End of Side Trip

8.7   Devils Canyon turnoff (repeated from above).

The main route arcs northwest under the railroad and parallels the tracks to join Dos Cabezas Road at crossover #2 at mile 10.3. A northeast (left) turn will reach Hwy S-2 at about...

16.0   Junction of Dos Cabezas Road and Hwy S-2 (BM 673').

This point is about four miles west of Ocotillo.

Alternate Route Out from Devils Canyon (4WD route)

A sandy route proceeds northeast down Devils Canyon Wash to Sugarloaf Mountain (actually a hillock), where it turns north (left) to cross the RR tracks and join the Dos Cabezas Road near Hwy S-2. Beware of major sand traps on this alternate.

Buckhorn cholla

AREA 7-SOUTHEASTERN:
Interstate-8, Hwys S-80 and 98

T he southeastern section hugs the international border and is the most isolated and the least visited area in this book. The political boundary was
created as a result of the Treaty of Guadalupe-Hidalgo in February 1848.
It is a generally unmarked boundary and it cuts through topography that is the
same on both sides. Therefore one needs to carefully study the map. For the
Kumeyaay, it was an artificial boundary that suddenly divided their families
and groups one day in the last century. Brothers and sisters and uncles and
aunts to the north were suddenly "Americans," and mothers and fathers who
were visiting cousins to the south were "Mexicans." They were legally divided,
not only from each other, but also from their traditional gathering and ceremonial areas.

Because of the mountain barrier, the main wagon route to California did not
heavily impact this border area. The Southern Emigrant Trail and the
Butterfield Overland Mail stage basically followed a northwesterly course
from Calexico to Plaster City and on to Carrizo Creek. The early non-Indian
history of this area largely involves the establishment of a later wagon road
from Yuma directly to San Diego via Yuha Well, Coyote Wells, Devils Canyon
to Mountain Springs, and Jacumba.

TRIP 7A:
Jacumba to Seeley Via I-8

From: Jacumba (San Diego County)
To: Seeley (Imperial County)
Via: I-8 (paved)

Connecting Trips:

6A–Earthquake Valley to Ocotillo via Hwy S-2
7B–Ocotillo to Superstition Mountain via Hwy S-80
7C–Ocotillo to Yuha Basin via Hwy 98

Points of Interest and Side Trips:

Table Mountain, Smugglers Cave, Valley of the Moon, Jacumba Wilderness, Boulder Creek, Myer Valley.

Summary:

This is the southern gateway to the Anza-Borrego region. I-8 post miles commence at I-5 in San Diego and increase to the east to mile 77.77 at the county line. Imperial County post miles start at zero here and increase to the east. Odometer mileage is given starting at 0.0 at the Jacumba off-ramp, which is 57 miles east of El Cajon (Hwy 67).

POST MILES FROM:
San Diego

0.0   I-5/I-8 intersection in San Diego.

74.0   Jacumba/I-8 off-ramp (elev. 2800′).

The bright lights of these Shell and Texaco station/mini-marts are welcome late-night sights, being the only 24-hour stops near the freeway for about forty miles east or west.

Jacumba is Kumeyaay for "hut by the water." Its hot springs are additional evidence of geothermal activity along the Elsinore/Sierra Juarez fault zone, midway between the hot springs of Agua Caliente to the north (Trip 6A) and Guadalupe Canyon to the south.

Side Trip to Table Mountain (dirt road, seasonally 4WD)

Table Mountain is important for its cultural resources and biological diversity. It is designated by the BLM as an Area of Critical Environmental Concern (ACEC). There are over 200 prehistoric sites linked to the ancestors of today's Kumeyaay. Table Mountain was important as a home, a gathering area, and a ceremonial area, and also figures in certain creation myths. The mountain was and continues to be sacred to the Kumeyaay. Some Kumeyaay refer to it as *Mat Kwisyaay* (witch mountain). Shamans (*Kusevaays*) would watch the movement of the sun from the top and tell people when it was time for their annual activities.

Because Table Mountain is in a transition zone between desert and mountain, the diversity of plants and animals is noteworthy. A survey of resources conducted by BLM in the 1980s indicated that 42 different species of animals were observed in the area and an additional 179 species were considered potentially within the area. Noteworthy species include the Peninsular bighorn sheep, the golden eagle, and the mule deer. The vegetative community is complex and diverse, and includes some rare and/or endangered species such as Jacumba milkvetch, Mountain Springs bush lupine, San Jacinto beardtongue, and the Jacumba monkey flower.

There has been little development in the area because of the absence of surface water. Mining is the primary historical activity in the area. Sand and gravel, feldspar, and semi-precious gems were extracted from the area from the turn of the century to the 1940s.

0.0   74.0 Jacumba/I-8 off-ramp (repeated from above).

Drive southeast toward Jacumba about a mile to the old Hwy 80 junction, which is Old Hwy 80 post mile 36.5. Turn east (left). Common high-desert vegetation here is creosote, juniper, lycium, yucca, prickly pear, agave, and flat-top buckwheat. The area is nicely mapped for jeepers in *Smugglers Cave and Table Mountain* by Sidekick, although new ABDSP and BLM wilderness closures don't show on the Sidekick map. Almost any crossing of the ABDSP boundary in this area enters a designated wilderness where vehicles are prohibited—it's time for old shanks mare.

3.3   Pass under the powerline at Old Hwy 80 post mile 38.5.

Turn north (left) onto a dirt road, jog left and right under the freeway at mile 3.8, and drive north to the BLM interpretive marker at mile 4.1.

TABLE MOUNTAIN AREA

This is a transitional zone between low [desert] chaparral and mountain chaparral; creosote and cholla versus juniper and buckwheat. Prehistoric Kumeyaay were attracted by stone-tool manufacturing from local volcanic rocks. Early Indians collected abundant quantities of yucca, beavertail, jojoba, desert apricots, chia, and scrub oak acorns. Agave was the principal and favored food staple. Descendants of the Kumeyaay still consider Table Mountain sacred because of earlier religious and healing activities.

—Funds for this sign donated by Harriet Allen.

The old mining roads visible to the northwest (left), climbing up onto Table Mountain, are closed to vehicles now but offer excellent hikes with superb views from the 4000' summit. It is clear from here that Table Mountain consists of a thick volcanic flow overlying sandstones and conglomerates. This pattern correlates to several other sites in the southern Anza-Borrego region, including Volcanic Hills, Fossil Canyon, Carrizo Impact Area, and Cerro Colorado, just over the border from Skull Valley. That the Table Mountain flow is some 3000' higher than similar flows on the nearby desert floor is clear evidence of the Laguna escarpment uplift in the last few million years. These andesitic and basaltic flows are dated to some 18 million years ago, coincident with the earliest stages of the rifting of peninsular California from the Mexican mainland.

4.3   Mica Gem mill site on the right. Maps show this incorrectly as the actual mine, which is about a mile northeast (see below). Sheets, or "books", of muscovite mica, mostly in a matrix of quartz diorite, were the prize here. Such "isinglass" was used extensively in high-temperature applications requiring transparency such as ovens and lanterns.

Continue north past a locked right fork, which leads to the Marden deposit of coarse-grained feldspar. Bear left up a creekbed to a BLM ACEC sign at mile 5.1.

5.6 "3 Way Crossing" at UTM 5-82.0E 36-13.4N. This is a key junction.

The road east (right) goes a short distance into ABDSP to several abandoned mining prospects. The Little Randsburg mine is a few hundred feet southeast of the intersection. It produced about $2,000 worth of tungsten and some scheelite. The main site of the Mica Gem muscovite mine is about a one-quarter mile in, within a large pegmatite dike.

The jeep road north (straight ahead) becomes hike-only when it enters ABDSP. The trail drops down the historic Mountain Springs wagon road to a dead-end at I-8 after a couple of miles at some stone ruins.

The road northwest (left) works up onto the ridge in section 26, past two microwave towers (go right around the second tower) and arcs left, west, descending into the beautiful and remote high-desert valley between Jacumba Peak to the north and Table Mountain to the south. Points of interest along this ridge road include: a BLM wildlife guzzler at mile 6.2 on the right; a short right fork at mile 6.8 into ABDSP and the "Atomic Flat" uranium prospect reported in 1957.

7.9 "Valley Fork" at 3350' (UTM 5-79.6E 36-14.7N) is on the boundary of sections 22 and 27. This is the center of the valley, with abundant exploration and camping opportunities. Options here are:

1. The northwest (right) fork goes about a mile into section 21, where mining prospects, wildlife guzzlers, and secluded camp sites are featured. An ornate stone cabin with a corrugated iron roof is just north of the center of section 21, between a creek and the road. The sense of the place is that of the well-known Yaquitepec on Anza-Borrego's Ghost Mountain. It was probably a mining camp for the Circle Group deposit of vermiculite, a soil additive. The tunnels and trenches of this deposit can be seen to the north. Vermiculite is a shiny, green, fibrous mineral, which occurs here in inclusions of dark gabbro in light-colored quartz diorite. Related minerals include pyroxene, amphibole, chlorite, chrysotile, and biotite (the usual suspects in basic dark-colored granitic rocks). Old mineral maps show the area as an asbestos mine. 4WD roads fan out to other prospects north and west. A hiking trail turns south to complete the loop with the southwest road fork described below.

2. The southwest (left) fork from Valley Fork goes past another BLM ACEC sign about a half mile to a nice campsite, nestled in giant boulders, along the creek. The prospect on a hillock just north of the campsite is the Overlook deposit, a pegmatite vein with very large feldspar and quartz crystals. Mountain bikers can proceed a couple of miles east (left) up the creekbed and up a very steep hill to the second microwave tower noted above.

The 4WD road continues in the creekbed west down the valley. The closed jeep road at mile 8.7 is now a hiking route which goes southeast (left) about three miles over the saddle between Table Mountain (left) and

Gray Mountain (right) to the Mica Gem mine mill. This offers an obvious shuttle opportunity for hikers to walk out and be picked up at Mica Gem. The hiking trail branching right at mile 9.0 goes about a mile north to the vermiculite mining area noted above. About halfway on this hiking trail, in the SW quarter of Section 21, walk west on the ridge to explore the old trenches of the White Cloud deposit, a tungsten prospect of tactite (skarn) in quartz diorite with garnet crystals.

The southwest fork continues west about three miles into ABDSP. It is hike-only from the park boundary but the reward is a magnificent overlook at the Carrizo Canyon tungsten deposit, which was a 25-foot mine tunnel near the SD&IV (SD&AE) railroad.
End of Side Trip

When returning from Table Mountain to I-8 an alternate easy exit is to turn east (left) on a dirt road after crossing under the freeway and going a half mile to old Hwy 80 and another mile east on pavement to the In-Ko-Pah on-ramps, east or west. This dirt road/old Hwy 80 junction is at the brake-inspection area noted below.

74.0 Jacumba/I-8 off-ramp (elev. 2800', repeated from above).
Drive east on I-8, climbing slowly, and cross into BLM's California Desert Conservation Area. A truck brake-inspection area (telephone and interpretive sign) is marked by a 9-mile, 6%-downgrade sign. There being no alternative, bicyclists can ride the shoulder of I-8 from here down to the desert. Caution— this is a fast, steep descent, often buffeted by high, gusty winds and sometimes high, gutsy drivers.

Post mile 77.0 (BM 3201') is Mountain Springs Pass, dividing the Carrizo drainage to the north and the Coyote Wash drainage to the east.

77.6 In-Ko-Pah Park Road (elev. BM 3098').
The name for this now-closed county park is Kumeyaay for "place of mountain people." The Desert Tower, a 1922 structure built by Bert Vaughn of Jacumba, is northeast (right) on old Hwy 80 about one mile into Boulder Park. Both the view and the hospitality are excellent.

An alternate entrance to the Table Mountain area from this off-ramp goes west about a mile on Old Hwy 80 to the brake-inspection area, then bears right onto a dirt road, paralleling the freeway for another half mile to bridge #57-603 underneath I-8 (see above).

Side Trip into Smugglers Cave and Valley of the Moon (4WD road/hike)
Smugglers Cave is a tumble-jumble of granitic boulders which has attracted and protected licit and illicit travelers since prehistoric times. The cave is almost 30 feet deep and is a perfect shelter. A January 1940 article in *Desert Magazine* recounts some of the more interesting occupants through the years. The earliest incident involved one of the bandits who robbed Silas and Lumen Gaskill's Campo store in 1875. It is believed that the posse tracked the wounded robber to the cave and shot him there. About 1900, Chinese opium smugglers were reported to be using the cave

until border patrolmen set up regular mounted patrols of the area. A border raider named Turso de la Toba also used the cave in 1911. After he was apprehended in Jacumba, lawmen followed his tracks back to the cave, where they found "considerable loot, saddles and bridles, sacks of beans, and a few horses."

0.0 In-Ko-Pah Park Road.

Jog slightly southwest (right) and pick up the dirt road (BLM Rt Y2219), which crosses the county line and runs clearly east (left) up the ridge. This road services a microwave tower, so it is fairly well maintained until...

1.5 Saddle (elev. 3850').

This is the jumping-off place into the Elliot Mine area as well as the Jacumba

In the Valley of the Moon

Wilderness which contains Smugglers Cave and the Valley of the Moon. Hikers can go northeast; vehicles must go southwest.

Hikers can descend the northeast (left) fork about a half-mile down to Smugglers Cave. The hiking trail turns right and goes southeast over two low ridges 0.3 mile to "Riders' Cabin Wash" and another one-quarter mile beyond to rejoin the southwest fork (below). Riders' Cabin and outlying structures can be explored just a few yards east of the trail down Riders' Cabin Wash in the west-center of section 5 at UTM 5-85.5E 36-10.6N, midway between peaks "Quirk" (BM 4031') and "Gold" (3866'). Rick Russell (Sidekick) reports this as an 1880s outpost for U.S. marshals patrolling the U.S. borderlands.

The southwest (right) fork goes along the ridge. Just a few hundred yards beyond the saddle noted at mile 1.5 above (elev. 3850') is another fork. Climbing straight ahead leads to the microwave tower, a mining prospect, and an alternate descent west to old Hwy 80 after several miles. The southeast (left) fork is 4WD only and drops around the south side of peak "Quirk" into the valley which is the...

2.8 South fork of Boulder Creek. Enticing destinations for hikers, riders, and backpackers just ahead include the Elliott Mine, Valley of the Moon (headwaters of Pinto Canyon), and the Jacumba Wilderness. It just doesn't get any better than this for training and practice in orienteering, map and compass work, and GPS because of the abundance of named checkpoints, known in Baja Spanish as "picachos," in all directions: Quirk, Gold, Tahe, Blue Angels Peak, Whip, and Nopal.

See Schad or Foster (Appendix 1) for details of the area.
End Of Side Trip

77.6 In-Ko-Pah Park Road (elev. BM 3098', repeated from above).

77.77/0.0   County line. Post miles start over at zero. I-8 crosses Boulder Creek, curves left and descends rapidly. The county line is crossed several times in two miles here.

POST MILES FROM:
San Diego/Imperial County Line

3.0   Mountain Springs offramps, eastbound and westbound (elev. 2292').

The old McDonald service station and general store closed in the 1930s. A cluster of palms, which mark a historic spring site and CHL No.194, can be seen to the southwest, above and beyond the old buildings, on the slope below I-8. This is all private property now—no trespassing.

Westbound travelers on I-8 can pull off at the radiator water barrel at the large curve to the south at post mile 2.3 and visit the site of Mountain Palm Springs toll station and spring on the west side of I-8. Ruins of building foundations and rock corrals mark the site, which serviced teams working the rugged grade up from Devils Canyon to Jacumba from 1865 to 1913. This was also a station on the U.S. Military Telegraph Line. Hikers can climb the old road from the site about three miles west and south into ABDSP for a pickup at "3-Way Crossing" (see Table Mountain side trip above.)

Side Trip into Boulder Canyon

0.0   Take Mountain Springs offramp. Turn toward the center area between the eastbound and westbound lanes of the freeway. Go east on a dirt road to the narrow concrete trace of the earliest Hwy 80, which bypassed treacherous Devils Canyon. (See Trip 6F for a description of a hiking route through Devils Canyon from the desert floor to this point.)

Since California statehood in 1850, there have been four incarnations of roads up the challenging Mountain Springs grade: Devils Canyon; concrete Hwy 80, up In-Ko-Pah Gorge, which was completed in April 1913; two-lane, asphalt "Old" Hwy 80, which was completed in the 1930s and is still used throughout much of San Diego and Imperial counties; and I-8 which was completed here in 1964.

Drive under powerlines to...

1.4   Access to Boulder Creek (elev. BM 1922'). Clamber down-slope and work left to Myer Creek and its tunnel under the freeway. Pass through the tunnel and hike west upstream a few hundred yards, past a huge granitic slab on the left, to a wash on the left leading into a natural amphitheater. On the southwest edge of this bowl is a stone and corrugated-iron cabin, called by some the "Recluse Cabin," at UTM 5-86.0E 36-

15.2N, said to have been built by a sheepherder from Holtville in the late 1940s or early 1950s. Morteros and abundant vegetation upstream, a hundred yards southeast of here, suggest that this site has been useful to people for a very long time. Boulder Creek is a desert transition area that includes desert transitional chaparral (desert apricot, nolina, and scrub oak); pinyon-juniper (both one-leaf pinyon and four-leaf pinyon, juniper, and scrub oak); and creosote bush scrub (creosote and burroweed). About 50 palms are found along the creek.

Schad (see Appendix 1) describes a clockwise loop hike from this point east and south through Myer Valley that returns down Boulder Creek to the Myer Creek junction.

The more common route, used by BLM naturalist hikes and SDNHM outings, goes a tenth of a mile west to the Myer Creek/Boulder Creek junction and then south up Boulder Creek into BLM's Jacumba Wilderness.

A variety of long-day hike or backpack options present themselves, including southwest up to Valley of the Moon, south to Recluse Springs, and southeast into Myer Valley. Details of this little known corner of BLM wilderness paradise are available from BLM or hardy veterans of the San Diego Chapter of the Sierra Club.

The seasonal stream, natural palm groves, abundant Native American sites, and superb desert/mountain transitional vegetation make this area most attractive, although little known and visited. Spring and early-summer wildflower displays are almost guaranteed in Boulder Creek.

End Of Side Trip

3.0 Mountain Springs (repeated from above).

Continue east down the interstate, past the runaway truck offramp at elev. 2000', and over the Myer Creek tunnel referenced above in the Boulder Creek side trip, descending In-Ko-Pah Gorge.

At mile 9.0, a trail, lined with white rocks, leads up the hill to the south (right) opposite the site of the original Miller's Garage to "Iron Springs," where Miller's gullible customers would hike while awaiting repairs. Over the ridge they found a pair of bed springs, conveniently out of sight of the unsuspecting hikers! This was also the site of Shepard's Bridge, which marked the beginning of the In-Ko-Pah Gorge grade on the 1913 road. At this site Myer Creek, raging from fierce late-summer-hurricane rains, has ravaged I-8 and the railroad more than once in the recent past. Repeat performances are unpredictable but inevitable.

The "Hwy 98/Calexico" offramp is mile 0.0 for Trip 7D, "Yuha Desert," below. New Miller's Garage (abandoned) is at mile 10.6. For many years Miller's was the last chance/first chance outpost for vehicles laboring on the rugged Mountain Springs grade.

The "Ocotillo/Imperial Hwy/Desert Parks" sign announces...

11.9 Ocotillo (elev. 400') at the bridge over Imperial Highway/S-2.

The new Imperial Valley College Museum (IVCM) is rising out of the desert just southwest of the I-8/S-2 intersection. The focus of IVCM will be the rich archaeological and cultural heritage of the Yuha Desert region.

I-8 continues east, bridging the railroad at the old Coyote Wells station and water tower (post mile 13.9) and the South Fork of Coyote Wash at post mile 14.5, to climb onto the Yuha Rim. Coyote Wells was once a stop on the San Diego road between Yuha Well and Mountain Springs via Devils Canyon.

23.5 Dunaway Road (elev. 40').

A slow descent to Dunaway Road provides alternate direct access to Plaster City and Trip 7B (Superstition Mountain) north and Trip 7C (Yuha Buttes and Basin) to the southwest. The open space on the south side of the Dunaway offramp is called the Dunaway Staging Area. It is about 4 miles southwest to the Yuha Buttes and Shell Beds area via BLM Rt Y1950.

Dunaway's interpretive significance derives from its location between the 40' and sea-level contours. Prehistoric Lake Cahuilla's approximate high-stand waterline was at 40', as is the elevation of the Colorado River delta dam south of Mexicali (elev. 0). Only this natural dam prevents the Gulf of California from inundating the below-sea-level Imperial and Coachella valleys. Remnant "tombolos" (near-shore sand spits and bars) are scattered across the desert here, bearing witness to the earlier shoreline environment. After crossing the sea-level contour just east of Dunaway, one enters the largest below-sea-level basin (over 2,000 square miles) in the Western Hemisphere. But for a couple of missing feet at the bottom of the Salton Sea, it would be also the deepest basin, being exceeded only by the narrow rift of Death Valley at Badwater (-282'). (The -1,200' Dead Sea rift basin takes the global crown for land below-sea-level.)

29.9 Seeley (elev. -40') at Drew Road (Hwy S-29).

(This town is off the east edge of the backpocket map but is readily identifiable from the text following and signage.)

Developed camping is available here on either side of the highway at Rio Bend RV Resort or Sunbeam Lake County Park.

This off-ramp also provides alternate access to Wheeler Road into Superstition Mountain. Go a mile north on Drew Road, and another mile west on Hwy S-80 to Huff Road. Turn north (right) on Huff Road and pick up Trip 7A.

The New River channel through this area was gouged out during the 1904-1907 floods, which formed the Salton Sea and swallowed up the nearby town of Silsbee (see Pepper's *Desert Lore* in Appendix 1).

A most fitting story for this area, in these years of California's Gold Rush Sesquicentennial, is that of "The Miracle of New River." Since the story is also a reminder of proper preparation for safe desert travel, so much the better.

The true tale begins hundreds of miles to the north at 7:30 a.m. on Monday, January 26, 1848, when one James Marshall recounts:

*I then collected four or five pieces and went up to Mr. Scott. "What is it?"
inquired Scott. "Gold," I answered. "Oh! no," returned Scott, "that can't be." I
replied positively,—"I know it to be nothing else." Mr. Scott was the second person who saw the gold.*

The rest is history, major history, the launching of one of the largest
human migrations in history. In any case, within one and a half years, thousands of thirst-crazed emigrants and dying animals were far beyond the point
of no return when crossing the inferno of the Colorado Desert in the heat of
summer. This waterless stretch had very nearly doomed the armies of Kearny
and Cooke over a year earlier in the winter. How much more likely was this
outcome for the inexperienced Argonauts of the summer of '49?

Enter the miracle—the crest from a major snow melt in the Rockies that
spring of 1849 caused the Colorado to overflow its banks in late June south of
Yuma, and the New River was born (or born again) to run fresh and free for
several years until the emigrant tide waned, as did the New River itself.
Journalist William H. Chamberlin, starting from moon rise at 2:00 a.m. on
Tuesday, August 14, 1849, offers this:

*Our canteens now contain our entire stock of water. This place is a perfect
Golgotha—the bones of thousands of animals lie strewed about in every direction;
and a great number of horses and mules that have died lately, pollute the atmosphere. Deserted wagons, harness, saddles, etc., add to this destructive and sick-
ening scene.*

*By 11 a.m. our water was entirely gone. Our joy can scarcely be imagined when,
after traveling a short distance, we came upon a stream of water. We have since
learned that it was "New River," a stream that miraculously opened up in this
desert waste during this summer.*

*But for this God-send, hundreds of emigrants must have perished, many of
whom, like ourselves, were very poorly supplied with suitable water vessels.*

On Monday, August 20, 1849, Major W.H. Emory, of the U.S. Topograph-
ical Engineers, reports:

*The first parties that came in by the Gila route arrived in San Diego about the
20th June. Amongst them were many intelligent persons who passed over the
route of the Army of the West 1846 and who saw no river in the desert and suffered dreadfully with thirst. The parties that came in the fourth of July first stated this remarkable circumstance; and of encountering a river where none before
existed.*

Finally Lt. Cave Couts, working for the Mexico/U.S. Boundary Commission, reports on Sunday, September 23, 1849:

*I was much astonished about dusk to find myself here on the prettiest grazing I
ever saw. All this with the river, have sprung up since we passed last fall, though
the river is probably as old as the desert...as though it had been the same since the
days of Noah.*

That the unprecedented rains last winter and spring can have increased it, is very probable. This particular place of the river, favored with such luxuriant grass can only be the work of an invisible hand to aid the thousands of distressed emigrants. I have called it Camp Salvation.

TRIP 7B:
Ocotillo to Superstition Mountain via Hwy S-80

From: Ocotillo (Imperial County)
To: Superstition Mountain
Via: Hwy S-80 and 4WD roads

Connecting Trips:
6A–Earthquake Valley to Ocotillo via Hwy S-2
7A–Jacumba to Seeley via I-8
7C–Ocotillo to Yuha Basin via Hwy 98

Points Of Interest and Side Trips:
East Coyote Mountains, Painted Gorge, Plaster City, West Mesa.

Summary:
From Plaster City there are two routes into Superstition Mountain. The easier-to-follow but longer route goes into Seeley and then north and west via Huff and Wheeler roads. The other route (BLM Rt SF404) departs from Hwy S-80 just east of Plaster City and goes north via West Mesa. They meet at the Superstition Mountain staging area near Rock House (site).

(The backpocket map ends before Seeley and Huff Road but these are readily identifiable from the following text and en route signage.)

MILES FROM:
Ocotillo

0.0   Ocotillo (elev. 395').
Junction of Hwys S-2 and S-80 just north of the I-8 off ramps. Drive east on Hwy S-80 (Evan Hewes Hwy) past the abandoned Coyote Wells service station and restaurant.

The bridge at mile 3.5 was washed out by Hurricane Kathleen in 1976 and not restored for more than a year. Just south of here, the railroad tracks were suspended in mid-air where the Coyote Wash trestle was washed out. Just north of this bridge is the confluence of Palm Canyon Wash, which drains the huge Devils Canyon/Dos Cabezas/Mortero Canyon watershed, and Coyote Wash, which drains the In-ko-Pah Gorge/Myer Valley/Davies Valley watershed. Hurricane floods from these watersheds in the late summers of both 1976 and 1977 severed Interstate 8 in several places, the SD&AE Railroad in many places, and all secondary highways connecting southwest Imperial County and San Diego County.

4.2 Painted Gorge turnoff from Hwy S-80.

Side Trip Into Painted Gorge (dirt road becoming 4WD road)

0.0   Turnoff north on S-80, 4.8 miles west of Plaster City. Bear right and then left, descending to cross multiple channels of Coyote Wash on a northwesterly course. Pass right of rock and gravel quarries and under transmission lines at mile 2.5. (The jeep trail along the powerlines leads four miles west to join the Fossil Canyon road noted in Trip 6A.)

The multi-hued palette of the Painted Gorge area now starts to manifest itself with yellow mudhills of the marine Imperial Formation mixed in with rich reds, greens, and steely blues of the Alverson volcanics and granitics stained with iron, copper, and sulfur oxides. The road tops a saddle and drops into...

5.3   Painted Gorge bowl (525') UTM 5-96.3E 36-31.0N

Much of this area is now designated wilderness, vehicles not permitted. Older maps still show now-closed routes as open. Be attentive to BLM signs.

Side Trip Down Northeast Fork (4WD road)

The northeast (right, jeep trail) fork goes down the canyon and east across broken country to intersect the Butterfield Overland Mail Stage route after five miles. It is another six miles southeast from this intersection to Plaster City.

Just after you turn right onto this northeast fork, an old mining trail climbs north (left) out of the gorge leading a couple of miles to tilted coquina beds in Section 31 for sweeping views to the north across the Carrizo Impact Area. Minor mud caves, the only ones known in marine material in this region, are to be found in these coquina beds.

Painted Gorge

A mile and a half after you turn right onto the northeast fork, a rough 4WD route. It goes about six miles north from UTM 5-97.6E 36-32.2N to intersect Carrizo Wash at UTM 5-97.0E 36-30.0N with access out to Split Mountain Road via the U.S. Gypsum Railroad (see Trip 5B). This route, which runs along the east boundary of the Carrizo Impact Area, can be very confusing. Use detailed BLM or USGS maps carefully. This and other military impact areas in the desert contain live ordnance left over from World War 2 and the Korean War.

End Of Side Trip

5.3   Painted Gorge bowl (525′, repeated from above).

The west fork (left, dirt road) leads into Painted Gorge. Watch for wilderness boundary signs.

6.4   Old Mining Trail turnoff.

Hike up Old Mining Trail

This old mining trail (hike-only) climbs steeply up the bank to the north (right) from the southeast quarter of the northeast quarter of Section 1, UTM 5-94.8E 36-30.3N. The trail hugs the brink of the canyon and goes to a silica prospect just past hill 1002′. The trail continues on about a mile to another prospect in the east center of Section 36, southeast of peak 993′. From here it arcs to the northeast to join the complex of old jeep routes at the coquina beds in Section 31 described above. This makes an excellent round-trip hike of about three miles on eroded old jeep trails.

End of Hike

7.1   Fork (700′). The left fork stays in the canyon and dead-ends after one-half mile in fossiliferous marine sandstone units worthy of exploration. The right fork lurches steeply up a hill and goes over a very uncomfortable pitch that angles down sideways to a 100-foot vertical drop. *Yecch.* This Jeep Wrangler says park and hike from here into the complex of old mining trails in the Coyote Mountains Wilderness. It is about two miles northwest to the summit of Carrizo Mountain (BM 2408′), highest in the Coyote Mountains. An 1800′ peak, circled by an old jeep road, is an obvious landmark en route. The route is intuitive—when it forks, go up.

Some years ago, a motorcyclist reported to the author that the biker had ridden west from the 1800′ peak into Fossil Canyon. While it is certainly illegal now, the route looks very plausible for an interesting hike-shuttle pickup in Fossil Canyon. An old jeep road runs southwest almost to the east edge of Section 3, from where an easy traverse can be made to the saddle in the middle of Section 3. This saddle is described above in the Fossil Canyon side trip in Trip 6A.

Similar old mining roads in the Coyotes are described by George Leetch in the 3rd edition of Horace Parker's classic guide to Anza-Borrego.

End Of Side Trip

4.2   Painted Gorge turnoff from Hwy S-80 (repeated from above).

Drive east on Hwy S-80. A BLM monument marks the entrance to the West Pit portion of Plaster City Open Area, which, combined with the East Pit portion, offers 41,000 acres of OHV playground between Hwy S-80 and the Naval Reservation to the north. Carefully observe boundary markers within the Open Area.

9.1   Plaster City (elev. 100').

There are no facilities for the traveler, only the nation's largest plant fabricating wallboard from gypsum. The school and residences here were closed many years ago.

The narrow-gauge U.S. Gypsum Mining Railroad interchanges with the standard gauge SD&IV railroad here. The dirt road paralleling the narrow gauge railroad can be followed from the east side of the plant about 25 miles north and west to the Split Mountain area (see Trip 5B). Respect the warning signs when traveling through the Naval Reservation.

10.1   East Pit turnoff (elev. 42').

A route runs due north from here, through the Plaster City Open Area and, via BLM Rt SF404 between live bombing targets 101 and 103, about nine miles to the Superstition Mountain staging area southwest of the Rock House (site).

The recommended route continues east on Hwy S-80, descending below sea level at Dunaway Road two miles east. Cross over the West Side Main Canal and Dixieland (Wind n' Sand Cafe) at mile 14.0, past Westmorland Road to...

16.6   Huff Road, a couple of miles west of the New River, Seeley, and Drew Road. Turn north (left) toward Superstition Mountain.

22.9   Wheeler/Huff Road intersection.

This is past Worthington Road and just over the Filaree branch of the West Side Main Canal.

Three miles north of here, in the curve where Huff turns east to become Imler Road, is the visible trace of the 1967 M6.5 Superstition Hills earthquake. Upthrust "flatirons" and ground rupture can be seen on both sides of Imler just west of the road into the Navy facility.

Reset Odometer to Zero.

0.0   Wheeler/Huff Road intersection.

This dirt road will downgrade to 4WD road after several miles. Drive west on the dirt road, between the low hills to the north and the green fields to the south, past the Imperial Valley Rifle and Pistol Association (IVRPA) firing range and into the Superstition Mountain OHV area at mile 1.6.

2.2   Cross west under the transmission line with BLM Rt SF272 paralleling it to the northwest. BLM Rt391 goes due north from here, then arcs to the northwest to the former Rock House (site) after about four miles (see above). Wheeler Road turns northwest along the shore of ...

3.0   Mesquite Dry Lake (elev. 39'), also called "Ancient Dry Lake."

In March 1993 this lake was full, covering almost two square miles. A low natural sand dam at elev. 42', expanded with an artificial dirt dike, runs along the southeast side with an outlet to the south into the Coyote Wash system. When prehistoric Lake Cahuilla was at its high point during the time of the Crusades, little Mesquite Lake would have been an estuary tucked behind Superstition Mountain. In that lusher, more moist age, it can very well have been a seasonal home to desert dwellers. In any case, Mesquite Lake, with its little sand dam (elev. 42'), is a miniature version of Lake Cahuilla, which had (and has) its own giant alluvial dam (elev. 42') south of Mexicali.

6.8   Wheeler Road junction (elev. 103') at section corner 22/23/26/27,

UTM 6-11.0E 36-43.8N. This unmarked but important point is the staging area for exploring the Superstition Mountain OHV Open Area. The Open Area is focused around "The Sand Dam" to the northwest and "The Rock House (site)" to the southeast. Mixed and changing management boundaries between BLM and Navy land can be confusing in this area. Check with BLM in El Centro for latest information (see Appendix 2).

Drive northeast across Section 23, climbing toward the saddle.

8.0   "The Rock House (site)."

This is the heart of the southwest Superstition Mountain OHV Area. The Rock House, removed in 1995, is said to have been a facility for convicts working the rock quarry about one-quarter mile northwest.

BLM Rt SF274 departs northwest from here, providing access to the northwest part of the Superstition Mountain OHV Area and "The Sand Dam" area about three miles away.

Continue east over the saddle a couple of miles to BLM Rt SF391, which delineates the northeast boundary of the Superstition OHV Open Area and the live bombing area on the Naval Reservation. Turn northwest (left) toward the "Sand Dam" area or southeast (right), working back to Wheeler Road. Continue east on Wheeler to Huff Road. The Wheeler/Huff road intersection is about six miles southeast of the Rock House area via this route.

Superstition Mountain is an isolated, fault-bounded granitic mountain block, seven miles long and two miles wide, trending northwest/southeast. As such, it mimics in miniature its much larger cousins in the mountain blocks of southern California such as the Coyote Mountains, the Peninsular Ranges, and the Chocolate Mountains. The Federal Writers Project (1939) notes that "the Indians say it is inhabited by evil spirits whose voices used to make weird rumblings." Choral Pepper in *Desert Lore* presents the notion of Superstition Mountain as a strong contender for "Aztlan", the legendary home of the Aztecs.

TRIP 7C:
Ocotillo to Yuha Basin via Hwy 98

From: Ocotillo
To: Yuha Basin
Via: Hwy 98 (paved with dirt-road and 4WD side trips)

Connecting Trips:
 6A–Earthquake Valley to Ocotillo via Hwy S-2
 7A–Jacumba to Seeley via I-8
 7B–Ocotillo to Superstition Mountain via Hwy S-80

Points Of Interest and Side Trips:
Davies Valley, Yuha Well, Yuha Buttes, Shell Beds, Geoglyphs, Crucifixion Thorn, Skull Valley.

Summary:
Hwy 98 (post mile 0.0) "The Yuha Cutoff" begins just west of Ocotillo on I-8. Hwy 98 can also be reached from the Ocotillo turnoff via The Imperial Highway, south of Desert Kitchen restaurant. Post mileage is utilized below for the paved highway. Odometer mileage is used off-road.

 Four gateways, or entry points, help to define the complex 4WD road system in the 41,000-acre Yuha Desert Management Unit: Clark Lane/Coyote Wells, Anza Trail (Loop) Road, Pinto Wash, and Dunaway Road/I-8 (Dunaway Staging Area). The first three of these are described as side trips off Hwy 98 eastbound. The Dunaway entry point was described in Trip 7A, 12 miles east of Ocotillo on I-8 at post mile 23.5.

 The BLM route-numbering system is utilized as presented in BLM's Desert Access Guide (DAG) map series. While there is talk of changing this system, it will probably remain in the field for some years to come. If it's updated, likewise will this book be.

POST MILES FROM:
Hwy 98/I-8

0.0   Hwy 98/I-8 offramp, 1.7 miles west of Ocotillo (elev. 680').

 A dirt road at mile 0.5 leads southwest (right), about a mile up Coyote Wash to the boundary of the Jacumba Wilderness. From here a hiking route leads about two miles south to a saddle (elev. 1220') UTM 5-91.2E 36-17.6N southwest of peak 1297'. Descend a half mile southeast into section 13 to join the northern Davies Valley hike below.

1.5   Hwy 98/Imperial Highway (S-2) junction.

 I-8 is 0.7 mile north (left), over the railroad tracks, past Desert Kitchen/ Fuel Stop.

3.0   Clark Lane (elev. 345').

Side Trip Into Davies Valley (dirt road, hiking route)

0.0   Drive southwest (right) on Clark Lane (BLM Rt Y235) to the boundary of the Jacumba Wilderness. A fork at mile 1.6 (elev. 585') provides hiking routes west and south, into northern Davies Valley and southern Davies Valley respectively. Soloing is not recommended as the southern end of the valley leads directly into Mexico and has been an area of illicit activity.

The south (left) fork enters Davies Canyon and forks again after another mile at elev. 690'. The southwest (right) fork here pitches steeply up Davies Canyon and reaches the northern valley at about mile 4.0 (elev. 1000'). The southeast (left) fork follows an old mining trail, past numerous prospects, and works south and west to reach central Davies Valley after several rugged miles.

The west (right) fork was the main 4WD route into Davies Valley. It works around the north end of a volcanic buttress and goes southwest up an alluvial fan and through an andesitic canyon where the White Hope limestone deposit was being worked.

4.5   Northern Davies Valley.

This southeast-trending valley has been described as one of the giant "stair-step valleys" which walk down the east escarpment of the Laguna Mountains along the I-8 corridor. BLM literature uses this term to describe these valleys, in order from west to east and higher to lower, which are McCain, Moon, Myer, Davies, and Skull. Elevations range from over 4000' at the top to 830' in the depression of Skull Valley to the east. Such stair-stepping fits well with the relatively new detachment faulting theory, now widely accepted to account for the structure and dynamics of the Laguna escarpment.

About three miles southeast is peak "Kirk" (elev. 1425'), a Miocene-age volcanic remnant correlated with the Alverson andesite encountered so frequently in the southern Anza-Borrego/Jacumba region.

9.0   Pinto Canyon.

Pinto Canyon enters southern Davies Valley from the west just north of the international border. Pinto Canyon rises in the Valley of the Moon, many miles north and west (see Trip 7A). Rock art, a seasonal stream, and palm groves just west of Davies Valley are the attractions here. Details of the groves are described by Palm Springs Museum Curator Jim Cornett in Foster (see Appendix 1).

End Of Side Trip

3.0   Clark Lane (repeated from above).

Continue southeast on Hwy 98 through the community of "No Mirage."

Side Trip To Coyote Wells (dirt road)

Molitar Road at mile 3.5 goes about a mile north to the original Coyote Wells (BM 267'), a railroad siding with a water tower that serviced steam engines. The dry lake to the east of the site served as a Navy emergency landing field in World War 2.

BLM Rt Y1852 (dirt road) starts from Coyote Wells and goes east, generally paralleling the freeway and climbing onto the Yuha Rim to reach the Dunaway Staging Area about 11 miles to the east. Several 4WD routes branch off south from Y1852 en route to provide access into the Yuha Basin.

End of Side Trip

Continue southeast on Hwy 98 from the Molitar Rd turnoff. At mile 5.8 BLM Rt Y2311 turns off north (left) down South Fork Coyote Wash. At mile 7.0 Hwy 98 goes past a ranch and hummock on the north (left) over a slight rise to...

7.4   Anza Trail Road (west entrance, elev. 375') UTM 6-01.8E 36-16.6N.

This road, aka Hocker Drive, is the primary and most popular gateway into the Yuha area. The Yuha Rim describes a rough horseshoe around the Yuha Basin with the opening of the horseshoe to the northeast. Yuha Well is in the basin to the northeast with Yuha Buttes and Shell Beds beyond. The Dunaway Staging Area, at Dunaway Road on I-8, is beyond the Buttes.

The following two side trips start from Anza Trail Road (west) and go opposite directions around the Yuha Rim with both trips coming together at a point we call "Yuha Buttes Overlook." There are two basic choices at the Yuha Buttes: one, complete a loop by returning southwest to the start point; two, exit the Yuha Basin to the northeast via Dunaway Road and I-8.

Side Trip to Yuha Well and Buttes via Vista de Anza (4WD road)

(This is part of a counter-clockwise loop around the Yuha Basin.)

0.0   Turnoff from Hwy 98 at BLM route Y1928. Drive north (left) to...

0.9   Fork of BLM routes Y1928 (north, left) and Y2739 (east, right).

(Left fork goes to the geoglyphs as described in the next side trip.) Go right and climb to...

1.6   Vista de Anza monument.

The view overlooks the Yuha Basin, technically a valley. Valleys are caused by water erosion while basins are fault-bounded features of tectonic subsidence. Yuha, like many of the recesses into the sediments and alluvium along the west side of Imperial County, is a headward-, westward-eroding valley.

DE ANZA OVERLOOK

Juan Bautista de Anza led two groups of Spanish explorers and settlers across this portion of the Colorado Desert from northern Mexico to San Francisco Bay. During each tortuous passage, the Spanish camped below here in Yuha Wash. The passage in 1774, which explored and pioneered the first overland route into upper California, consisted of only a small group of soldiers and two missionaries, Fathers Garces and Diaz.

A second trip in 1776 brought settlers to the coast of California. Spain felt that its tenuous hold on the New World was threatened by Russian settlements to the north. The Spanish missions were struggling to survive and needed a reliable supply route to ensure military, political, and religious success.

This expedition contained 240 people, including Captain de Anza, 38 soldiers, 16 muleteers, 136 colonists, several Indian guides, and Father Pedro Font, as chronicler. There were over 800 head of livestock which included pack mules, horses, and cattle. The settlers became founders of what would become San Francisco. (Monument erected by BLM in cooperation with Imperial County Pioneers Historical Society, dedicated January 1990.)

Just past the monument (southeast) is the fork of BLM Rts Y1995 (left) and Y2739 (right), mile 1.8 at UTM 6-03.0E 36-17.5N.

(The right fork Y2739 works along the Yuha Rim to the southeast, passing an abandoned World War 2 radar station and the Yuha man site to reach Hwy 98 after a couple of miles.) Yuha man was, for awhile, one of the most exciting archaeological finds in the Western Hemisphere. At first, he was dated at 21,500 years from caliche (calcium-carbonate) deposits on bone fragments. However, in recent years, a new method of dating with a mass spectrometer has established a date of about 3,000 years.

1.8   Turn northeast (left) onto route Y1995 and drop down a sandy wash filled with sandstone concretions into Yuha Basin. Yuha Wash joins from the left at mile 3.2. Turn northeast (right) and drive down-wash as smoke trees, tamarisk, and mesquite begin to appear, heralding water near the surface.

4.6   Wash junction and fork of BLM Rts Y1995 (right) and Y1950 (left) at UTM 6-05.7E 36-20.0N.

The route straight ahead, down Yuha Wash on Y1995, leads several miles along the south edge of the Shell Beds to the Y1964 pole line. The pole line road leads a couple of miles northwest (left) to I-8 at the Dunaway Road Staging Area or several miles southeast (right) to Hwy 98 at Pinto Wash.

Turn northwest (left) and drive up-wash 0.2 mile to...

4.8   Yuha Well (elev. 220′) at UTM 6-05.3E 36-20.2N.

The historic Yuha Well site today is marked by remnants of four water-development structures: a vertical concrete pipe with a roof, a wooden-sided well casing, a vertical iron boiler, and a horizontal galvanized tank. A very weathered wooden sign, origin unknown, reads:

YUHA WELL (Santa Rosa de las Lajas)

Used by the Kamias (sic) Indians who showed it to Anza's scouts on March 8, 1774. The second Anza Expedition passed here on December 11, 1775. Later an important water source on the trail from Yuma to San Diego.

Anza described the six wells, dug several feet into the sand, as having the "finest water." It was at this point in 1774 that both Father Francisco Garces and Sebastian Tarabal became confident of the direction they needed to travel to arrive at San Gabriel.

Lt. W.H. Emory, who traveled with Kearny's Army of the West in 1846, mentions a *laguna* ("lake") which may have been Yuha Well. Roscoe and Margaret Conkling, researching the Butterfield Overland Mail in the 1930s, noted that the road to San Diego, via Coyote Wells and Mountain

Springs, branches from the Butterfield road at "Laguna." The Bancroft map of California in 1868 and the Rand McNally map of 1876 also show this junction at Yuha Well.

Retrace the route down-wash 0.1 mile east to...

4.9 BLM Rt Y1950 climbs out of the wash to the northeast (left) and crosses sandy mudhills covered with black, basaltic cobbles.

5.9 "Section Corner Fork" at BM 218', UTM 6-06.6E 36-21.3N.

This is the NE corner of Section 6 and the NW corner of Section 5. The two sets of Yuha Buttes are obvious now, defining the north and south sides of this valley, with the Shell Beds beyond to the southeast (right). The less-traveled east (right) fork leads into the valley to a serene camping and exploring area. Please respect signs which protect sensitive natural resources. The Shell Beds are composed of abundant fossil oyster and other mollusk shells from the early Pliocene epoch, 4-5 million years ago. Similar oyster shells and "reefs" are in the Coyote Mountains, Fish Creek Badlands, and OWSVRA. The well-traveled north (left) fork goes to...

6.2 Fork in "Yuha Buttes Valley" UTM 6-06.8E 36-21.7N.

Rt Y1950 goes northeast (right), through the Yuha Buttes Valley, about 4 miles to the Dunaway Staging Area.

Rt Y1928 climbs northwest (left), gaining the Yuha Rim at...

7.0 "Yuha Buttes Overlook," UTM 6-05.7E 36-22.3N, approximately in the center of Section 31. The dirt road works its way along the Yuha Rim to the southwest, past the geoglyphs, to reach Hwy 98 at Anza Trail Road (west) after about 5 more miles.

End of Side Trip

7.4 Anza Trail Road (west entrance, elev. 375', repeated from above).

Side Trip to "Yuha Buttes Overlook" via Geoglyphs (dirt road)

(This is part of a clockwise loop around the Yuha Basin.)

0.0 Turnoff from Hwy 98 at BLM route Y1928. Drive north (left) to...

0.9 Fork of BLM routes.

(Right fork goes to Vista de Anza as described in the previous side trip.) Go north (left) on BLM Rt Y1928 to...

2.0 Desert Restoration Project.

Three BLM routes fork from here.

Y2312 goes west (left) to Coyote Wells.

Y1929 and Y2314 go north just over a mile to the Power Geoglyph Site, which is fenced with an interpretive marker at UTM 6-02.4E 36-21.1N (elev. 390').

Y1928 bears northeast (right) toward the Yuha Rim. Continue northeast to...

2.5 Yuha Geoglyphs UTM 6-02.9E 36-20.2N (elev.415').

GEOGLYPHS, GROUND FIGURES, OR INTAGLIOS (BLM Interpretive Panel)

The geoglyphs located nearby are an extremely rare legacy from the Native Americans who once lived here. Preserved by the arid climate and absence of man, these ground figures were scraped into the desert pavement hundreds or thousands of years ago.

Some archaeologists believe that they were created by a shaman (or medicine man) to contact the spirit world. Geoglyphs can be a link to prehistoric mythology. Other archaeologists believe that some figures were actually a response to a deteriorating environment which led to today's desert conditions. Geoglyphs, which mean earth carving, remain enigmatic features.

YUHA GEOGLYPH (BLM Interpretive Panel)

This geoglyph or intaglio is one of the most elaborate ground figures in the southwest. It is a unique and unusual aspect of aboriginal Native American culture. The meaning of these prehistoric ground drawings is unknown, but can be related to boundary markings, fertility rites, or shamanistic (medicine man) activities.

Geoglyphs are also found along the Colorado River near Blythe and in four other sites in the Borrego area.

The side trip continues on Y1928 to the northeast along the Yuha Rim, past a 4WD trail at mile 3.2 which drops to the southeast (right) directly one mile to Yuha Well. Continue along the Yuha Rim to...

4.9   "Yuha Buttes Overlook," UTM 6-05.7E 36-22.3N, approximately in the center of Section 31. There are three basic choices from here.

1. Complete the clockwise loop by dropping down into Yuha Buttes Valley (see 4WD side trip above in reverse.)

2. Work northeast about 5 miles to Dunaway Road and I-8 via dirt roads, heeding BLM directional signs.

3. Reverse route back to the southwest and the geoglyphs along the Yuha Rim.

9.5   Option #2 above is the dirt road through-route which takes you to Dunaway Staging Area at I-8.

End of Side Trip

7.4   Anza Trail Road (west entrance, repeated from above).

Continue southeast on Hwy 98.

9.5   Crucifixion Thorn Natural Area, Coyote Road #2 southwest (right).

This unique stand of plant, located in a natural depression, is surrounded by a barbed-wire fence with one entry. This site has the largest known concentration of this intricately branched plant in California. The plant (*Castela emoryi*, formerly called *Holocantha e.*) is relatively common in the desert basins of Arizona and Sonora but rare in California. It is found only in the deserts of North America and is similar to the biblical "Crown of Thorns," associated with the crucifixion of Jesus.

Side Trip to Skull Valley (dirt road, hike)

From Hwy 98 drive 1.9 miles southwest up Coyote Road 2 (BLM Rt Y286) and veer west another one-half mile to park north of a gravel pit. Commence hiking northwest around a prominent ridge, then turn south in the NW corner of Section 23 into a wash (elev. 600') about a mile from the parking area. GPS fix at the south turn is UTM 5-99.9E 36-14.4N. Ascend the wash another mile and climb west over a minor ridge (elev. 900') into the Skull Valley basin which covers about two square miles, centered on Section 27. Total distance to the center of the sink is about three miles.

Skull Valley is the lowest of the "stair-step" valleys, at elev. 830'. Its precipitous west ridge and gentler east slope is consistent with the half-graben characteristic of detachment faulting. BLM Planner Arnie Schoeck reported thick green grass ankle-deep after hurricane rains in the early fall of 1997. Honeybean mesquite and crucifixion thorn are also found here.

The macabre origin of the name is unknown although a gorge five miles south is named Cañon de los Muertos ("Canyon of the Dead"). Be aware that the international border crosses the south edge of the sink and that the lowest opening of the basin is south into Mexico.

End of side trip

10.0 Anza Trail Road (east entrance) Y2739.

This route loops several miles northwest along the Yuha Rim, past the radar tower and Vista de Anza Historical Marker to Anza Trail Road (west entrance).

This area is home to the flat-tailed horned lizard (Phrynosoma m'callii) which is fully protected by the California Dept. of Fish and Game. It is an uncommon lizard that is threatened by human and vehicular activity—in particular, soil compaction by OHVs. It measures about 4" long, and is distinguished by a dark stripe running down its back, a broad flat tail, and a long, slender, spined crown head. The lizard is diurnal, and its diet consists 95% of harvester ants. The horned lizard is found in sandy flats where it will bury into the loose sand to avoid its predators and the hot rays of the sun, which can heat the ground surface to over 150°F. The lizards' defense mechanisms are limited. They use cryptic coloration to blend with their surroundings. They will die in captivity without their special dietary and habitat requirements being met. Do not collect, for their sake and because it is the law.

12.3 Sunrise Butte (elev. 387'), survey point "Cross," occasional site of Easter sunrise services.

19.5 Pinto Wash (elev. 100').

BLM Rt Y2812 goes southwest up Pinto Wash along the Mexican border to the Jacumba Mountains near Skull Valley.

BLM Rt Y1851 goes northwest, generally along a pole line, about 19 miles to West Mesa and the Dunaway Staging Area.

In conclusion, a true tale that seems worthy of the annual Pegleg yarn-spinning contest: Since the 1800s, government and commercial dreamers have preferred the notion of a canal for ocean-going vessels to connect the Sea of Cortez with the Yuha Desert at this very point where Pinto Wash crosses Hwy 98. In 1967 a bi-national commission proposed a canal 300 feet wide and 75 feet deep, connecting sea-level Laguna Salada with Pinto Wash via locks through the international border. A local elected board is currently promoting a similar concept. (The lost Spanish galleon of the desert sails again! Or is it those wayward Vikings?)

APPENDIX 1
Recommended Reading—Books In Print

ANZA-BORREGO AND WESTERN COLORADO DESERT REGION

The following publications are currently in print (1998) and are available at major bookstores and natural history visitor centers in southern California. Contact Sunbelt Publications, telephone (619) 258-4911, for availability. Many of these books have bibliographies for further research. Plant guides, referenced in Appendix 5, are not repeated here.

Abbott, Patrick L., ed., *Sturzstroms and Detachment Faults, Anza-Borrego Desert State Park*. Santa Ana: South Coast Geological Society, 1996. This volume focuses on the geology of the midriff of ABDSP along Hwy 78 and the Vallecito Mtns. Includes classic works by Blake (1853) and Dibblee (1954).

American Automobile Association Southern California, *Desert Area*. Los Angeles: AAA Southern California, 1996. A complete motoring guide to California's desert areas.

Balls, Edward, *Early Uses of California Plants*. Berkeley: University of California Press, 1962. This book outlines plant sources of food, drink, clothing, utensils and tools by Indians and early Californians.

Bean, Lowell, Sylvia Brakke Vane, and Jackson Young, *Cahuilla Landscape*. Menlo Park: Ballena Press, 1991. This book explores Cahuilla place names and legends associated with Santa Rosa and San Jacinto mountain sites and some linking trails.

_____, and Katherine Siva Saubel, *Temalpakh: Cahuilla Indian Knowledge and Usage of Plants*. Morongo Indian Reservation: Malki Museum Press, 1972. This ethnobotany represents 10 years of meticulous field work by the authors to document the usage of plants among the Cahuilla Indians who inhabited the northern section of ABDSP including 250 different plants.

Beauchamp, R. Mitchel, *A Flora of San Diego County, California*. National City: Sweetwater River Press, 1986. This is the authoritative catalog listing of the plants of San Diego County. The introductory material includes a description of the various plant communities found in the county.

Belzer, Thomas, *Roadside Plants of Southern California*. Missoula, MT: Mountain Press, 1984. This book has 242 color plates of plants, many of which are commonly found in the desert and mountain areas of ABDSP.

Bowers, John and Emily, *100 Desert Wildflowers*. Tucson: Southwest Parks and Monuments Association, 1989. The most familiar wildflowers of the desert southwest are featured in this guidebook.

Brooks, Joan, Tom Budlong, *Desert Magazine Index*. Spokane: Arthur H.Clarke Co., 1997. Covers the 534 issues of Desert from Nov. 1937 to July 1985 and the 5 issues of American Desert Magazine from Nov. 1992 to Sept. 1993.

Burns, Diane, ed., Hal Clifford, Ted Bergen, and Steven Spear, *The Geology of San Diego County*. San Diego: Sunbelt Publications, 1996. This chronicle of the county's geological past, present, and future helps the outdoor enthusiast to understand the creation and changing face of San Diego's diverse landscape.

Corones, Joe, *Colorado Desert and Salton Trough Geology*. San Diego Association of Geologists (SDAG), 1993. Volume contains scientific papers and maps including the Superstition Hills earthquake, evolution of the Vallecito Mountains, and major landslides in the eastern Peninsular Ranges.

Cornett, Jim, *Indian Uses of Desert Plants*. Palm Springs: Nature Trails Press, 1995. This book focuses on 16 plants considered by Native Americans to be among the most important and widespread in the arid Southwest.

Cunningham, Bill, and Polly Burke, *Hiking California's Desert Parks*. Helena: Falcon Press, 1997. The best 111 hikes in the California deserts are outlined in this book, including 25 hikes in the Anza-Borrego area. Hikes include maps, mileages, elevation gain/loss, and trail conditions.

Foster, Lynne, *Adventuring in the California Desert*. San Francisco: Sierra Club, 1987. The single best reference to the natural history and destinations in the local deserts including numerous walks and drives in Anza-Borrego, Yuha Desert, and Salton Sea.

Ganci, Dave, *Basic Essentials of Desert Survival*. Merrillville, IN: ICS Books, 1996. All the information you need on desert survival techniques is in this portable, easy-to-read book.

_____, *Desert Hiking*. Berkeley: Wilderness Press, 1993. This excellent general handbook is for anyone interested in hiking desert terrain. Covers planning, vehicle use, clothing, first aid, desert environment, and water.

Greenstadt, Daniel, *San Diego Mountain Bike Guide*. San Diego: Sunbelt Publications, 1998. This comprehensive trail guide has 32 great rides ranging from coastal plains to the foothills, mountains, and deserts of the county. All rides are in public lands and are ranked for various skill and experience levels. Illustrated with photos and maps.

Harrison, Tom, *Recreation Map San Diego Backcountry*. San Rafael: Tom Harrison, 1997. A superb full color map for outdoor enthusiasts and naturalists who need East County's mountains and deserts on one handy and frequently updated map. Features topographic information, water features, roads and trails, campsites. The map is gridded for GPS/UTM.

Huegel, Tony, *California Desert Byways*. Idaho Falls: Post Company, 1995. This book features backcountry drives in southern California's deserts, including nine trips in the Anza-Borrego area. Emphasis on family trips.

Johnson, Paul, Mark Jorgensen, and Harry Daniel, *Anza-Borrego Desert State Park*. Borrego Springs: Anza-Borrego Desert Natural History Association (ABDNHA), 1992. A book of color photographs with text that captures the geology, scenery, and shifting moods of Anza-Borrego's varied landscape.

_____, *Cacti, Shrubs and Trees of Anza-Borrego: An Amateur's Key to Identifying Desert Plants*. Borrego Springs: ABDNHA, 1990. This slim volume will benefit even the seasoned naturalist. Its easy-to-use system helps to identify perennial plants native to the Anza-Borrego area when no blooms are present, which is most of the year.

_____, *Weekenders Guide to Anza-Borrego*. 2nd ed. Borrego Springs: ABDNHA, 1992. Walks along desert roads and trails with geological and natural history highlights are discussed and mapped by a veteran desert naturalist and professional photographer.

Knaak, Manfred, *Forgotten Artist: Indians of Anza-Borrego and Their Rock Art*. Borrego Springs: ABDNHA, 1988. The rock art of the native Cahuilla and Kumeyaay Indians of Anza-Borrego is discussed, including the possible origin and meaning of this art form, and includes photographs.

Larson, Leo and Helen Larson, *Anza-Borrego Desert Recreation Map*. Eureka, CA: Earthwalk Press, 1994. This is an excellent topographic map of San Diego's diverse backcountry, including ABDSP, Cuyamaca Rancho State Park, and the Laguna Mountains. Text includes campgrounds, trails, and permits.

Lee, Milicent, *Indians of the Oaks*. San Diego: San Diego Museum of Man, 1989. A delightfully written fictitious, but historically accurate, account of life among the Kumeyaay Indians whose villages were in the foothills of San Diego County. Reveals agave gathering techniques used in the desert.

Lehman, Charles, *Desert Survival Handbook*. Phoenix: Primer, 1996. The desert is not a gentle environment, and it is imperative for outdoor enthusiasts on foot or in off-road vehicles to know how to survive if stranded or temporarily lost.

Lewellyn, Harry, *Backroad Trips & Tips to Unpaved Southern California*. Anaheim: Glovebox Publications, 1993. The Glovebox Guide to off-roading in southern California includes several off-road trips in the Anza-Borrego area. It also includes excellent introductory material on off-roading.

MacMahon, James, *Audubon Society Nature Guides: Deserts*. New York: Alfred A. Knopf, 1985. This comprehensive natural history field guide to the major ecological zones of North America includes extensive color plates and descriptive text for flowers, birds, reptiles, insects, and landscape.

McKinney, John, *Walking California's Desert Parks*. Santa Barbara: Olympus Press, 1996. A day hiker's guide to California's deserts, including 16 walks in the Anza-Borrego area.

Peik, Leander and Rosalie Peik, *Camper's Guide to San Diego County*, 21st ed. San Diego: Peik Enterprises, 1992. A concise but comprehensive guide to San Diego County campgrounds in federal, state, and county parks, and on BLM land. Includes directions, maps, facilities, points of interest.

Pepper, Choral, *Desert Lore of Southern California*, 2nd ed. San Diego: Sunbelt Publications, 1998. Former Desert Magazine publisher Choral Pepper evokes the mystery and magic of southern California's desert, weaving fancy and fact into a tapestry woven of prospectors, lost mines and Indian myths.

Pryde, Philip, *San Diego: An Introduction to the Region*, 3rd ed. Dubuque, IA: Kendall Hunt, 1992. This is the most comprehensive compendium of the natural environments and cultural patterns of the county. Numerous charts, photos, and maps.

Reed, Lester, *Old Time Cattlemen and Other Pioneers of the Anza-Borrego Area*. 3rd ed. Borrego Springs: ABDNHA, 1986. Reed knew first-hand most of the old-timers of Anza-Borrego. His family was one of the earliest settlers and cattle ranchers of the area after the Civil War.

Remeika, Paul, and Lowell Lindsay, *Geology of Anza-Borrego: Edge of Creation*. San Diego: Sunbelt Publications, 1992. This non-technical guide introduces the southern California desert enthusiast to one of the most active geologic regions in North America. Eight field trips journey through deep time in the desert with numerous maps, photos, and charts.

_____, and Anne Sturz, *Paleontology and Geology of the Western Salton Trough, Anza-Borrego Desert State Park.* San Diego: SGAG, 1995. This book contains two volumes: V.1 contains geology roadlogs to the Vallecito Badlands, Split Mountain, and the Borrego Badlands; V.2 is a detailed bibliography of earth sciences in the region.

Reynolds, Robert and Jennifer, eds., *Ashes, Faults and Basins.* San Bernardino County Museum Publication 93-1, 1993. Papers include Wonderstone Wash (M.C. Van Buskirk), Coyote Mountains fossils (T.A. Demere), Vallecito Badlands fossils (E.H. Lindsay and J.S. White), Borrego Badlands (P.A. Remeika and G.T. Jefferson), Anza-Borrego fish fossils (M.A. Roeder).

Roberts, Norman, *Baja California Plant Field Guide,* 2nd ed. La Jolla: Natural History Publishing Association, 1989. Contains an excellent introduction to Baja's plant environment with discussions on geography, geology, and climate of the peninsula of which the Anza-Borrego region is geologically and biologically a part.

Schad, Jerry, *Afoot and Afield in San Diego County,* 3rd ed. Berkeley: Wilderness Press, 1998. Over one-third of this guide is allocated to desert and desert mountain hikes.

Schaffer, Jeffrey P. et al, *The Pacific Crest Trail,* Volume 1, 4th edition. Berkeley: Wilderness Press, 1995. The PCT passes through two of Anza-Borrego's three montane areas. Co-author Ben Schifrin supplies precise detail of the PCT in these areas including updated topographics.

Sidekick, *Los Coyotes Indian Reservation.* Chino, CA: Sidekick, n.d.

_____, *Smugglers Cave & Table Mountain.* Chino, CA: Sidekick, n.d. This is the most complete off-road map of this area near Jacumba.

Winnett, Thomas, *Backpacking Basics,* 4th ed. Berkeley: Wilderness Press, 1994. Compact guide containing a full-bookshelf of information on a broad range of outdoor skills and equipment, including appendices on suppliers, packing checklist, and conservation organizations.

Jimson weed (Datura), used by Mountain Cahuillas in Toloache ceremony

APPENDIX 2
Desert Directory: Anza-Borrego and Western Colorado Desert Region

Area code (760) unless otherwise noted
All emergency calls: 911
Information current as of August 1998
Fax updates to (619) 258-4916 (Sunbelt Publications)

GOVERNMENT AGENCIES
Bureau Of Land Management (BLM):
El Centro Resource Area Office 337-4400
1661 South 4th St., El Centro, CA 92243
Palm Springs/South Coast Resource Area Office 323-4421
400 So. Farrell Dr., Palm Springs CA 92262

California State Parks:
Anza-Borrego Desert State Park
200 Palm Canyon Drive, Borrego Springs, CA 92004
Visitor Center 767-4205
Administrative Office 767-5311
ABDSP Wildflower Hotline 767-4684
For seasonal information, send self-addressed, stamped
postcard to:
Wildflowers, 200 Palm Canyon Drive, Borrego Springs, CA 92004.
Response will be sent approximately 2 weeks prior to peak bloom.
Cuyamaca Rancho State Park 765-0755
12551 Hwy 79, Descanso, CA 91916
Ocotillo Wells State Vehicular Recreation Area (OWSVRA) 767-5391
P.O. Box 360, Borrego Springs, CA 92004
California State Parks camping reservations (Call individual
parks for appropriate number.)

Imperial County Parks Dept
1002 State Street, El Centro, CA 92243 339-4384
San Diego County Dept. Of Parks & Recreation
5201 Ruffin Road, San Diego, CA 92123 .... (619) 565-3600
(reservations for Agua Caliente, Vallecito, William Heise
Regional Parks)

Cleveland Nat'l Forest, Laguna Mtn Recreation Area
3348 Alpine Blvd, Alpine, CA 91901 . . . . (619) 445-6235
Visitor Center Mt. Laguna (weekends only) . . . . (619) 473-8547

LAW ENFORCEMENT (NON-EMERGENCY)
California Highway Patrol . . . . (619) 296-6661
San Diego County Sheriff, Borrego Springs 767-5656
San Diego County Sheriff, Boulevard/Jacumba . . . . (619) 766-4585
San Diego County Sheriff, Julian 765-0503
San Diego County Sheriff . . . . (619) 565-5200
Imperial County Sheriff 452-2051

EMERGENCIES—Dial 911 for life-threatening emergencies
Automobile Club of Southern California . . . . (800) 400-4222
Borrego Medical Center 767-5051
    4343 Yaqui Pass Road, P.O. Box 2369, Borrego Springs, CA 92004
    (24 hour emergency medical service)
Calexico Hospital 357-1191
    450 Birch Street, Calexico, CA 92231
    (24 hour emergency medical service)
El Centro Regional Medical Center 339-7100
    1415 Ross Avenue, El Centro, CA 92243
    (24 hour emergency medical service)
Pioneers' Memorial Health Care District (hospital) 344-2120
    207 W. Legion Road, Brawley, CA 92227
    (24 hr emergency medical service)

CB COMMUNICATION
REACT Monitor . . . . Citizens' Band Channel 9
Burro Bend REACT (Ocotillo Wells) . . . . Citizens' Band Channel 20
Desert Ironwoods REACT . . . . Citizens' Band Channel 7

PUBLIC INTEREST AGENCIES AND ORGANIZATIONS
Anza-Borrego Desert Natural History Association 767-3052
    POB 310, Borrego Springs, CA 92004
Anza-Borrego Foundation 767-0446
    POB 2001 Borrego Springs CA 92004
Borrego Springs road conditions 767-7623
Borrego Valley Airport 767-7415
    POB 2401, Borrego Springs, CA 92004
Imperial County Historical Society 352-1165
Imperial Valley College Desert Museum 358-7016
Julian Pioneer Museum 765-0227
Mountain Empire Historical Society, Campo . . . . (619) 478-5707
Natural History Museum (San Diego) . . . . (619) 232-3821
Northeast Rural Bus Service 767-4287

Connects La Mesa/El Cajon and Escondido with Julian,
Borrego Springs, Agua Caliente and other rural east county
stops. Carries bicycles.
Road/highway conditions from CALTRANS (recorded) .... (800) 427-7623
Sierra Club .... (619) 299-1743
Southeast Rural Bus Service .... (619) 478-5875
    Connects La Mesa/El Cajon with Jacumba. Bicycles carried.
Theodore Payne Foundation Wildflower Hotline .... (818) 768-3533
USNPS, BLM, USFS Wildflower Hotline .... (800) 354-4595
Weather forecast (recorded) .... (619) 289-1212

PRIVATE CAMPGROUNDS, RV PARKS, MOTELS/HOTELS, CONDOS & RESORT HOMES

Banner Store and Recreation Ranch (campground & RV park) 765-0813
    36342 Highway 78, Julian, CA 92036
Blu-In Park .... no phone
    2189 Highway 78, Borrego Springs, CA 92004
Borrego Springs Resort Hotel 767-5700
    1112 Tilting T Drive, Borrego Springs, CA 92004 .... (888) 826-7734
Borrego Valley Inn 767-4356
    405 Palm Canyon Drive, Borrego Springs, CA 92004
Butterfield Ranch (mobile home & RV park in Mason Valley) 765-1463
    14925 Great Southern Overland Stage Route of 1849
    Julian, CA 92036
Club Cirle Resort Apartments 767-5944
    POB 2130, Borrego Springs, CA 92004
Coldwell Banker First Borrego Springs Properties 767-4521
    POB 951, Borrego Springs, CA 92004
Desert Ironwoods RV Park & Motel 767-5670
    4875 Highway 78 (Ocotillo Wells)
    Borrego Springs, CA 92004 .... CB Channel 7
Desert Sands (mobile home & RV park) 767-5554
    277 Palm Canyon Dr. (POB 247), Borrego Springs, CA 92004
Hacienda del Sol Motel 767-5442
    610 Palm Canyon Dr. (POB 366), Borrego Springs, CA 92004
Holiday Home (mobile home and RV park) 767-5590
    351 Palm Canyon Dr. (POB 1978), Borrego Springs, CA 92004
Kamp Anza RV Resort .... (909) 763-4819
    41560 Terwilliger Rd, Anza, CA 92539
La Casa del Zorro Resort Hotel 767-5323
    3845 Yaqui Pass Rd. (POB 227), Borrego Springs, CA 92004 ..... (800) 824-1884
    (corner Yaqui Pass & Borrego Springs Rd)
Leapin' Lizard RV Ranch 767-4526
    5929 Kunkler Lane, Borrego Springs, CA 92004
Leisure LifeStyle (property rental office) 767-5891
    POB 666, Borrego Springs, CA 92004

Los Coyotes Indian Reservation (campground) 782-0711
    POB 249, Warner Springs, CA 92086
Oasis Motel 767-5409
    610 Palm Canyon Dr. (POB 226), Borrego Springs, CA 92004
Ocotillo Motel & RV Park 358-7559
    14 East Agate Road (POB 99), Ocotillo, CA 92259
Palm Canyon Resort (RV park, hotel, and restaurant) 767-5341
    221 Palm Canyon Dr. (POB 956), Borrego Springs, CA 92004   (800) 242-0044
The Palms at Indian Head (bed & breakfast) 767-7788
    2220 Hoberg Road (POB 525), Borrego Springs, CA 92004   (800) 519-2624
Rio Bend RV Resort Ranch 352-7061
    1589 Drew Road, Seeley, CA 92243
Ram's Hill Properties 767-5595
    1675 Las Casitas Drive, Borrego Springs, CA 92004
Salton City Spa & RV Park 394-4333
    End of Sea View at Salton Bay (POB 5375), Salton City, CA 92275
Split Mountain Park & Country Store 767-3811
    5525 Split Mountain Road (Ocotillo Wells), Borrego Springs, CA 92004
Stagecoach Trail RV and Equestrian Resort (Shelter Valley) 765-2197
    7878 Great Southern Overland Stage Route of 1849, Julian, CA 92036
Stanlunds Resort Motel 767-5501
    2771 Borrego Springs Road (POB 278), Borrego Springs, CA 92004
Villas Borrego Resort Apartments 767-5371
    3134 Club Circle (POB 185), Borrego Springs, CA 92004   (800) 700-5944
Whispering Sands Desert Spa Resort 767-3322
    2376 Borrego Springs Road (POB 2156), Borrego Springs, CA 92004

CHAMBERS OF COMMERCE

Borrego Springs Chamber of Commerce
P.O. Box 420
Borrego Springs, CA 92004
767-5555 or (800) 559-5524

Indio Chamber of Commerce
P.O. Box TTT
Indio, CA 92201
347-0676

Julian Chamber of Commerce
Box 413
Julian, CA 92036
765-1857

Brawley Chamber of Commerce P.O.
P.O. Box 218
Brawley, CA 92227
344-3160

Salton City Chamber of Commerce
North Marina Drive
Salton City, CA 92274
394-4112

El Centro Chamber of Commerce
P.O. Box 1141
El Centro, CA 92243
352-3681

MISCELLANEOUS
ABDSP Tour Concessionaires:

Naturalist Services - Paul Johnson 676-5179
    POB 1555, Borrego Springs, CA 92004
    (4-wheel drive interpretive tours)

Desert Jeep Tours - Paul Ford .... (619) 295-3332
    3111 Camino del Rio North, Suite 400, San Diego, CA 92108   (888) 295-3377
Agua Caliente Store 765-1875
    39545 Great Southern Overland Stage Route, Julian, CA 92036
Borrego Sun 767-5338
    POB 249, Borrego Springs, CA 92020
Carrizo Bikes (bike rentals) 767-3872
    648 Palm Canyon Dr., Borrego Springs, CA 92004
Coffee & Book Store 767-5080
    590 Palm Canyon Dr., Borrego Springs, CA 92004
Desert Fuel Stop (and store) 328-7329
Desert Kitchen 358-7731
    1071 Imperial Highway, Ocotillo, CA 92259
Ocotillo Treasures Unlimited (OTU) - store and fuel stop 358-7324
    1182 Imperial Highway, Ocotillo, CA 92259
Ranchita Store 782-3800
San Diego Association of Geologists .... (619) 697-6212
    POB 92159-1126, San Diego, CA 92159-1126
Sunbelt Publications .... (619) 258-4911
    1250 Fayette St., El Cajon, CA 92020-1511
Wilderness Press .... (510) 558-1666
    1200 5th Street, Berkeley, CA 94710   (800) 443-7227

INTERNET SITES FOR MORE INFORMATION

    http://www.anzaborrego.statepark.org
    http://www.desertusa.com
    http://www.cal-parks.ca.gov
    http://www.borregosprings.com
    http://www.borregosprings.org
    http://www.theabf.org
    http://www.california-desert.org

APPENDIX 3
Recommended Trips By Mode Of Travel

AREA 1- WESTERN:
WEST HWY S-22/

NW S-2	Natr Walk	Trail Hike	X-Co Hike	Back Pack	Horse Trail	Mtn Bike	Pavd Road	Dirt Road	4WD Road*
Montezuma Mine								X	
Jasper Trail						X		X	
Culp Val/Pena Spring	X	X							
Hellhole Ridge Trail			X		X				
Paroli Homesite	X					X		X	
Pinyon Ridge/Wilson Trl		X							
Hellhole Canyon			X		X				
Flat Cat Flat/Canyon			X						
ABDSP Visitor Center	X								
Borrego Palm Canyon	X		X						
BPC NoFk to Indian Can				X					

AREA 2- NORTHWEST:

COYOTE CANYON	Natr Walk	Trail Hike	X-Co Hike	Back Pack	Horse Trail	Mtn Bike	Pavd Road	Dirt Road	4WD Road*
Henderson Canyon			X						
Horse Camp					X			X	
DiGiorgio Rd. to 2nd	X				X	X		X	
Alcoholic Pass		X							
Desert Gardens	X								
2nd X to Lower Willows					X	X			X
Lower Willows/3rd X	X				X				
Box Canyon			X						
3rd X to Collins Vly						X			X*
Sheep,Indian,Cougar Cans			X	X					
Salvador Can/Yucca Val			X						
Collins Vly to Midl Wil.			X	X	X				X
Midl Wil to Uppr Willows			X	X	X	X			
Upper Wil to Terwilliger					X	X			X*
Alder,Parks,Tule Cans			X	X					
Horse Canyon/White Wash			X	X	X				
Tule Spr/Tabl Mtn via PCT	X	X	X	X					
Terwilliger Valley to Anza						X		X	

AREA 3- NORTHEAST:
EAST HWY S-22/

NORTH HWY 86	Natr Walk	Trail Hike	X-Co Hike	Back Pack	Horse Trail	Mtn Bike	Pavd Road	Dirt Road	4WD Road*
Coyote Mtn		X							
Beckman Wash									X
Clark Valley						X		X	
Rockhouse Can/Hidden Spr		X							
Rockhouse Valley		X	X						
Inspiration Wash/Pt									X
Fonts Pt/Short Wash									X
Thimble Trl/V.del Malpais						X			X
Lute Ridge EQ view	X								
Villager Pk/Rattlsnk Can				X					
Palo Verde/Smoke Tree Cans			X						
Coachwhip Can/Ella Wash						X			X
Arr Salado/17 Palms									X
Truckhaven Rocks	X								
Calcite Mine			X			X			X*
Sheep Tanks/Palm Wash									X
Wonderstone Wash						X			X
Travertine Palms			X						
Trav Pt to Palo Verde Can				X					

AREA 4- CENTRAL:
CENT HWY 78/

HWY S-3	Natr Walk	Trail Hike	X-Co Hike	Back Pack	Horse Trail	Mtn Bike	Pavd Road	Dirt Road	4WD Road*
Sentenac Cienega	X								
Plum/Grapevine Canyons						X			X
Yaqui Well	X					X			X
Tamarisk Grove	X								
Yaqui Pass/Kenyon O'lk	X								
Glorieta Canyon						X			X
Mine Canyon						X		X	
Pinyon/Nolina Washes						X			X
Sunset Mtn/Pinyon Canyon			X						
The San Felipe Narrows	X								
Nude Wash/Old Bor Val Rd						X		X	
Texas Dip	X								
Cactus Gdns/Old K.S.Rd.	X					X		X	
Harper Canyon			X						X
Borrego Mtn/Buttes Pass						X		X	
Hawk Can/West Butte			X			X		X	
Borrego Mtn Dropoff									X*
Borrego Mtn/East Butte									X
Goat Trail/Blow Sand Can						X			X
Blow Sand Hill									X*
So Bor Badlns/San Gregorio									X

AREA 5- EAST: EAST HWY 78, CENT HWY 86

	Natr Walk	Trail Hike	X-Co Hike	Back Pack	Horse Trail	Mtn Bike	Pavd Road	Dirt Road	4WD Road*
Elephant Trees Trail	X								
Gypsum Railroad						X		X	
Split Mtn	X		X			X		X	
Fish Creek/Hapaha Flat									X
Harper Flat **			X			X			X*
OWSVRA Devils Slide									X
Barrel Spring	X					X			
Shell Reef Expressway									X
Old Mine Rd						X		X	
Harpers Well,O.K.Spr Rd						X			
San Sebastian Marsh		X							X
San Fel Hills/Gas Domes						X			X

AREA 6-SOUTHWEST: HWYS S-1/S-2

	Natr Walk	Trail Hike	X-Co Hike	Back Pack	Horse Trail	Mtn Bike	Pavd Road	Dirt Road	4WD Road*
Kwaaymii Pt/PCT/Fages Mon.	X								
North and main Pinyon Mtns						X		X	
Whale Peak			X						
Squeeze and P.M.Dropoff						X			X*
Blair/Li'l Blair Valleys						X		X	
Ghost Mtn		X							
Morteros	X								
Smuggler Canyon	X								
Box Canyon	X								
Mason Val Cactus Gdns	X								
Oriflamme/Chariot Cans						X		X	
Rainbow Canyon			X						
Vallecito	X								
Agua Caliente		X							
June Wash									X
Val./Carrizo Badlands									X
Palm Spring/Mesq.Oasis	X					X		X	
Arroyos Tapiado/Diablo									X
Diablo Dropoff									X*
Carrizo Cienega/Stage Sta									X
Indian Gorge/Mtn Palm Spr		X				X		X	
Bow Willow Canyon		X				X		X	
Carrizo Gorge			X						X
Canyon Sin Nombre						X			X
Jojoba Wash/Volc Hills									X
Mortero Wash/Dos Cabezas						X			X
Devils Canyon			X						
Fossil Canyon			X						X

AREA 7-SOUTHEAST:

I-8/HWYS S-80/98	Natr Walk	Trail Hike	X-Co Hike	Back Pack	Horse Trail	Mtn Bike	Pavd Road	Dirt Road	4WD Road*
Table Mountain		X				X			X
Smugglers Cave/Val of Moon		X	X			X			X
Jacumba Wild/Myers Valley			X	X					
Boulder Creek			X						
Painted Gorge			X			X		X	
Plaster City/West Mesa									X
Superstition Mtn									X
Davies Valley			X						
Yuha Rim/Geoglyphs	X					X		X	
Yuha Basin									X
Crucifixion Thorn	X								

* = 4WD route which has a difficult, perhaps dangerous segment.

** = Harper Flat closed to vehicles. 4WD Rd in extreme SW corner.

APPENDIX 4
Backpocket Map Key to Topographic Maps

The large, regional map in the backpocket of this guidebook is divided into a 7.5′ grid, each quadrangle of which is a named USGS topographic map per the following list and the map of Anza-Borrego Topographic Coverage (see table of contents, list of maps). Sites on the regional map, or in its alphabetical index on the back, can thus be located on their corresponding detailed topographic map (e.g., "Smugglers Cave" in grid H6, on the regional map and in the alphabetic index, is on the detailed "In-Ko-Pah Gorge" 7.5′ topographic map.) Each of the forty 7.5′ topos is about the same size as the large map. See Chapter 3 for additional discussion of maps in the Anza-Borrego region.

Map Index Number	Corresponding 7.5′ Topographic Map	Map Index Number	Corresponding 7.5′ Topographic Map
B2	Bucksnort Mountain	E4	Whale Peak
B3	Collins Valley	E5	Harper Canyon
B4	Clark Lake NE	E6	Borrego Mountain SE
B5	Rabbit Peak	E7	Harpers Well
B6	Oasis	E8 .	Kane Spring
C2	Hot Springs Mountain	F2	Cuyamaca Peak
C3	Borrego Palm Canyon	F3	Monument Peak
C4	Clark Lake	F4	Agua Caliente Spring
C5	Fonts Point	F5	Arroyo Tapiado
C6	Seventeen Palms	F6	Carrizo Mountain NE
C7	Truckhaven	F7	Plaster City NW
D2	Ranchita	F8	Superstition Mountain
D3	Tubb Canyon	G5	Sweeney Pass
D4	Borrego Sink	G6	Carrizo Mountain
D5	Borrego Mountain	G7	Painted Gorge
D6	Shell Reef	G8	Plaster City
D7	Kane Spring NW	H5	Jacumba
D8	Kane Spring NE	H6	In-Ko-Pah Gorge
E2	Julian	H7	Coyote Wells
E3	Earthquake Valley	H8	Yuha Basin

Appendix 5

100 Common Plants in Anza-Borrego by Family

Includes page numbers to major plant field guide references listed in the chart in the following order (– denotes no page reference in book):

A/P — Plant is either an annual (A) or perennial (P). If AP, plant species appear as both an annual *and* a perennial.

DO — Dole, Jim W. and Rose, Betty B. *An Amateur Botanist's Identification Manual for the Shrubs and Trees of the Southern California Deserts.* North Hill, CA: Foot-loose Press, 1996.

TE — Bean, Lowell John and Saubel, Katherine Siva. *Temalpakh: Cahuilla Indian Knowledge and Usage of Plants.* Morongo Indian Reservation, CA: 1987.

AB — *Wildflowers of Anza-Borrego Desert State Park.* Borrego Springs, CA: Anza-Borrego Desert Natural History Association, 1997.

BE — Belzer, Thomas J. *Roadside Plants of Southern California.* Missoula, MT: Mountain Press Publishing Company, 1986.

BO — Bowers, Janice Emily. *100 Desert Wildflowers of the Southwest.* Tucson: Southwest Parks and Monuments Association, 1994.

JA — Jaeger, Edmund C. *Desert Wild Flowers.* Stanford: Stanford University Press, 1941.

MU — Munz, Philip A. *California Desert Wildflowers.* Berkeley: University of California Press, 1962.

ST — Stewart, Jon Mark. *Colorado Desert Wildflowers.* Palm Desert, CA: Jon Stewart Photography, 1993.

JO — Johnson, Paul R. *Cacti, Shrubs and Trees of Anza-Borrego.* Borrego Springs, CA: Anza-Borrego Desert Natural History Association, 1990.

WI — Collins, Barbara J. *Key to Wildflowers of the Deserts of Southern California.* Thousand Oaks, CA: California Lutheran College, 1979.

CO — _____. *Key to Trees and Shrubs of the Deserts of Southern California.* Thousand Oaks, CA: California Lutheran College, 1976.

JE — Hickman, James C., ed. *The Jepson Manual: Higher Plants of California.* Berkeley: University of California Press, 1993.

MB — Beauchamp, R. Mitchel. *A Flora of San Diego County, California.* National City: Sweetwater River Press, 1986.

SCIENTIFIC FAMILY	COMMON FAMILY	GENUS/SPECIES	COMMON NAME	A/P	DO	TE	AB	BE	BO	JA	MU	ST	JO	WI	CO	JE	MB
ACANTHACEAE	ACANTHUS	Justicia californica (Beloperone)	CHUPAROSA, HUMMINGBIRD FLOWER	P	92	47	12	108	68	245	23	65	22	--	9	125	79
ANACARDIACEAE	SUMAC	Rhus ovata	SUGAR BUSH	P	68	131	--	72	--	--	--	--	--	--	--	135	82
ARECACEAE	PALM	Washingtonia filifera	CALIFORNIA FAN PALM	P	53	145	--	106	--	6	28	--	9	--	111	110	45
ASCLEPIADACEAE	MILKWEED	Asclepius subulata	MILKWEED, AJAMETE, RUSH/LEAFLESS MILKWEED	P	--	43	--	126	21	184	74	--	16	--	--	172	87
ASTERACEAE	SUNFLOWER	Ambrosia dumosa (Franseria)	BURROBUSH, BURROWEED, BURSAGE	P	100	--	--	110	--	279	106	90	24	--	74	194	94
ASTERACEAE	SUNFLOWER	Artemisia tridentata	SAGEBRUSH, GREAT BASIN SAGEBRUSH	P	104	43	--	--	--	302	--	--	--	--	70	205	95

SCIENTIFIC FAMILY	COMMON FAMILY	GENUS/SPECIES	COMMON NAME	A/P	DO	TE	AB	BE	BO	JA	MU	ST	JO	WI	CO	JE	MB
ASTERACEAE	SUNFLOWER	Baccharis salicifolia (glutinosa)	MULE FAT, SEEP-WILLOW, WATER MOTTIE/WALLY	P	110	46	-	76	-	-	78	-	-	-	86	210	96
		Baccharis sarothroides	CHAPPARAL BROOM, BROOM BACCHARIS	p	110	-	-	-	-	-	-	-	-	-	77	274	96
		Chaenactis fremontii	FREMONT/DESERT PINCUSHION	A	-	52	34	-	28	295	78	21	-	103	-	224	98
		Chrysothamnus paniculatus	RABBITBRUSH, BLACKBANDED RABBITBRUSH	P	106	-	24	76	-	263	103	-	17	-	79	230	99
		Encelia farinosa	BRITTLEBUSH, INCIENSO	P	94	69	24	78	53	286	105	49	25	94	83	249	102
		Eriophyllum spp.	GOLDEN YARROW, WOOLLY SUNFLOWER	A	-	-	-	118	-	291	55	52	-	-	73	261	104
		Geraea canescens	DESERT SUNFLOWER	A	100	76	54	-	51	286	104	50	-	96	-	270	105
		Helianthus niveus ssp. canescens	DUNE/GRAY SUNFLOWER	AP	-	-	53	-	50	283	-	48	-	93	-	278	107
		Hymenoclea salsola	CHEESEBUSH, WHITE BURRO BUSH	P	100	-	-	110	-	282	54	90	19	-	76	291	108
		Layia glandulosa	TIDY TIPS	A	-	-	38	-	-	287	54	19	-	99	-	302	110
		Malacothrix glabrata	DESERT DANDELION	A	-	141	52	-	30	757	57	57	-	109	-	315	111
		Monoptilon bellioides	DESERT STAR, MOJAVE DESERT STAR	A	-	-	37	-	24	270	77	18	-	98	-	319	112
		Palafoxia arida (linearis)	SPANISH NEEDLES	A	-	-	40	-	-	291	24	92	-	107	-	322	113
		Perityle emoryi	ROCK DAISY	A	-	-	36	-	-	291	107	20	-	98	-	323	113
		Peucephyllum schottii	DESERT FIR, PIGMY CEDAR	P	101	-	-	78	-	303	109	-	17	-	78	324	113
		Pluchea sericea	ARROW WEED, DESERT ARROW WEED	P	112	105	-	-	-	275	-	-	27	-	86	326	-
		Rafinesquia neomexicana	DESERT CHICORY	A	-	-	33	-	-	310	79	23	-	110	-	332	114
		Stephanomeria pauciflora	DESERT STRAW, WREATH PLANT	P	-	-	-	-	-	310	-	95	-	-	71	348	115
		Trixis californica	TRIXIS	P	99	-	22	-	58	307	110	-	26	-	84	355	116
		Xylorhiza orcuttii (Machaeranthera)	DESERT/ORCUTT'S/BORREGO ASTER	P	-	-	16	-	95	267	-	-	-	-	-	360	117
BIGNONIACEAE	BIGNONIA	Chilopsis linearis ssp. arcuata	DESERT WILLOW, CATALPA	P	87	53	14	30	85	245	23	-	11	-	4	366	118

SCIENTIFIC FAMILY	COMMON FAMILY	GENUS/SPECIES	COMMON NAME	A/P	DO	TE	AB	BE	BO	JA	MU	ST	JO	WI	CO	JE	MB
BORAGINACEAE	BORAGE	Amsinckia tessellata	FIDDLENECK	A	--	--	55	116	46	211	101	46	--	62	--	368	119
		Cryptantha spp.	FORGET-ME-NOT, POPCORN FLOWER	A	--	--	--	--	22	211	75	16	--	73	--	369	119
BURSERACEAE	TORCHWOOD	Bursera microphylla	ELEPHANT TREE, TOROTE	P	62	48	--	80	--	142	--	--	12	--	4	448	131
CACTACEAE	CACTUS	Echinocereus engelmannii	HEDGEHOG, PURPLE-FLOWERED HEDGEHOG	P	--	--	5	96	79	162	41	111	7	--	107	451	131
		Ferocactus cylindraceus (acanthodes)	BARREL CACTUS, BISNAGA	P	139	67	8	96	63	168	--	115	7	--	104	452	132
		Mammillaria dioica	FISHHOOK CACTUS	P	--	--	1	--	--	--	--	112	6	--	--	452	132
		Opuntia basilaris	BEAVERTAIL CACTUS	P	137	95	4	96	81	159	40	109	6	--	100	454	132
		Opuntia bigelovii	TEDDYBEAR/JUMPING/BALL CHOLLA	P	134	96	7	--	16	155	39	108	8	--	103	454	132
		Opuntia phaeacantha	PRICKLY PEAR CACTUS	P	--	97	3	98	--	--	--	--	--	--	--	456	132
		Opuntia ramosissima	PENCIL/DIAMOND/DARNING NEEDLE CHOLLA	P	134	97	2	--	--	158	--	105	7	--	102	456	132
		Opuntia spp. (O.echinocarpa & O.ganderi)	SILVER/GOLDEN CHOLLA & GANDER'S CHOLLA	P	134	--	--	--	--	158	39	106	8	--	103	455	132
CAPPARACEAE	CAPER	Isomeris arborea (Cleome isomeris)	BLADDER POD	P	66	79	21	36	--	71	33	33	22	--	--	470	136
CHENIPODIACEAE	GOOSEFOOT	Atriplex canescens	FOURWING SALTBUSH, SHAD-SCALE, WINGSCALE	P	118	45		--	--	53	--	--	--	--	35	503	141
		Atriplex hymenelytra	DESERT HOLLY	P	102	--	--	--	--	54	63	--	24	--	35	504	141
CRASSULACEAE	STONECROP	Dudleya pulverulenta ssp.	LIVE-FOREVER, DESERT CHALK LETTUCE	P	--	67	--	106	--	84	34	34	--	51	--	525	147
CUCURBITACEAE	GOURD	Cucurbita palmata	COYOTE MELON, COYOTE GOURD	P	--	--	57	--	48	252	--	30	23	--	--	536	147
CUPRESSACEAE	CYPRESS	Juniperus californica	CALIFORNIA JUNIPER	P	132	81	--	18	--	1	63	--	11	--	1	114	40
CUSCUTACEAE	DODDER	Cuscuta californica	CALIFORNIA DODDER, WITCH'S HAIR	P	--	59	--	92	--	138	--	--	--	119	--	539	144
EPHEDRACEAE	EPHEDRA	Ephedra spp.	MORMON/DESERT/MINER'S/MEXICAN TEA, JOINT FIR	P	130	70	--	16	--	5	10	--	16	--	2	115	41
EUPHORBIACEAE	SPURGE	Croton californicus	CROTON, DESERT CROTON	P	--	56	--	--	--	277	70	--	28	27	--	572	151

SCIENTIFIC FAMILY	COMMON FAMILY	GENUS/SPECIES	COMMON NAME	A/P	DO	TE	AB	BE	BO	JA	MU	ST	JO	WI	CO	JE	MB
FABACEAE	PEA	Acacia greggii	CATCLAW, ACACIA, WAIT-A-MINUTE BUSH	P	74	29	--	56	11	97	95	35	9	--	11	582	154
		Astragalus spp.	LOCOWEED, MILKVETCH, RATTLEWEED	AP	--	44	49	--	74	241	17	77	--	78	--	583	154
		Cercidium floridum	BLUE PALO VERDE	P	73	52	20	54	37	93	36	37	9	--	5	606	156
		Lotus rigidus	DEERWEED, ROCK-PEA, BROOM LOTUS	P	--	--	--	--	--	102	96	--	--	77	--	620	157
		Lupinus arizonicus	ARIZONA LUPINE	A	--	87	50	140	72	106	16	75	10	74	--	627	160
		Olneya tesota	IRONWOOD	P	77	94	--	58	73	114	84	76	10	--	14	638	163
		Prosopis glandulosa (juliflora)	HONEY MESQUITE	P	72	107	--	56	--	96	35	--	10	--	6	642	163
		Prosopis pubescens	SCREWBEAN MESQUITE	P	72	118	--	56	--	93	96	--	10	--	13	642	163
		Psorothamnus schottii (Dalea)	INDIGO BUSH, MESA INDIGO, DALEA	P	76	59	17	--	--	107	83	100	14	--	32	643	164
		Psorothamnus spinosus (Dalea)	SMOKE TREE	P	75	--	--	56	87	114	83	99	8	--	5	643	164
		Senna armata (Cassia)	CASSIA, DESERT CASSIA, SENNA	P	71	--	23	--	--	102	36	33	16	--	8	644	164
FAGACEAE	OAK	Quercus cornelius-mulleri	SCRUB OAK, MULLER'S OAK	P	128	--	--	--	--	--	--	--	--	--	--	661	166
FOUQUIERIACEAE	OCOTILLO	Fouquieria splendens	OCOTILLO, CANDLEWOOD, COACHWHIP	P	82	74	13	98	65	147	20	62	14	--	5	664	167
GERANIACEAE	GERANIUM	Erodium texanum	FILAREE	A	--	72	45	--	76	123	18	79	--	36	--	672	169
HYDROPHYLLACEAE	WATERLEAF	Nama demissum	PURPLE MAT	A	--	--	44	--	82	202	22	86	--	68	--	688	171
		Phacelia campanularia	DESERT CANTERBURY BELL	A	--	--	--	--	--	199	47	101	--	61	--	697	172
		Phacelia crenulata	HELIOTROPE/NOTCH-LEAFED PHACELIA	A	--	--	48	--	--	202	46	85	--	61	--	698	172
		Phacelia distans	WILD HELIOTROPE, PHACELIA, BLUE PHACELIA	A	--	--	47	--	99	199	85	102	--	60	--	698	172
KRAMERIACEAE	KRAMERIA	Krameria spp. (K.grayi & K.erecta)	KRAMERIA, RHATANY	P	81	--	--	--	75	110	17	--	14	--	30	710	175
LAMIACEAE	MINT	Hyptis emoryi	DESERT LAVENDER; BEE SAGE	P	91	79	15	100	92	223	87	--	23	--	19	714	176
		Salvia apiana	WHITE SAGE	P	90	136	11	100	--	--	--	--	23	--	--	726	177
		Salvia columbariae	CHIA	A	--	136	51	--	100	226	--	87	--	81	--	728	177
LILIACEAE	LILY	Agave deserti	AGAVE	P	57	31	19	104	31	22	29	3	13	--	112	117	42
		Hesperocallis undulata	DESERT LILY	P	--	77	28	--	--	9	27	2	--	114	--	119	54